"In the 21st century, peo~~~~~~~~~~~ a path to your door if you don't tell them where you live—especially on the Internet. *Poor Richard's Branding Yourself Online* gives you the smart steps you need to take to promote yourself and increase awareness of who you are and what you do. Don't get lost in cyberspace. **Let Bob Baker show you the way.**"

—Raleigh Pinskey, author of 101 Ways to Promote Yourself
http://www.promoteyourself.com/

"Predictable—that is the impression that comes to mind when reading *Poor Richard's Branding Yourself Online*. You expect (predict) a book published through Top Floor to be **informative**, **thoroughly researched**, and **well written**. As with all the other titles, you are not disappointed. Author Bob Baker focuses on a topic that is sure to become the next buzzword in Internet marketing. He details the process so well, that I suggest wearing a football helmet when reading it. This way when you slap yourself in the head with a hearty 'I should have thought of that!' you won't injure yourself."

—Gary Clark, Content Writer, Web Presence Provider,
http://marketing.ww-net.net/ and http://www.ww-net.net/

"**Highly recommended!** *Poor Richard's Branding Yourself Online* is a **great read**. The content is rich, the easy-to-read writing style is refreshing and the many resources listed are very helpful. Anyone who reads this book and applies the lessons will be a success both online and off."

—Reg Rygus, The Idea Generator, http://www.eideagenerator.com/

"WOW, *Poor Richard's Branding Yourself Online* is **required reading** for anyone who wants their website to generate substantial traffic by standing out from the crowd. This not only tells you what and how to do it, but it's **chock full of resources** to make your job easier!"

—Joel Weiner, Webmaster, http://www.LogoSpot.com/

"I was greatly impressed with *Poor Richard's Branding Yourself Online*. This **accessible** and **comprehensive** book is the prefect guide for anyone who wants to establish an online presence. As with all the *Poor Richard's* series, the language is geek-free and assumes almost no computer expertise on the part of the reader. And yet there is no sacrifice of depth for the sake of simplicity. The more technically attuned reader may find himself skimming through certain sections of the book, only to stumble upon some gem of wisdom, gleaned from Bob Baker's years of online experience. I would recommend this book to anyone who is wanting to make a personal impact in the Internet community."

—Rev. David B. Smith B.A., B.Th, Dip. A., http://www.Fighting-Fathers.com/

"**Great book! Contains sensible and valuable advice**, which is easy to put into practice. Bob certainly knows his stuff. I especially like the small 'tip' feature."

—Paul East, http://www.pyramidmultimediaconsulting.com/

"**Outstanding!** Top Floor's done it again. *Poor Richard's Branding Yourself Online* is exactly what I've been searching for in the lackluster quagmire of Internet marketing literature. True to the spirit of the publisher, *Branding* succeeds at containing encyclopedic amounts of information in a very concise, easy-to-implement format. Unlike many Internet authors and marketing gurus I've experienced, Bob Baker's expertise in the subject obviously comes from massive personal experience. **This is the type of book the *For Dummies* series aspires to, but never reaches.** From initial concept, to web design, to online publicity, to integrating your online and offline marketing, this book shows you how to make your business the most recognized, and sought-after, resource in your field, all using little or no money. This is clearly **one of the best business investments you'll ever make!**"
—Seth Cauthorne, author of *HOW TO RAKE IN THE TIPS in Any Service Profession*

"I thought I knew all the 'off the wall' marketing ideas to promote my web community. I was wrong! You have **a wealth of ideas** I will be implementing because I had made the decision long ago that we would not go into debt for this project. Your book has confirmed my belief that much can be accomplished **without a huge outlay of money.** Thank you!"
—Maureen Sullivan, http://www.OurFortWorth.com/

"A **great** book for beginners to learn how to market themselves online. Like anything else in life people aren't going to knock your door down unless they know where you are and think you can help them. This book will certainly teach the reader how to tell people who you are and how to find your Web site."
—Branch Whitney, www.HikingLasVegas.com/

"The joy of the *Poor Richard's* series is that each volume serves up **a perfect combination of philosophy and practicality, along with a healthy dollop of humour.** Bob Baker's *Branding* is no exception: be inspired, have your thoughts provoked—and then use the tool-kit to build yourself a brand."
—Holly Ellson, Online Marketing Officer, WWF, the conservation organization

"**Packed with up to the minute examples** of dot.com successes, this book provides a wealth of 'best practice,' links to useful resources, and informed, practical commentary. Another worthy addition to my bookshelf!"
—Mike Price, Chief Executive Officer, http://www.cozmikshirts.co.uk/

"Bob Baker's book *Poor Richard's Branding Yourself Online* is a **fun, energetic** journey through the arena of personal branding via Internet marketing. Baker has a personal, loose writing style that begs you to follow him on this journey. **His passion for the subject is contagious** and you can't help but become as eager to follow, as he is to lead you through the adventure. It is truly a wonder today to receive more—in this case, far more—than you feel you have paid for. No wonder Bob Baker is the 'expert' in creating raving fans. He has another one right here!"
—Karen M. McCamy, President and CEO, *ExecPlanet.com*

"**It's a blueprint!** I love the concept—it's what I think the web is all about, be it homepage or corporate site. So many gurus on the net for this stuff and so many answers, but nothing concrete. And when there are answers, they never tell you *why* you are doing what they suggest. This book seems to have excellent answers, a concrete order for implementing a plan and tells you *why*—and *why not* too! It's also **well-written, friendly and sensible**, broken down into orderly and useful steps that keep the overall goal in mind but also provide the details that most website marketing plans leave out.

—Diane Offill, Re:Collections.net (Coming soon to a website near you!)

"*Poor Richard's Branding Yourself Online* **re-affirms everything that I have learned the hard way, over years of trial and error.** If I had this book a few hours ago, I would have been where I am much sooner."

—Matt Mickiewicz, Co-Founder, http://www.SitePoint.com/

"You're special. You have something unique to offer the world. Unfortunately, only you know it. However, by the time you finish reading *Poor Richard's Branding Yourself Online* you'll have **a clear map to guide you in getting the word out.** *Poor Richard's Branding Yourself Online* isn't just another book about online promotions. Author Bob Baker understands the Internet, and doesn't minimize the time and effort it takes to create a 'brand called you.' He offers a clear step by step guide to creating an identifiable image to build your reputation and get you noticed."

—Angela Booth, Web content writer/ editor/ copywriter, http://www.angelabooth.zip.com.au/

"I **thoroughly enjoyed the book and found many ideas** which will help me to pursue my own online identity. If (and when) I follow all the steps in this book, I look forward to the prosperity and enjoyment having created my own brand and identity will bring (and will send you a note on my success)!"

—Kara Tersen, President, CNETCanada Ltd., http://www.cnetcanada.com/

"**Baker says we must make a personal connection with our customers to be successful and he has done just that with his readers through his book.** If you want to start a business on the web or if you are an experienced marketing/PR professional making the transition to online marketing, *Poor Richard's Branding Yourself Online* is the quintessential tool for you. Bob Baker has it all in this resource book, that will be dog-eared from the first chapter."

—Marcia J. Williams Marketing/Public Relations Specialist for 20+ years, http://mjwwords.com/

"Get out your highlighter. You'll find **hundreds of tips** throughout the pages of *Poor Richard's Branding Yourself Online* and you'll want to refer to them again and again."

—Andrea Reynolds, http://www.AndreaReynolds.com/

POOR RICHARD'S BRANDING YOURSELF ONLINE

How to Use the Internet to Become a Celebrity or Expert in Your Field

by
Bob Baker

To Kelli-Rae, a little girl who has forever
branded me as one happy daddy.

Poor Richard's Branding Yourself Online:
How to Use the Internet to Become a Celebrity or Expert in Your Field

SAN#: 299-4550
Top Floor Publishing
8790 W. Colfax #107
Lakewood, CO 80215

Feedback to the author: feedback@topfloor.com
Sales information: sales@topfloor.com
The Top Floor Publishing Web Site: http://TopFloor.com/
The Poor Richard Web Site: http://PoorRichard.com/
Cover design/illustration by Marty Petersen, http://www.artymarty.com

ISBN: 1-930082-14-2

03   02   01   6 5 4 3 2 1

ACKNOWLEDGMENTS

So many people to thank; so little time. First, a special thanks to Top Floor publisher Missy Ramey, who recognized the match between my background and the topic of this book. Thanks also to Top Floor owner Peter Kent for agreeing to include me among the stable of fine Top Floor authors.

While the author usually gets credit for the success of a book, it takes a team of dedicated people to crank out a good title. The team I worked with on *Branding Yourself Online* was top-notch. Project manager Jerry Olsen's attention to detail challenged me and made this book a far better resource for readers. Sydney Jones' rock-solid copyediting skills and encouraging words made her a joy to work with. Proofreader and indexer Joann Woy served as an excellent fourth pair of eyes that fine-tuned the words in this book.

These acknowledgments would be incomplete without a nod to my aunt, Verla Baker, one of my biggest supporters. Verla is indirectly responsible for my involvement with this book. She took me on a trip during which I read my first Top Floor book, *Poor Richard's E-mail Publishing*, which led to my first connection with Missy. Who knows what might have happened had I not taken that book on that trip?

Thanks to the authors, experts, and successful online branders who contributed quotes and anecdotes. Hats off to my *Buzz Factor* and *Quick Tips for Creative People* e-zine subscribers, who encourage and inspire me every week. Thanks also to Kathy, Pat, Chad, Maureen, Libby, and Corey for making my initiation to the corporate writing world an enjoyable one, and to my wonderful band mates Dave, Jim, and Lela.

Most of all, I want to express my love and appreciation for Lynn Zeller, who encourages me and adds meaning to my life (while putting up with the guy who spends so many hours on the computer). Thanks also to Alyssa (who gives up her online time to the guy who spends so many hours on the computer), Angela, and Joey. Finally, I must acknowledge the positive influence that Juanita Baker continues to have on my life. This one's for you, Mom!

ABOUT THE AUTHOR

Bob Baker is a writer, webmaster, speaker, and consultant who provides inspiration and low-cost marketing ideas for musicians, writers, artists, and other creative people. He is the author of *Ignite Your Creative Passion*, *The Guerrilla Music Marketing Handbook*, and *Turn Your Creativity Into Cash: A 28-Day Workshop*.

For 10 years, Bob was the managing editor of *Spotlight*, the Midwest music magazine he founded in 1987. In 1995, he began publishing *The Buzz Factor* (http://TheBuzzFactor.com/), a free e-mail newsletter and Web site that established his identity as a music-marketing resource for aspiring songwriters, musicians, and bands. Over the years, Bob has been covered in such magazines as *Music Connection*, *Keyboard*, *American Artist*, and *Windplayer*.

In addition to his reputation in the online music community, Bob has established a related presence through **Quick Tips for Creative People** (http://Bob-Baker.com/qt/), an e-zine and Web site that provides advice for artists, writers, crafters, and other people pursuing a creative passion. He also oversees Branding Yourself Online, (http://BrandingYourselfOnline.com/), a companion Web site and e-zine to this book.

CONTENTS AT A GLANCE

TABLE OF CONTENTS

INTRODUCTION

A s I began writing this book in the summer of 2000, a phenomenon was taking place on American television. A program called *Survivor* was setting new records as millions of people tuned in to watch the weekly show over the course of a 15-week period.

As you may remember, *Survivor* gathered together a group of 16 "average" people and plopped them on a remote island in the South China Sea for 39 days. At regular intervals the castaways were subjected to challenges that tested them physically and mentally. They were then required to vote each other off the island one at a time. The last remaining survivor won a million dollars. More than 50 million people watched the final episode, second only to the Super Bowl in ratings.

Each castaway received a certain amount of cash to compensate them for their time on the island; but many of them profited in other ways. Some appeared in commercials, sitcoms, and movies. Others endorsed products and were featured on magazine covers. Some wrote books or hit the road to cash in on public speaking engagements.

Why did these people do so well? Had they trained for years to live a life in the public spotlight? Not likely. They were in such demand because, through this TV show, millions of people had come to know them and identify in some way with who they are.

The Professor and Mary Ann ...

These castaways were hardly cookie-cutter images of each other. Like their *Gilligan's Island* predecessors, they were a varied cast of characters: the conniving corporate trainer, the crusty old Navy seal, the redneck truck-driver, the dim-witted doctor, the cute pixie girl, the emotional mother, and so on.

Each had his or her own distinct personal identity, and more importantly, millions of people knew who they were. In essence, these people suddenly had reams of opportunity because they had each embedded their personal brand image into the minds of millions of people.

That message is at the heart of this book: When lots of people know who you are and what image and message you stand for, you are put in an incredible position to better your life and profit from your notoriety. The Internet provides an excellent, cost-effective tool to accomplish that end, whether you want to become a celebrity or expert in your field, or simply hope to promote a new business, idea, or cause.

You may not have the opportunity to star in a blockbuster television series, but you most definitely have the power to hone a strong personal brand identity and then use the Internet to reach tens of thousands of people (or more) with your focused message.

Your Journey Begins Now

The good news is, you won't have to spend 39 days on a deserted island to become a recognized figure in your chosen field. Using the online branding tactics in this book, you'll be in control of determining who you are and how you want to be portrayed to your potential customers and fans. You'll decide what specific messages are sent out into the world and through what avenues those messages will travel.

The key to establishing a personal brand identity in the cyber world is focusing on who you are and what you stand for and then getting the word out through a variety of Internet channels that are frequented by the people most likely to be interested in your message.

As people start seeing your name and the benefit you offer, an impression begins to form. At first, ten people will be attracted to you and what you do ... then 50, and then 100. Before you know it, thousands of people will not only know who you are, but will come to view you as the resource of choice on your particular subject.

As your circle of online influence grows, a multiplying effect takes place and your notoriety suddenly starts growing in bursts. A critical mass occurs, and before long, you find yourself in the enviable position of being an online celebrity of sorts, or at least a well-known expert among people who are immersed in the topic, craft, industry, or idea you represent.

If the Internet Gives the Individual So Much Power, Why Isn't Everyone Using It?

The answer to this question is simple: Given all the opportunities the online world offers, most people just don't use the Internet in the most effective ways. Worse yet, many ambitious folks who try to establish a business online actually do themselves more harm than good. Here are just some of the ways people defeat themselves online:

- They use offline strategies that don't work on the Internet.
- They spend too much money getting set up online (or move too slowly because they believe having an Internet presence is an expensive process).
- They unknowingly engage in marketing activities that not only fail, but make people angry.
- They send out mixed messages about who they are and what they offer— and end up confusing people.
- They don't follow up consistently enough, and they give up before their efforts have had time to take hold.

Since so many people don't know how to use the Internet effectively, you're left with a world of opportunity to hone your image and your message and create a personal brand that will cut through the clutter and raise you to a higher level of recognition and success.

What's In this Book for You?

Over the next dozen or so chapters, I supply you with the tips and tools you'll need to effectively create a brand name for yourself online. First, we talk about what personal branding is, why you need it, and how successful people are using it right now to further their careers. We also discuss the best ways for you to determine the perfect brand image for you, as well as methods for hammering home that image so that it makes the most impact in the least amount of time.

This book points out the right ways and wrong ways to use e-mail, shows you what options you have for setting up your Web site, and reveals the best ways to publish a brand-building newsletter online. You also get the lowdown on networking through other people's Web sites, newsletters, and online forums.

On top of that, I cover the best ways to get free publicity on the Internet and go over a lengthy potpourri of effective online and offline strategies for driving your brand image and identity onto the computer screens and into the consciousness of the masses.

Most importantly, you learn that branding yourself online can be accomplished on an extremely low budget. In fact, many of the tools you'll use to promote yourself are available at no cost whatsoever.

There's a thrilling journey ahead of us within these pages. Let's get started.

—Bob Baker

CHAPTER ONE

The Brand Called *You*

Let's get right to the heart of the matter. If you're reading this book because you want to know more about corporate strategy, market penetration, paradigm shifts, business models, strategic partnerships, or any other business buzz word flavor of the week, you may be in for a big letdown. Here's a revelation: This book isn't about learning how to use the Internet to promote your product, your service, or even your small business. Nope. It's all about promoting *you*. That's right, *you*!

You may have excellent products or services to offer, and the steps outlined in this book can help you sell more of them online, but the approach I recommend involves *you* taking center stage, *not* the product, service, or business itself.

Before you get the wrong idea, personal branding has nothing to do with bragging or being self-centered. As we discuss throughout this book, the focus should always be on the customer or person whose attention you're trying to grab, but the way you present yourself is deeply rooted in who you are as a person.

Why Brand Yourself in the First Place?

You may be asking, "Why do I need to brand myself online? How does it benefit me?" The answer is that branding allows you to take control of your online identity and influence the impression that people have of you in their minds, which helps you accomplish any number of the following things:

- Establish yourself as an expert in your field
- Connect with like-minded people on a large scale
- Focus your energies on feeding your life's purpose
- Build a solid reputation within your industry
- Become self-employed doing something you enjoy (or gain credibility and be in a better position to land the job you really want)
- Increase your notoriety and improve your perceived value in the marketplace

- Develop your circle of influence within a particular business niche
- Earn praise and recognition from a growing number of people who embrace your message
- Become a celebrity in your chosen field

As you can see, the reasons people brand themselves are many and varied. If you're an artist, branding will help you connect your name with your technique and attract more fans (and more paying customers). If you're a Web designer, branding allows you to mix your attitude and distinct perspective with your technical skills so that more people hire you. If you're a writer, branding paves the way to reaching a loyal readership without having to kiss the...er, feet of a major publisher.

Not everyone has the same end-goals in mind, but there's one aspect that is consistent for everyone who successfully brands himself or herself online: interweaving an individual's name and personality directly with the product, service, or idea being promoted.

In this chapter, we look at some real-world examples of people who have effectively branded themselves and examine the reasons why their approaches work. I detail how I have used branding techniques successfully in my own career. We also discuss some of the obstacles you face concerning Internet identity issues and how to overcome them. Finally, we address the attitude and mindset you need to fully brand yourself online.

What Dave Teaches Us About Personal Style

While doing research for this book, I read an article that pointed out how the fast-food business was flat. Even though many "hamburger and fries" companies were spending millions on TV and print advertising, only one was at that time showing an increase in market share. It was Wendy's, which always features owner Dave Thomas in its commercials. He may be low-key, but he also projects a familiar, guy-next-door appeal that strikes a chord with customers. While his competitors were using theme songs from popular boy bands and focusing on menu items, there was Thomas humbly telling us about Wendy's.

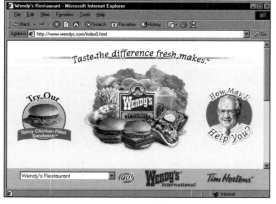

FIGURE 1.1: Wendy's owner Dave Thomas serves as a good example of using a personal brand identity to promote a business.

Even the Wendy's Web site (shown in Figure 1.1) reflects that personal style. Pay a visit to **Wendy's**

Restaurant at http://www.wendys.com/index0.html and you'll find a picture of Thomas in the top right corner along with this text: "Thanks for stopping by Wendy's restaurant. Use the menu bar below to get your fill of fun, information, and entertainment. If you ever need help, click on Dave. You'll find him at the top of every page. Please note, this site is best viewed with a hearty appetite." Now that's a great example of creating a warm, human atmosphere on the Internet.

When it comes to promoting on the Internet, a personal approach is the ideal route to take. Although glitzy advertising may still work in the offline world, when people go online, they don't connect with logos, theme songs, or mission statements. They connect with people, and starting today, I want to help you become one of those people with whom a growing number of Web surfers connect on a regular basis.

Playing the Name Game—*Many of the most successful companies use the appeal of a real person to sell the brand name. When you think of popcorn, who comes to mind? Most likely, the late Orville Reddenbacher and his distinct nerdish look. Remember Victor Kiam? He was the guy who liked Norelco electric shavers so much, he bought the company and for years appeared in its TV commercials. The fashion world is filled with the names of top designers: Tommy Hilfiger, Donna Karan, Calvin Klein, and so on. Even local car dealers have been playing the branding game well for years. Their commercials may be schmaltzy at times; but you can't deny they're filled with the personality the owner brings to the table. Most people prefer visiting a car dealer named Ernie Hudson Chevrolet over a place with a generic name like Midtown Auto Mall.*

Advertising Doesn't Pay Online

You may have heard that advertising on the Web (through banner ads, pop-up windows, and other display ad marketing) has been a dismal failure. With passive media such as TV and radio, people often let ads wash over them between programs and songs; but in the interactive arena of the online world, the user is in control, and users have made it abundantly clear they don't care to interact with advertising.

When most people power up their computers and log on, it's usually to get specific information or to accomplish a predetermined task: check e-mail, research a topic of interest, purchase a book, download a favorite band's song, see people without clothes on (yes, it happens), or get up-to-the-minute news. To achieve these goals, people routinely ignore anything that resembles advertising. They scan the screen in search of something that piques their interest. Then they move on.

It can be a cold, mechanical world online. The challenge is to make the experience warm and inviting—to create the feeling that a real human is on the other end of that product, service, article, newsletter, or Web site. That's why creating an honest and personal connection with people online is so crucial.

You Are the Brand

The concept of branding yourself as an individual is not completely new. A fall 1997 cover of *Fast Company* magazine screamed "The Brand Called You" in large type. Business guru Tom Peters wrote the main article, which carried the tag line "Big companies understand the importance of brands. Today, in the Age of the Individual, you have to be your own brand." I encourage you to read the article, which you can find online at **The Brand Called You**, http://www.fastcompany.com/online/10/brandyou.html.

In the article, Peters encourages business people to start thinking of themselves as "the CEO of Me Inc." To create a brand name for yourself, he suggests you evaluate your strengths and track record and ask yourself, "What about me makes me different?"

What's Your Definition of Branding?—*In his book* Circle of Innovation, *Tom Peters writes, "Branding means nothing more (and nothing less) than creating a distinct personality ... and telling the world about it."*

Why Tom Peters Is Successful

Peters was the ideal author to write the aforementioned article. Ever since his best-selling book, *In Search of Excellence*, was published in 1982, he's hammered home his identity as a forward-thinking, passionate troubadour in the modern business world. The guru also has a site devoted to ... who else? Himself. You'll find it at **TomPeters! Online**, http://www.tompeters.com/, and displayed in Figure 1.2.

One look at his home page reveals several common factors used by people who successfully brand themselves online. For starters, his Web address is his own name. Additionally, his site features the following sections:

- Tom's Latest Observations
- Who's/Where's Tom?
- Tom's Ideas
- Tom in the Media
- Subscribe to Tom's Newsletter
- Tom's Latest Cool Friend

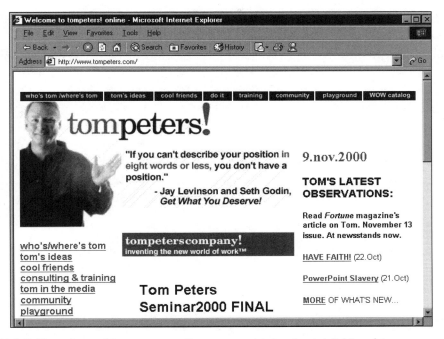

FIGURE 1.2: Tom Peters' home page does a good job of establishing his name as a brand name.

Branding Draws People Like Magnets

It may seem a bit self-centered, but reinforcing your own name is key to creating a brand name for yourself. Once you fill a niche and provide a unique perspective on your area of expertise—and once people are drawn to what you offer—they continue to return to you not only because of what you do, but also because of who you are and what you bring to the subject.

There are thousands of business guru wanna-bes who serve up advice similar to Peters', but there's only one Tom Peters. His ideas are written in a staccato, rapid-fire, almost stream-of-consciousness style. It's far from your typical business writing, and that's why he gets a disproportionate amount of attention—because he earned it by establishing his own personal brand identity.

Being Branded on Your Own Terms

While it's true that Peters has a lot of good advice on personal branding, his books are filled primarily with tips on building your identity while maneuvering within an organization or company—in other words, while working for someone else. The purpose of the book you hold in your hands, however, is to give you the tools you'll need to develop a personal brand that stands on its own.

You aren't attached to a company or a product line. You don't have to hide behind a logo or separate business entity.

The goal is for you to be known entirely for who you are as a person and what you stand for. You aren't just another generic consultant, freelance writer, artist, musician, graphic designer, or whatever your chosen vocation is. Instead, you establish yourself as (insert your name here), a (insert your specialty here) who is known for (insert your unique perspective here). When you play the Internet branding game correctly, you set yourself apart by attaching to your name a quality that's unlike anyone else's in your field.

The Web Can Make You a Star—*Gina Imperato, writing in* Fast Company *magazine, perhaps summed up branding online best when she said, "Some people think of the Web as a cavernous online library. Others consider it an electronic global village. But the Web is also the world's biggest stage. If you're an expert in a field that people care about, if you're connected to people whom others want to meet, or if you have a sense of style that lots of people enjoy, you can reach a potential audience of millions—and have impact around the world. You can become a star." Read Gina's entire article at* **The Web Can Make You a Star***,* http://www.fastcompany.com/online/12/webstar.html.

How Branding Propelled My Career

You may be wondering if it's really conceivable to create a brand name for yourself without a big advertising budget or the support of a large organization. I'm living proof that it is quite possible. Years ago I made a decision to find a way to make a living doing something related to my love of music, art, and writing. Branding allowed me to do just that.

Since I was a teenager (in the mid 1970s), I've played in pop and rock bands as a guitarist, singer, and songwriter—and put out three independently released albums. In 1987, I combined my passion for music with my interest in journalism and launched a music magazine called *Spotlight* in my hometown of St. Louis, MO. Like many musicians in my area, I was frustrated by the lack of coverage the media gave to local artists. My magazine filled that void. An early branding lesson was learned: Find a weakness in what the competition is doing and exploit that niche.

I didn't have a journalism degree or a financial backer—just an old Mac Plus (talk about the Dark Ages) and a desire to make it work. Advice: Never let a lack of traditional resources stop you from pursuing your goals. I've always made the best use of whatever I had to work with at the time—a trait that proved invaluable when I got involved with marketing myself on the Internet.

Taking on the Role of "Expert"

By 1992, *Spotlight* magazine had developed a solid identity as the voice of the St. Louis music scene. I was appearing regularly on local radio and gaining a reputation as a local music expert. That year I also hooked up with a publishing company that put out my first book, *101 Ways to Make Money in the Music Business*. Now I was not only Bob Baker, the St. Louis music news guy, I was also a published author and music business expert. A year later, I became an internationally published author when the Japanese version of the book was released. Cool beans, huh?

It was during these years that I honed my skills as a marketer. Whether I was seeking exposure for my music magazine or national coverage for my book, I became fascinated by publicity and the art of using clever marketing angles to establish a name and identity. I read every PR book and article I could get my hands on, and it paid off. Over the years, I've not only been covered by the media in St. Louis, but got plugs in national magazines such as *Keyboard*, *Windplayer*, and *Music Connection*.

Because of my interest in PR, I decided to narrow my identity within the music business category to music marketing and publicity topics only—and, more specifically, to marketing ideas for independent bands (meaning bands not yet signed to a recording contract). Another branding lesson: You can't be all things to all people. Narrowing your focus often strengthens your identity. In 1995, I self-published *The Guerrilla Music Marketing Handbook*, a manual I not only sell consistently, but also use as a tool to further solidify my brand name within this category.

Marketing in the Trenches—*Jay Levinson's excellent "Guerrilla Marketing" series of books was the inspiration for my self-published* Guerrilla Music Marketing Handbook. *Visit Jay's site at* http://www.gmarketing.com/ *and soak up some of his advice.*

Entering the Wired World

Another important step took place in 1995 when I signed up for an AOL account and joined the online community. The prospect of reaching thousands of people without the expense of printing or postage was intoxicating. One of the first things I did was start a music marketing e-mail newsletter called *The Buzz Factor*—one of the first of its kind on the Internet. Another lesson: Being one of the first in your category—especially in a new medium—is a tremendous advantage.

In 1996, I took my interests in the visual and performing arts and launched a second e-mail newsletter, called *Quick Tips for Creative People*. With it, I took the same marketing ideas I offered to musicians and applied them to people in creative fields of all kinds. I immediately started building a separate e-mail subscriber list made up of artists, writers, crafters, photographers, actors, and more. Branding lesson: The best approach is to stay focused on one core identity; however, if you are compelled to pursue other interests, don't broaden your original brand image. Doing so will only water down the appeal of that identity. Instead, launch a separate name, site, newsletter, message, etc. for the other brand.

Following this advice, I first registered the name of my music-marketing newsletter, *The Buzz Factor*, as a domain name—and http://www.thebuzzfactor.com/ was born (shown in Figure 1.3). The home page clearly indicates who the site is for and what benefit it offers, plus it makes a plea for every visitor to sign up for my free weekly e-mail newsletter (a topic we cover in-depth in Chapter 5).

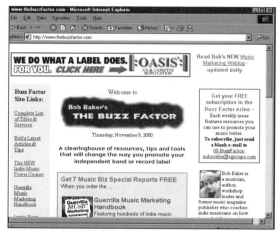

FIGURE 1.3: My independent music-marketing site, The Buzz Factor, helps establish my identity as someone who can help bands and record labels promote their music.

As I mentioned, I made *Quick Tips for Creative People* a separate identity; but that domain name would have been far too long. I wondered what Web address I should use. The solution was easy: my own name. Soon after, I launched http://www.bob-baker.com/ (seen in Figure 1.4), a site with a design similar to The Buzz Factor—but for a different target audience, as the home page greeting indicates.

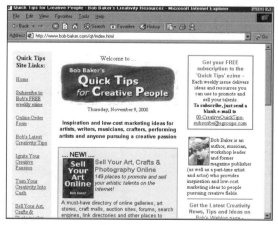

FIGURE 1.4: A look at the home page of my Quick Tips for Creative People site. Notice how my name and the purpose of the site are established early.

The Internet Becomes the Great Equalizer

In 1997, I hit some speed bumps. After 10 years of running my local magazine, I ceased publication to pursue my music and creativity-related publishing goals, but I soon faced some financial obstacles (a nice way to say I was up to my ears in debt). At that time, I was still using a good amount of direct mail to promote my books and my name. I suddenly had no money to fund my career path. What then? Give up? Hardly. What I did have was an Internet connection, a couple thousand e-mail subscribers and a good idea, and that was all I needed to continue.

Since then, I have used the Internet almost exclusively to promote my Web sites, newsletters, and brand name (or names). Both sites have grown in popularity, racking up to 500 visitors a day as of this writing. The number of subscribers to both newsletters has increased more than five fold and continues to grow every month. The number of sales generated by both sites has also risen steadily.

The moral of this story is that branding myself online saved me from having to wander aimlessly in the offline world. While news of multimillion dollar Internet startups (and the crashes and burns that followed) bombarded newspaper headlines, I was spending about a buck a day to build my online identity and attract attention to my name and what I offered. I used low-cost, guerrilla tactics instead of a big ad budget. I used creativity instead of cash. It can be done. Are you ready to make that concept a reality for yourself?

Lessons from the Original Poor Richard

The book you're reading is part of Top Floor Publishing's "Poor Richard's" series. As you may know, the name is a reference to *Poor Richard's Almanack*, first published by Benjamin Franklin in 1732.

How appropriate that a modern book on Internet branding pays homage to one of the original practitioners of personal branding. More than two hundred years after his death, the identity of Benjamin Franklin is alive and well. The name and bespectacled image of the elderly statesman is indelibly etched into the consciousness of millions of people the world over.

As you may know, Franklin was one of the original signers of the *Declaration of Independence*, the inventor of bifocal eyeglasses, and the person who discovered, among other things, that lightning is electricity. He was the Leonardo da Vinci of his era, and he did a fine job of making a name for himself.

Franklin also took personal branding to a new level when he created the identity of "Poor Richard" Saunders, the fictitious publisher of his almanacs.

Every annual issue was filled with weather forecasts, jokes, recipes, and sayings that have since become part of the American psyche.

***Benjamin Franklin's Legacy**—The man also known as "Poor Richard" Saunders is credited with founding the first post office in the United States, starting the first hospital in America, being the first person to identify industrial lead poisoning, discovering ocean currents, improving the way streetlights operate, and much more. Not a bad list of accomplishments to have one's name linked to.*

This history lesson demonstrates the uncanny parallels between Benjamin Franklin's life in the 1700s and today's Information Age. Franklin believed in the following:

- Having a central source of information accessible to everyone
- Sharing information and interacting with others in lively discussions
- Using mottos and simple phrases to communicate meaningful ideas
- Compiling useful how-to information and publishing it so that others could profit from it (while he profited from it as well)
- Using a sense of humor and personal style to communicate with the masses

All of these traits are essential to your success in branding yourself online. I believe the use of "Poor Richard" in the title of this series serves a commendable purpose. It's a tribute to a man who more than 250 years ago—long before the power of electricity was even harnessed—combined the workings of his brain with the need to discover and share information in new and profound ways. Benjamin Franklin was a pioneer in communicating his ideas via the best means available in his era.

The Internet Identity Crisis

The online world is an exciting frontier. The Internet presents so many opportunities and countless ways to accomplish personal goals with far more ease than at any time in human history. However, it's also a mysterious and confusing terrain for many people. More and more news headlines are filled with stories about security breaches, hackers, credit card fraud, and copyright infringement. It's not surprising that millions of people are leery and cynical about fully embracing the Web. As someone who is now dedicated to branding yourself online, it's important to be aware of this stigma and—as we discuss in a moment—know how you fit into the picture.

One of the reasons the Internet has become such a vibrant melting pot of ideas is because people feel less intimidated when expressing themselves online. The cyberworld creates an electronic barrier between a person sending a message and the individuals receiving it. People feel as if they're protected when communicating in the anonymous environment of e-mail, message boards, chat rooms, and more.

This syndrome is so prevalent that many people assume new identities altogether while online, as if they were attending a giant cyberspace masquerade ball. Men pose as women, teenagers pretend to be adults, older folks act like children, and unscrupulous con men dupe innocent people into revealing personal information. This quandary creates a lot of skepticism among people who venture onto the Web.

Cyberspace Theater—"On the Net, protected by a mask of anonymity, people can be quite dramatic because their identity is hidden," says theater director Elyse Singer in Rock Diva Online. "They create characters and play roles just like in a theater space, but their stage is cyberspace." Read the full article at http://www.cyber24.com/htm2/6_112.htm.

Out of fear of being ripped off, Web surfers now use extra caution to protect themselves. You've most likely heard the advice before: Don't give out your password; don't enter credit card numbers on unsecure servers; don't open an attached file from someone you don't know; and don't post your phone number on message boards. In other words, when you're on the Internet, watch your back and look out for the bad guys, who could be lurking just around the corner in the next e-mail you open or Web site you visit.

It's Time to Expose Your Identity

Right in the middle of this distrustful online atmosphere comes your new commitment to brand yourself on the Web. That means you not only reveal yourself online, you go out of your way to make anyone who will listen aware of who you are and what you do. Unlike many folks who communicate behind a veil on the Internet, you are honest and forthcoming—perhaps even a little extroverted and controversial. But you don't express yourself behind the haze of a fishy e-mail name. Instead, you state your case confidently and make it clear who is sending your message—because, after all, you *are* the message. Let's take a look at some of the key branding attributes that will help you stake a claim in these murky Internet waters.

How to Overcome Online Identity Obstacles

Although we delve into some of the following topics in more depth in other chapters of this book, here, in a nutshell, is how building your personal brand online is essential when dealing with consumer insecurities on the Internet. To succeed online, you must do the following:

Build trust—Not only must people know who you are, they also need to feel certain that you conduct yourself honestly and with integrity. You build trust with everything you do—and don't do. If you promise a response within two days, make sure you don't let more than 48 hours slip by without responding. If you offer a weekly newsletter, stick to that schedule (I've made the mistake of straying from a publishing schedule—and I can tell you, business is better when you deliver what you promise).

Have a consistent theme—Being clear about who you are and what you offer instills confidence in the people who are attracted to your message. If you create confusion as to what you represent, it leads to uneasiness and skepticism in the people you're trying to win over. For example, Terri Lonier's **Working Solo** Web site, at http://www.workingsolo.com/, (shown in Figure 1.5) does a good job of telling visitors what they're in for when they arrive.

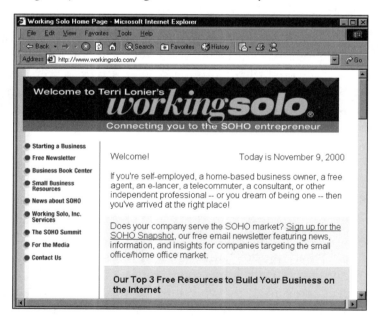

FIGURE 1.5: Terri Lonier's Working Solo site is clear about who she is and what she does. Clarity conveys confidence.

Use repetition—The best way to build trust is to become a recognizable name that stands for something specific. Consider this scenario: You're hiring a Web site designer. You receive e-mail pitches from two designers. You've been receiving one designer's e-mail newsletter twice a month for the last six months, but the other designer is contacting you for the first time.

Based on samples at their Web sites, both appear to be equally talented. Which one are you most likely to go with?

Be available—People stay away from Internet marketers who appear to be hiding something. To brand yourself online, you absolutely must come out of the shadows and stand proudly in the direct sunlight. That means on your Web site and in your e-mail newsletters you must include options for contacting you, including an e-mail address, physical address, and phone number. (A fax number is helpful, but optional.) Even if people never use them, it demonstrates that you're not afraid to be available. If you don't want to use your home contact info, rent a post office box and use a business voice mail number, as I've done for many years. I don't get many business-related phone calls, but I still spend $8 a month for voice mail so that I can display the number on my Web sites.

Assure people you won't abuse their personal info—This practice is pretty common these days, and for good reason. People are concerned that their e-mail addresses and other personal data will be sold or rented to other companies, and that they'll be bombarded with unwanted e-mail messages (known as *spam*). However, it's also important to collect e-mail addresses and other information from people who are interested in who you are. Therefore, whenever you ask for personal details, let people know how that information will be used. Then stick to using that info as you promised.

Your Privacy Statement—*If you ask people for their e-mail addresses, include a statement like this near the sign-up form: "I do not sell, rent, trade, or give away e-mail addresses. Your information is safe and secure, and will only be used by me to send information you asked for."*

Why Branding Yourself Is the Best Solution

Using the personal online branding techniques in this book is the best way to overcome the paranoia so prevalent among people who venture onto the Internet. Building a laser-focused identity and solid reputation quickly evaporates the natural skepticism your potential fans and customers have when they first hear of you. Here are a few more branding concepts you should keep in mind as you establish your identity online:

Touch people—Unscrupulous Internet marketers are out to make a sale by any means necessary. On the other hand, people who effectively brand themselves online are interested in making personal connections with a particular group of people. Make it your job to do some or all of the following on a regular basis: inspire people; reveal memorable personal experiences; express your gratitude; take a stand on a current issue; stir things up; vent your anger toward a common obstacle you share with your audience; recount your success stories; and make people feel good about themselves.

Teach people—I can't think of a field whose practitioners wouldn't benefit from educating their target audience. Copywriter **Bob Bly** (http://www.bly.com/) has not only written several books on the craft of writing marketing and PR copy, he also offers free articles on how to hire a copywriter and, once hired, how to best work with one. The benefit of offering this free information, of course, is to position Bob Bly as the best person to hire when a copywriter is needed. Teach your customers something that helps establish you as the most knowledgeable person in your field.

Exploit third-party endorsements—You telling people how great you are is one thing. Having an objective party (whether it's a customer, media outlet, or respected expert) say you're cool, now that's something to brag about. When you win an award, get a raving review, receive a comment from a happy customer, or get a recommendation from an authority in your field, it validates your contribution to your area of expertise and builds your personal brand and reputation as a person to be reckoned with in your field.

Maintain your visibility—By the time you finish reading this book, you'll have a full arsenal of tools to help you keep your name and brand identity in front of your target audience. It's vitally important that you make consistent visibility your goal. Whether it's contributing an article to a Web site, being interviewed on the radio, arranging a cross-promotion with a company or other expert, or being quoted in a magazine feature, the more your name and message is embedded into the public consciousness, the more you will be respected, admired, and trusted.

The Online Branding Balancing Act

Building an online brand can be confusing. Where do you put the focus? On you, or on the type of customer or fan you're trying to attract? As children, we're taught to think of other's needs before our own. We're scolded whenever we act in any manner that resembles being self-centered. However, any adult who has ever read a self-help book on positive thinking knows that the prevailing advice is to love yourself and take care of your own needs first. Talk about an identity crisis!

The same goes for personal branding. Focus too much on yourself and what you offer and you're "branded" as being an egomaniac; but if you cater so much to the customer that your personality fades to the background, you end up being just another generic online peddler. The answer lies in finding the right balance.

The objective of branding yourself online doesn't mean you stand on a hilltop and shout, "Hey, look at me! Don't you think I'm cool?" Instead, successful branders discover what avenues they need to use to reach the people most likely to be interested in their message. Then they use those avenues to confidently say, "Hello, this is my name and this is what I do. Now here's what I think about it and here's how I can help you pursue this particular path." The most successful people (online and offline) don't have to twist arms to convince other people that they are worthy. The quality of who they are surges through everything they do. It's a natural byproduct of the image they project and the information they distribute.

At the same time, it's not unusual to have some self-doubt. You may have some reservations as to whether you're truly worthy to take on a brand identity, but people who are successful in branding themselves feel confident that they are deserving of attention. Make certain your chosen field is one that's right for you. Don't pursue it unless you're willing to attach your name to everything you do in an ongoing effort to increase your notoriety, and don't wait for someone to give you the green light before you assume your new role. An attitude of worthiness doesn't come from an outside source; it comes from within.

Marketing consultant **Dan Kennedy** (http://www.dankennedy.com/, shown in Figure 1.6) refers to this frame of mind as *self-appointment*. Instead of waiting for approval, a degree, a promotion, or reaching some predetermined level, truly successful people decide that they are already worthy of success and start acting like it. "Most people wait around for someone else to recognize them, to give them permission to be successful," Kennedy writes in his *Ultimate No B.S. Business Book*. "You don't need anybody's permission to be successful. If you wait for the establishment in any given field to grant you permission, you'll wait a long, long time."

Benjamin Franklin's Opinion—*"God helps them that help themselves."*
—*Poor Richard's Almanack*

Noted self-help author **Wayne Dyer** (http://SuccessLISTS.com/wayne-dyer/) has similar advice on the concept of success that can easily be applied to personal branding. Dyer contends that success is not a destination you reach. Instead, success is something that exists inside of you that you bring to everything you do. It's not something you go and get; it's something you make a decision to be and demonstrate through your actions. The bottom line is that your attitude of success can and should be displayed confidently without your feeling guilty for promoting yourself.

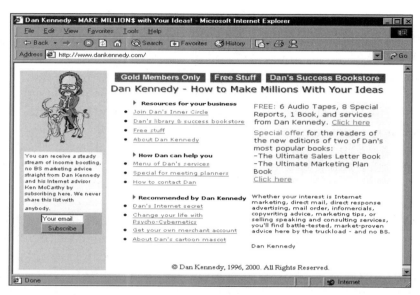

FIGURE 1.6: Dan Kennedy's home page demonstrates how he "self-appoints" himself to be a source of good marketing advice. Notice the clever use of his name, cartoon image, and confident (yet personal) writing style.

Are You a Self-Promotion Introvert?—*For more inspiration on how to overcome promotional shyness, read Dan Kennedy's article "How to Sell Your Way Through Life," available online at* http://www.dankennedy.com/dkartcl1.html.

Additional Resources for Your Branding Homework

Do you want a few different perspectives on building a brand name? Here are several articles from various Web sites that cover the subject well:

Building Your Brand Online
http://www.aibn.com/buildbrand.html

Tips on Creating a Brand Identity for Your Site
http://www.infoscavenger.com/brand.htm

How to Build an Online Brand
http://www.startitnow.com/book01/ch03/a04.htm

The Brand Called URL
http://www.fastcompany.com/online/resources/brandurl.html

You Are Your URL
http://www.fastcompany.com/online/04/urls.html

Build Your Marketing Muscle—*While this book gives you the tools you need to brand yourself online, you should absorb as much information as you can on the broader topic of marketing and promoting online. A great place to start is* Poor Richard's Internet Marketing and Promotions *(Second Edition) by Peter Kent and Tara Calishain, Top Floor Publishing. Get more details on this title at* http://topfloor.com/pr/promo/index.htm.

Build Your Brand with Online Resources
http://www.canadacomputes.com/v3/story/1,1017,1056,00.html?tag=81&sb=125

How to Build an Online Brand
http://www.fm.co.za/00/0929/admark/cam.htm

Web Site Promotion and Marketing Strategies
http://www.infoscavenger.com/promo.htm

Are you getting excited by the prospects of branding yourself online? Good. In the next chapter we get busy crafting the best brand identity for you.

CHAPTER TWO

Crafting Your Best Brand Identity

If you've read Chapter 1, "The Brand Called You," you're sold on the idea that branding yourself online is a good thing. You're pumped and ready to promote your brains out. But before you proceed, hold on! It's vitally important to have a solid idea of exactly what kind of identity you want to expose to the world. The last thing you want to do is start out with one message, switch to another, and then decide a third image is the one you really want. Once people get an initial impression of what you stand for, the thing that keeps them coming back—and turns them into loyal fans—is consistency.

In this chapter, we cover how to use a fan-club mentality to position your brand identity and why narrowing your focus is the best way to attract attention. We also talk about a list of questions and self-evaluations you must consider before embarking on your branding endeavors. Once your message is determined, we discuss the best ways to convey your image to the masses. Throughout the chapter, we look at examples of people who are successfully branding themselves online and off and how you can borrow their brand-building tactics to use in your own promotional efforts.

Develop a Fan-Club Mentality

Admit it, recognition is a wonderful thing. When people praise you for a product you create, an idea you express, or a service you render, it feels good. I've been playing in rock bands for years and know the satisfaction that comes with having fans. It's great to meet people who are touched in some positive way by what you do.

The term *fan* is typically associated with people in glamour fields—actors, athletes, rock stars, comedians, etc. Most people, though, circulate in nonglamour fields and are used to dealing with customers, buyers, and patrons. In fact, I used to describe people who complimented my articles and books as "happy readers," or if they purchased something, "satisfied customers." But since honing my online identity, I regularly receive e-mail messages from people who write something like "Hi, Bob. I've been a subscriber to your newsletter for six months. I'm a big fan." There's that glamour word again.

Sure, you could use your brand name to cultivate customers, visitors, members, users, or whatever you call people who are attracted to what you do, but your online efforts will be more effective (and a lot more fun) if you make creating *fans* your primary goal. *Patrons* are people who visit your Web site, subscribe to your newsletter, and pay for your services. *Fans*, on the other hand, cheer you on, rave about you to their friends, follow everything you do with interest, go to great lengths to attend your public appearances, and more. Which would you rather have?

Successfully pinpointing your online brand identity as an individual can mean the difference between attracting patrons and creating fans. Here are some examples to clarify this concept: *Self* magazine has readers; Oprah Winfrey's magazine is read by fans. The Republican National Committee has members; Rush Limbaugh has fans. The radio program *All Things Considered* has listeners; Howard Stern has fans. *Entertainment Tonight* has viewers; David Letterman has fans. The Dallas Cowboy Cheerleaders have admirers; Pamela Anderson has ... you guessed it, fans.

What Can Stephen King Teach Us?—*Stephen King maneuvered around his publisher when he sold previously unpublished novels to fans directly from his personal Web site. This bold move proves that the magnetism of a brand lies in the creator, not the company who sponsors him or her. The Internet allows talented people who aren't afraid to promote themselves to bypass the institutions they once depended on for success. Why go through the middleman when it's so easy to directly reach the public at large?*

Titles, business entities, and logos sometimes sneak into the public consciousness and become popular through massive advertising campaigns, but the real power of brands lies in the essence of an individual. Why else do so many companies hire Michael Jordan, Mark McGwire, Cindy Crawford, and other celebrities to hawk their wares? The magnetism of certain well-known individuals is so strong, companies hope some of that good-vibe attraction will rub off on their products. To find out more about celebrities in a variety of fields, take a look at **The Celebrity Cafe**, at http://www.thecelebritycafe.com/, shown in Figure 2.1.

What do you have to do to inspire people you don't know (yet) to become your fans? Here are some of the reasons people may enthusiastically connect with you, along with real-life examples of famous people who illustrate each reason:

FIGURE 2.1: The Celebrity Cafe site features interviews with countless celebrities in a variety of fields and is a good source for finding out how well-known people position themselves and take advantage of their appealing qualities.

- Fans strongly agree with your distinct point of view (Dr. Laura Schlessinger, Ross Perot)
- Fans are entertained by you (Chris Rock, Rosie O'Donnell)
- Fans respect your background and the experiences you've been through (Jesse Jackson, Sen. John Glenn)
- Fans admire your talents (Eric Clapton, Wayne Gretzky)
- Fans are inspired by you (Deepak Chopra, Brian Tracy)
- Fans are impressed by your reputation (Steve Jobs, Cal Ripken Jr.)
- Fans think you're attractive (Brad Pitt, Bo Derek)
- Fans are drawn to your outrageousness (Dennis Rodman, Richard Simmons)
- Fans are impressed by the people with whom you are associated (James Carville, Prince William)
- Fans enjoy your personality (Catie Couric, Regis Philbin)

Please note, though, that many people who attract fans do so for more than one reason. Consider pop star Madonna, one of the most prolific self-promoters of the past couple of decades. Her fans could easily claim all of the reasons listed previously to connect with her. Your appeal doesn't have to be one-dimensional (and you don't necessarily have to dance in a leather suit to be noticed), but your public identity must be focused for you to have any chance of widespread notoriety.

Positioning Is Important

Al Ries and Jack Trout coined the term "positioning" in the early 1980s in their book, *Positioning: The Battle for Your Mind*. Although a few years have passed since the book was released, the core ideas they express are just as true today. *Positioning* refers to the way a product, service, or person is presented to the buying public. To properly position yourself on the Internet, you must consider many factors:

- Your name
- Your Web address (URL)
- The benefits of what you offer
- Your personal strengths and weaknesses
- The strengths and weaknesses of your competition
- How people generally perceive the category in which you seek an impact

Ries and Trout contend that positioning is not something you do to a product, service, or to yourself. It's something you do to a human mind. It's all about perception and how you fit in—especially when compared to the other perceptions that already exist in each potential fan's brain. Crafting the best identity for you is an inside job. In other words, you shouldn't conjure up an image you feel would be cool and then mold yourself into that identity. The brand you create should be based on who you truly are as a human being. It should reflect your real skills and personality. Remember the pop duo Milli Vanilli and the fallout that occurred when it was discovered they didn't actually sing on their best-selling album? Faking it doesn't work.

The same goes for the person on the other end of the positioning equation—your potential fan. A person's preferences and view of the world are influenced mainly by the memories and attitudes that already exist in his or her mind, which explains why most people aren't easily swayed by dazzling advertising blitzes and publicity campaigns. If they were, every dotcom company that ran a Super Bowl ad would be prospering today. The truth is, they're not.

Remember the Pets.com sock puppet? The company used the mascot in a flurry of television ads in early 2000. Nine months later, when the Web site shut its doors, it was just another stray dog that had lost its way. The mistake Pets.com made was assuming that, since consumers were spending millions online buying books and airline tickets, people would also buy pet supplies in the same manner—if only the company got the word out on a grand enough scale. But people didn't bite for many reasons: They simply weren't ready to purchase pet products in the same way they purchased books, plus there were already a number of competitors in the pet category.

The Sock-Puppet Saga—The defunct Pets.com Web site may not have persuaded the public to buy pet supplies online, but it did do a great job of promoting its sock-puppet mascot, which was featured extensively in its television ad campaign. In fact, the puppet ended up being the site's top-selling product. When a toy for humans is one of the best-selling items in a store selling pet products, you know you're in trouble. Lesson: Clever gimmicks alone won't guarantee that your brand will succeed.

Bottom line: The mental perceptions that exist inside the minds of people who make up your target audience are just as important as your ideas about how you'd like to be perceived. Online book sales offer another example. In the mid 1990s, who was in the best position to sell a lot of books on the Internet? Perhaps brick-and-mortar behemoths Barnes & Noble or Borders? You'd think so. But who sells the most books online today? That's right, Amazon.com—the first book-selling identity to make a splash on the Internet.

For every 12 books sold online, 11 are purchased through Amazon—a company that in short order established itself as the online retailer of choice for people who want to buy books. Barnes & Noble and Borders have expended a lot of money and effort trying to play catch-up, but the mental perception has already been established that Amazon is the leader, and once ingrained, that perception is hard to undo.

Define Your Brand Focus

You may not be a corporation or big-name celebrity, but the lessons learned by examining high-profile names can help you craft your online brand identity. For instance, one of the key elements that propel successful brands—and successful people—is having a defined focus. After all, that's what a brand name does: It stands for something specific to a particular group of people you hope to transform into fans.

Let's look at an example on a smaller scale. Rebecca Kemp is an artist. Like thousands of artists, she is promoting herself through her Web site and other online avenues. To keep from being lost in the over-saturated cyberspace marketplace, she sets herself apart by focusing on her specialties: wildlife and fantasy art. Take a look at her Web site, **Becky's Wildlife & Fantasy Art**, at http://www.wildlife-fantasy.com/ (shown in Figure 2.2). She not only sells her artwork imprinted on T-shirts, coffee mugs, and mouse pads, Kemp also holds animal trivia contests, publishes an e-mail newsletter, exchanges links with other wildlife and fantasy artists, offers an affiliate program, and more.

FIGURE 2.2: Becky's Wildlife Art site provides a nice example of how a person can brand himself or herself as a specialist online.

At the top of her home page, she prominently displays the name of the site: "Becky's Wildlife and Fantasy Art," so there's no doubt about what type of art she enjoys and creates. Becky could have easily decided to be more generic with her marketing approach and call the site Becky's Art Site; but what is a Becky's Art Site besides a site that has something to do with art and is maintained by someone named Becky? Name recognition means nothing if the name isn't associated with something specific. Art is too broad a subject. Does it refer to abstract, still life, landscape, portrait, impressionistic, or what?

You need to supply your potential fans with a hook on which to hang your name. Becky could have zeroed in even tighter on her specialty by choosing either wildlife or fantasy to be her primary specialty. Plus, she might have specified a particular medium, such as Becky's Wildlife Watercolor Art or Becky's Fantasy Pastel Art. Still, her site serves as a good example of how one person can effectively home in on a specialty area and exploit it.

Regardless of what your general area of expertise is, you must focus on a particular slice of the pie and make certain your name is attached to it. Think of this concept as Nitro (your name) and Glycerin (your specialty). Either ingredient alone is powerless. Put them together and you have an explosive combination.

Imagine that you suddenly develop an interest in left-handed bowlers. Not knowing where to turn for more information, you head to your favorite Web search engine and type in the keywords "left-handed" and "bowler." After looking through a few uninformative links, you come across the name Harold Fernburger. One click later and you're at Harold's site looking over a cornucopia of articles, photo galleries, message boards, and links to all things left-handed bowler–related. You subscribe to Harold Fernburger's *Southpaw Strike* e-mail newsletter and vow to return to his site often, since he adds new information every week.

What just happened? Before you made this discovery, the name Harold Fernburger meant nothing to you. It was just another name is a sea of names. Before you stumbled upon his site, the topic of left-handed bowlers gave you no reference points or associations; it brought up a blank screen in your mind. Once you found his site, the two things—the name and the specialty—were not only connected, they were welded together in your brain. The next time you go looking for information on lefties who wear those funny shoes, you'll most likely head straight to Harold's site (or use the key words "Harold Fernburger" in a search). That's the difference between fuzzy branding and having your name and identity sharply in focus.

Be First, Be Fresh, Be Different—*To succeed at branding yourself, you need to be first in a category ... not just first in being associated with a product or service, but first in the mind of a fan. According to Laura Ries (who co-authored the book* The 11 Immutable Laws of Internet Branding *with her father, Al Ries), if you're not first in your category, you should strive to be the opposite of the leader. "If Coke is focusing on the older generation, Pepsi should focus on the younger generation. If McDonald's is focusing on kids, Burger King should focus on adults." Visit the authors' Web site, Ries & Ries, at* http://www.ries.com/.

Pop quiz: What's your primary goal as you move toward branding yourself online? That's right, to help people make the connection between your name and what it stands for. Getting your name out there is a noble goal, but it means nothing if your name gets out there without its loyal travel companion: your unique identity—the thing that sets you apart from other people in your general field. Here are a few examples of people carving out a defined niche on the Internet:

Sam Gugino—Gugino is a journalist who could probably write well on any number of subjects, but he uses his Web site to clarify his specialty. Gugino is a food writer and wine columnist who provides wine and nutrition guides, recipes, and more in a monthly e-mail newsletter. Also note how he has cleverly chosen his Web site address http://www.samcooks.com/

Bob Johnson's Auto Literature—Johnson's site obviously sells literature on cars and trucks, which is a niche category by itself, but Johnson further focuses his identity by specializing in factory literature: owner's manuals, repair guides, etc. http://www.autopaper.com/

Manfred Schmidt Collectible Cameras—As his home page explains, Schmidt took his passion for a particular aspect of photography and became a full-time dealer of antique and collectible cameras and accessories. His Web site spells that out for visitors. http://www.manfredschmidt.com/

Troy Hartman—If you're interested in skydiving and daredevil aerial feats, Hartman is your man. His site, depicted in Figure 2.3, is all about him and his many high-profile skydiving stunts. http://www.troyhartman.com/

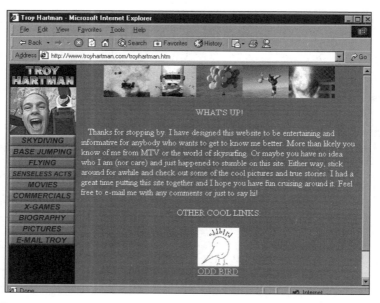

FIGURE 2.3: Troy Hartman's Web site focuses on his career as a skydiving stunt man. He doesn't confuse people by also covering any other interests he may have. It's all about Hartman and skydiving.

How to Determine Your Brand Identity

Before you run headlong into cyberspace to promote your brand, it's important that you have a rock-solid understanding of how your brand is presented—and why it's the best identity for you. What follows are a series of questions and self-evaluation exercises to help you uncover your ideal brand image. Even if you feel you already know who you are and what you stand for, these exercises will help refine your brand so that you'll have the best chance of success on the Internet.

My advice is don't just go through these questions in your head. Grab a notebook and write your answers and thoughts in a concrete form that will allow these concepts to sink in and be put to use.

What Are You Passionate About?

If you don't have a passion for your chosen area of expertise, your career will be filled with challenges. Many people pursue vocations because of family pressures or the urgings of school authority figures. Others decide to enter a career based on what they perceive as a hot trend or a guaranteed moneymaker. Unfortunately, the road to fame and fortune is littered with failures and unhappy business people who were sidetracked following a path that led to low satisfaction and lower self-esteem. Having a passion for the subject related to your brand identity is crucial.

To discover some of the things that really matter to you, write down answers to the following questions:

- If you won the lottery and never had to work another day in your life, what things would you want to accomplish?
- If you were told you had six months to live, how would you spend your time?
- At the end of your life, what would you most like to be known for?
- What reoccurring interests have you had since you were a child?

The most fulfilling careers allow you to make money doing something you'd do anyway for free. Before you start wondering if there's cash to be made by reclining on a couch and watching game shows or football, realize that most people have to dig a little deeper to find their true calling. We all have personal passions that creep up on us at regular intervals; activities we're drawn to whenever we have spare time. Those interests may hold the key to discovering your online brand.

It's also important to choose a brand identity that gives you a sense of contribution—a feeling that you are fulfilling a purpose and that your work will have an impact long after you have passed on. Additionally, successful people who follow their true calling can usually trace their skills and talents back to childhood. For instance, my fascination with music, writing, and art started when I was in early grade school. What interests have popped up regularly throughout your life? Have you ever given them serious thought or have you simply dismissed them? Instead of suppressing those inclinations, examine them with a more objective eye.

***Do What You Are**—Paul D. Tieger and Barbara Barron-Tieger, in their book* Do What You Are, *write: "The secret of career satisfaction lies in doing what you enjoy most. A few lucky people discover this secret early in life, but most of us are caught in a psychological wrestling match, torn between what we think we can do, what we (or others) feel we ought to do, and what we think we want to do ... Concentrate instead on who you are, and the rest will fall into place." Visit the authors' Web site, Personality Type, at* http://www.personalitytype.com/.

If you're reading this book, you probably already have a brand identity in mind. If that's the case, ask yourself the following questions:

- Will you feel good getting up every morning to work on this topic?
- Are you excited by the thought of being known for years to come as a specialist in this field?
- Will you feel proud describing your work to others?
- Are you optimistic about the prospect of succeeding in this field?

If you answered "yes" to all of these questions, you're on the right track.

What Are You Knowledgeable About?

When asked about the ingredients to a successful career, business consultant and author Tom Peters once commented, "You have to know a lot about something of significant value to a bunch of potential clients." That advice sounds simple enough. So, what do you know? Look in your notebook at the list of things you're passionate about and answer these questions:

- What do you already know about this subject?
- What direct experience have you had in this area?
- How easy is it to access experts and other information resources in this field?
- In what areas are you lacking information?
- What would you need to learn to feel comfortable saying you are an expert in this field?

The first thing you must do is determine whether the branding identity you are considering is based on a curious fascination with a topic or your first-hand experiences. I decided to become a music-marketing consultant for independent bands after years of playing in bands, interviewing musicians, circulating in the music business, and actively marketing my own interests. I had the experience to back up that career direction.

That doesn't mean you shouldn't pursue an identity about which you still have a lot to learn. Only you can determine how wide the gap is between your interest level and your ability to deliver what's expected of you in your chosen field. You must also decide how much time you're willing to spend to get educated on your topic. Regardless of how much you currently know about your area of expertise, you must commit to ongoing study and research. Attend conferences, read books, compile a list of online resources, and most importantly, maintain a sense of wide-eyed curiosity about your chosen field; because, if you lose interest in it, so will your fans.

What Solutions Do You Provide?

The word *solution* is overused in the business world these days. Look through the *Yellow Pages* ads and you'll find countless businesses with names like Computer Solutions, Furniture Solutions, and Gardening Solutions. What's next? Pizza Solutions? Beef Jerky Solutions? Resolution Solutions? The reason this word is so popular is because it speaks to a crucial marketing issue: The most successful people provide valuable solutions to problems.

Think about it. Diet experts offer solutions for people who have a problem with being overweight. Entertainers have the answer for people faced with having a potentially boring party. Real estate agents smooth the hardships involved with selling a house. No matter how positive an image you have, the real reason customers and fans are drawn to you is rooted somewhere in a problem that you solve.

People take action because they either want to move closer to pleasure or away from pain. Of the two reasons, pain is the greater motivator. For example, when you had a college term paper due, the idea of how much pleasure you'd have hanging out with your friends was stronger than the pain associated with not starting the paper. But as the deadline grew closer, the painful idea of a failing grade far outweighed any pleasure you might get from being sociable, so you got moving on the term paper. The prospect of pain is a motivator, and you'll have a much more effective brand identity if you consider how your expertise provides the solution to people's problems.

Benefits Versus Features—*People who successfully brand themselves know the difference between stressing features and benefits. A feature is an attribute or description of your product or service (blue, small, quiet, comfortable) while a benefit is how a customer personally gains from the feature (save time, save money, feel good, be respected). It's important to always attach a corresponding benefit to every feature you mention; for example: "With XYZ Web Hosting, you get 50 Megs of space, which means you'll have peace of mind knowing you won't run out of room."*

Narrowing Your Focus Equals Power

This may be the single most important piece of advice in this chapter: *You can't be all things to all people.* Many ambitious people who brand themselves online make the mistake of trying to appeal to too broad a range of potential fans. Don't get caught in this trap. To create an indelible brand name for yourself, you must stand for something specific and *not* be a generalist in a wide-open field. Let's see how this principle works with some celebrities:

Rush Limbaugh is not just another lively radio talk show host; he's a passionate character who preaches about conservative values and embraces the Republican Party. Does everyone agree with him? Absolutely not. Does he try to appeal to the widest possible audience? Not a chance. Whether or not you agree with his politics, he knows his niche and sticks with it.

Eric Clapton has etched his place in musical history by being closely associated with blues-based rock music. It's reasonable to assume that a man of his talents could also flawlessly play jazz songs, Irish jigs, Appalachian folk tunes, and more. However, the songs he writes and the albums he releases are consistently focused on the blues. Couldn't he sell more records if he played all styles of music? No, because fans embrace him for what he's known for.

Wayne Gretzky is one of the greatest hockey players of all time. He often endorses hockey-related products and events. Some may say, "But sports is sports, and Wayne should be a spokesman for athletic competition of all kinds." Not so fast. Gretzky is most effective when he sticks to the specific niche he's most associated with.

Attempting to be all things to all people may seem like it expands your potential market of fans, but it actually does just the opposite. The wider you cast your branding net, the more watered down your message becomes. Remember, the human brain works by recognizing patterns and making connections. The more specific your brand is (to a point), the better your chances of inspiring a connection.

You could try to position yourself as Pat Smith, the gourmet chef, but the generic category of gourmet chef is blurred by the existence of hundreds of cooking and food-related experts and Web sites. There's no glue to make that identity stick in someone's mind. On the other hand, if you are Pat Smith, author of *How to Prepare Low-Carb Gourmet Meals for Under $5 Per Person*, you've moved closer to occupying a distinct position in your fans' minds.

If given the choice between being a big dog in a small yard and a small dog in a big yard (my apologies to fish lovers for not using the traditional metaphor), smart online branders aim for being the big dog. Another thing that happens when you narrow your brand focus is that the people who are attracted to you tend to be more loyal. For instance, the controversial Goth band Marilyn Manson only appeals to a small sliver of the general public, but people who do appreciate them are often cultlike in their devotion. The thin slice of the music fan pie that they command is more than enough to allow them to make a living playing their brand of music.

Contrary to typical corporate strategy, as an individual, you don't have to win over a huge percentage of the population to be hugely successful. If you made your name and brand identity known to just one-tenth of one percent of the United States population, you'd have more than 280,000 admirers. That's enough to establish you as a bonafide celebrity; but you'll only reach that level if you carefully choose your brand niche and own the category.

"Okay, Bob," you say, "what if my brand niche—the one that I'm genuinely passionate about—is in a category that's overpopulated with brand name people who have already established themselves?" The solution (there's that word again) is to create a brand-new category.

Consider the area of exercise experts, which for years has been filled with high-profile names from Jack Lelane and Richard Simmons to Kathy Smith and Jane Fonda. How do you break into such an overcrowded category? You don't. Instead of fighting the mental perception battle on such a wide front, you create a new battleground altogether—one that you dominate exclusively. Billy Blanks was just another martial arts practitioner until he became known for Tae-Bo. He didn't produce a set of videos on aerobic exercise or weight training or stair stepping. He created a completely fresh category, and now he's the Tae-Bo king. What category can you create and turn into your kingdom?

Think about the narrow-focus branding concept as you look over this list of Web sites that have effectively defined their online niche:

Jobs 4 HR—Monster.com is the clear leader in the general job site category, so this smart company sets itself apart by specializing in one area: jobs for human resources professionals—all HR-related, all the time. http://www.jobs4hr.com/

Varsity Books—Why compete with Amazon.com and try to sell every kind of book imaginable when you can specialize? Varsity Books, shown in Figure 2.4, does just that in the college textbook market. http://www.varsitybooks.com/

Baby's Away—A lot of companies are in the rental business, from cars and moving vans to furniture and cleaning equipment. Baby's Away rents only one type of product: items that parents might need to care for their babies while traveling. http://www.babysaway.com/

FIGURE 2.4: Varsity Books doesn't try to sell all kinds of books to all kinds of people. Its brand identity lies strictly in offering college textbooks online.

Developing Your Brand Identity Statement

You've probably heard the phrase, "unique selling proposition," also known simply as USP. It's been around since the 1950s, when advertising agencies started using the phrase to describe how their clients should present the benefits they offer to potential customers. Well, it's a new millennium, so I've taken it upon myself to coin a fresh phrase for a new generation. Ladies and gentlemen, please welcome the Brand Identity Statement (BIS).

A BIS is a concise phrase or motto that sums up what you do, why you are different, and how you provide a benefit—in other words, it lets potential fans know why they should care to know more about you.

Developing your BIS allows you to take all the ideas we've discussed thus far in this chapter, mix them in a blender, and compress them into a short, snappy statement of no more than 10 or 15 words that describes who you are and what you stand for. That's a lot to ask of a dozen or so words, but it can be done.

Your BIS should be crafted to include not only a description of what you do, but also a benefit to your customers. M&M's classic "Melts in your mouth, not in your hands" (only eight words) is a great example. The BIS I use to promote my Buzz Factor Web site is "Resources, tips, and tools that will change the way you promote your independent band or record label." (Okay, I cheated and used 17 words, but you get the picture.)

A Source of Inspiration—*Not long ago I changed the BIS for my Buzz Factor Web site from "Resources, tips, and tools to help you promote your independent band or record label" to "Resources, tips, and tools that will change the way you promote your independent band or record label." It's a subtle change, but I think it adds more impact. I was inspired to make the alteration after reading Chris Pirillo's* Poor Richard's E-mail Publishing, *Top Floor Publishing. Get more details online at* http://topfloor.com/pr/email/.

The ideal BIS tightly focuses on exactly who you are, what you do, and how it benefits potential customers and fans. It should leave no doubt in the prospect's mind as to what he or she gets from you. You can use your BIS in two ways; one is internal, the other external.

Internal—A good BIS keeps you focused on your marketing message. Every time you send an e-mail, write a press release, post to a discussion group, or update your Web site, refer to your BIS. Doing so ensures that your brand image is crystal clear. You don't want your home page to convey humor while your e-mail newsletter is grim and serious. By constantly keeping your BIS in mind, you make sure the messages you send out over the Internet stay focused on what's going to establish your brand identity in the shortest amount of time.

External—You can also use your BIS as a personal slogan that appears on all your Web pages, banner ads, newsletters, press releases, e-mail messages, and more. That way, whenever someone hears or sees your name, he or she will be reminded of your core identity. Remember, your goal is to make mental connections that merge your name with what you stand for. Having your BIS appear every time your name appears online is one of the best ways to help people make that brand–identity connection.

Here are some real-life examples of Brand Identity Statements in action:

- Canada's Helios Design and Communications uses "Hard-hitting design, done right the first time."
- H&B Catalog of Jazz CDs claims to be "A mail order service for people who know jazz."
- Copywriter Luther Brock, who calls himself "The Letter Doctor," uses the phrase "High-response sales letters for firms on a limited budget."
- Chicago's Smart Studios promotes itself with the BIS "Great sounds. Cool people. Killer studio."

To make your online branding endeavors easier, keep your BIS message simple. Most people feel they need to fully explain themselves; that potential customers (fans) won't understand them and what they offer unless it's laid out in great detail. The reality is that people don't have time to absorb your whole story at first glance. Give them a simple message that quickly cuts through the clutter and leaves no doubt.

For instance, when Domino's Pizza was expanding and gaining notoriety decades ago, it could have tried to appeal to customers by telling them, "When you get home after a hard day at work, you and your family members are hungry. You want to eat a good, hot meal but don't have the time and energy to make it yourself. We can save you all that hassle and deliver a fresh pizza to you, and we'll do it within 30 minutes or less. If it takes longer than 30 minutes, we'll give you the pizza free." Well, people wouldn't have had the time and energy to muddle through the 72 words of that sales pitch. Instead, Domino's used 13 words to quickly convey its brand identity: "Fresh, hot pizza delivered to your door in 30 minutes or less, guaranteed." When creating a BIS, remember, less is more, so keep it short.

Don't Bore People to Death

I've lost count of the number of Web sites, e-mail newsletters, and online articles I've read while having to fight off yawns and wandering thoughts. I've seriously considered printing off some of the more mundane Internet promotions and placing copies in a drawer near my bed, just in case I ever suffer from insomnia. All it would take is a couple paragraphs of this dreck and I'd be sleeping like a baby.

Heed this lesson: When you communicate with people in an effort to promote your online brand image, you must be exciting, energetic, interesting, captivating, and intriguing. Whatever you do, don't bore people to tears with humdrum marketing materials. Let your personality shine through with everything you do. Don't be afraid to be conversational, to loosen up, and communicate with your fans as if they were sitting across a table from you. Be funny, be bold, be optimistic, and above all, be yourself.

A great example of light-hearted online branding principles in action is the Web site by illustrator Bob Staake, **BobStaake.com** at http://www.bobstaake.com/ (see Figure 2.5). Staake is an accomplished artist, author, and graphic designer. Over the years he's developed an inimitable, yet recognizable cartoon style of drawing. His illustrations have appeared in *MAD* magazine, on MTV and Nickelodeon, and in 26 children's books and how-to titles. Staake knows how to make good use of his name and personality online. Here are just some of the labels he uses for sections of his site:

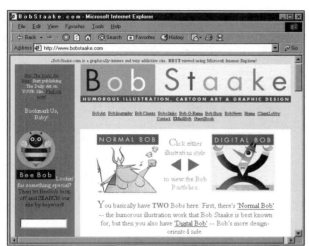

- Bob Art
- Bob News
- Bob Press
- The Daily Bob
- Bob-O-Rama
- Bobliography

FIGURE 2.5: Illustrator and graphic artist Bob Staake makes good use of his name and a light-hearted approach to promote his brand online.

What I like about Staake's site (besides the fact that it repeatedly uses *my* first name) is that he's filled it with tons of fun and informative content that reinforces who he is and what he does best. You can browse hundreds of examples of his artwork in any number of styles, take a step-by-step tour of how he creates some of his digital designs, get a sneak peek at children's books he's currently working on, send free Bob Staake greeting cards by e-mail, purchase some of his original art, and a lot more. If this isn't making good use of the Internet to build a personal and professional identity, I don't know what is.

Perhaps you feel the nature of your brand niche is perpetually void of personality. After all, how can you possibly be the life of the party if your specialty is accounting, tax preparation, dry cleaning, or plumbing? The same used to be said of car maintenance and repair. That is, until Tom and Ray Magliozzi made their mark on the world. Their *Car Talk* program on National Public Radio is heard by a throng of listeners every week in 450 cities; their newspaper column is syndicated to more than 300 newspapers; and their Web site, **Car Talk**, at http://cartalk.cars.com/, gets a lot of traffic. Why? Because the Magliozzi brothers bring warmth, humor, and personality to a useful subject that was previously thought of as dry and ... well, mechanical. Think seriously about how you can lighten up your brand identity and make it more interesting for your growing crop of fans.

Before you move to the next chapter, go through your notebook and nail down the ideal way you want to present your brand on the Internet. Next up: We gather the tools you need to launch your online branding attack.

CHAPTER THREE

Developing Your Branding Arsenal

This chapter gets down to the nitty-gritty of building your brand online. First, we must gather the troops and make sure you're armed with all the ammunition you'll need to make the biggest splash in the least amount of time. In this chapter, we cover the following topics:

- Making sure you understand computer and Internet basics
- Knowing where to turn to stay up to date on Web technology developments
- Choosing the all-important name you'll use to brand yourself online
- Introducing you to your new identity-building game plan
- Discussing how to compile your greatest branding weapon: your online database of targeted connections
- Getting into a marketing mind-set that allows you to repeatedly connect with your audience

By the time you finish this chapter, you'll be wired (both literally and figuratively) and ready to take your branding campaign into cyberspace. You'll be well on your way to choosing a brand name that works for your identity and you'll have a clear idea of how to hunt down the online sources that can best help you increase your notoriety. Armed with these tools, you'll be ready to set your corner of the Internet world on fire.

Getting Started

Chances are good that you already have a computer system and Internet access. If that's the case and you feel up to speed on how the Internet works, you may want to skim the next few pages and pick the discussion back up in the

"Choosing Your Brand Name" section. However, if you're just getting your feet wet in the wired world, or if you're considering a computer upgrade, this section should prove helpful.

You won't find any recommendations on specific makes and models here, but we do talk about some of the features you must consider. First, let's address the Macintosh versus Windows issue. I'll admit I was a Mac-only computer guy for many years. I still enjoy working on my Power PC and like the way the Macintosh operating system is set up, but there's no denying there are disadvantages to using a Mac exclusively. Microsoft's stronghold on the computer world has made Windows the system of choice for most people. However, many graphic designers and other computer pros swear by the Mac and find ways to make it work. The choice is up to you.

The Mac Minority—*Here are some sobering figures: According to StatMarket, at http://www.statmarket.com/, more than 92 percent of Internet users worldwide use a Windows operating system; whereas 3 percent use Macintosh. Talk about one operating system dominating the market!*

For more information on the operating system debate, check out the **Windows-Macintosh Feature Comparison** at http://www.execpc.com/~rjohnson/ics/features/index.html and About.com's **Mac vs. Windows** page of links at http://www.macos.about.com/compute/macos/cs/macvswin/.

Here are three online resources that explain what you need to know about computer systems:

The Basics of Buying a Personal Computer System
http://www.magicnet.net/~ericwat/buypc.htm

InfoHQ's Computer Buying Primer
http://www.infohq.com/Computer/computer-buying-primer.htm

Google Web Directory—Computer Buying Information
http://directory.google.com/Top/Computers/Shopping/Buying_Information/

Hardware from Hell—*Not only does **Trish's Escape from Hardware Hell**, at http://hardwarehell.com/ (shown in figure 3.1), provide an excellent directory of helpful computer-related links, it also serves as a good example of someone using her name to promote her expertise. There's that branding mantra again: Attach your name to an online description of who you are and then meld the two identities together.*

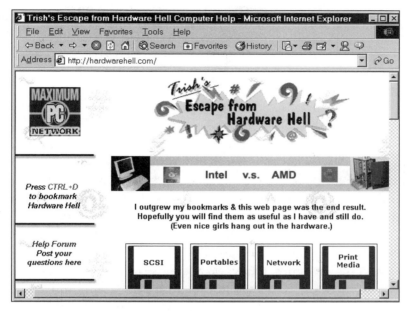

FIGURE 3.1: Trish's Escape from Hardware Hell is not only a good source for computer information, it's also a good example of a site that attaches a person's name to an identity.

Getting Connected to the Internet

Once you have a computer system in place, you must choose the method that will connect you to the Internet and the service provider that will allow you access. Here are the various connection options you have:

Telephone modem—A modem connects your computer to the Internet through the phone lines. Just about every new PC these days comes with a built-in 56K modem. 56K refers to 56 bits per second, a measure of how fast the modem can send and receive data. You can also buy an external modem and hook it up to your computer, which gives you flexibility in choosing the best modem for your needs. Resource: **56K.com** at http://www.56k.com/.

Cable—More and more cable TV companies are offering Internet access through cable wires. Cable connections are still not widely available in all areas and are sometimes a bear to install, but people who have them rave about their speed. Keep in mind that as the number of users in your vicinity increase, speed will decrease. Resources: **How Cable Modems Work** at http://www.howstuffworks.com/cable-modem.htm and **Cable Modem Help** at http://www.cablemodemhelp.com/.

DSL—Digital Subscriber Line is a service that phone companies have been aggressively marketing. DSL may be slower than cable but faster than your basic modem. Fortunately, the speed will remain constant as the number of users increases. Like cable, DSL is not available in all areas. Where it is available, the service usually comes packaged with Internet access and e-mail capabilities. Resources: **Everything DSL** at http://www.everythingdsl.com/ and **The DSL Zone** at http://thedslzone.com/.

ISDN—The next step down from DSL is asking the phone company to install an ISDN (Integrated Services Digital Network) line. However, the phone companies generally don't put much emphasis on this option, and therefore, the lines don't always work well. In fact, users joke that ISDN stands for *It Still Doesn't Work*; but it is another option to be aware of, especially in areas that don't currently offer alternatives. Resource: **ISDN Tutorial** at http://www.ralphb.net/ISDN/.

Satellite system—Hughes Network Systems and its competitors offer an Internet connection using satellite technology. The companies claim the hardware and service is available anywhere in the continental United States. Visit http://www.direcpc.com/ to find out more about how it works. Often, this option is the only choice among cable, ISDN, and satellite in rural areas, because ISDN and DSL are limited to customers within relatively short distances from their phone company's local switching office.

T1 and other options—The phone company and others may also be able to provide you with other services, such as a T1 line, fractional T1, or T3. These options usually carry a high price tag—more than most small business people and individuals care to pay. Resource: **All You Wanted to Know About T1 But Were Afraid to Ask** at http://www.dcbnet.com/notes/9611t1.html.

Internet Access Options

Even if you have a modem, cable, or other online connection, you still have to gain access to the Internet. The job of an Internet service provider (ISP) is to give you an onramp to the cyberspace highway. ISPs are similar to long-distance phone companies. Just because you have a phone doesn't mean you can immediately call your uncle in Montana. First you need to choose a long-distance provider (AT&T, MCI, Sprint, or any number of other companies). The same goes for ISPs. Here are the three basic types of ISPs:

- **True ISP**—These are companies that are primarily in business to provide Internet access and related services such as Web page design and Web hosting. True ISPs can range in size from local firms with a few hundred subscribers to national companies with hundreds of thousands.

- **Online service**—High-profile companies such as America Online (AOL), Microsoft Network (MSN), CompuServe (CSi), and Prodigy make up this category. They provide content and other features in addition to Internet access. You'll find news, weather, chat rooms, message boards, discussion groups, and a whole lot more. They offer more of a club membership feel than an ISP does while still connecting you to the Internet.

- **Phone or cable company**—A growing number of phone companies (including long-distance providers) are jumping into the ISP game. Cable companies are doing the same, so when you purchase a cable modem connection, you'll get Internet service thrown in with it. If you have DSL or an ISDN line installed, you'll probably be given the option of using the phone company as your ISP.

Are You Ready for WAP?—*Another option for logging onto the Web is using a cell phone-like wireless device. Wireless Application Protocol (WAP) allows manufacturers, networks, content providers, and application companies to develop compatible systems for handheld Internet devices. Don't get too excited, though, because there are only a limited number of WAP-enabled sites and only so much you can do with a palm-size screen. To make full use of the power of the Internet to brand yourself, you'll need a traditional computer system. Still, wireless is one aspect of technology to keep an eye on. For more information, visit **WAP.com** at* http://www.wap.com/.

Some experts feel that true ISPs offer the best customer service while the big online services allow for better access, since you can usually log on from whatever city you happen to be in. Again, the choice is yours. Here are a few online resources to help you become more informed on ISP issues:

ISPs—The Basics
http://www.connectyourfamily.com/Basics/isps.htm

How to Pick Your Internet Service Provider
http://www.pageland.com/isp/noframes/

Reviews of Internet Service Providers
http://www.epinions.com/cmsw-ISP

Find an ISP (searchable database of ISPs—shown in Figure 3.2)
http://www.findanisp.com/

Origins of the Web—*The World Wide Web was conceived in March 1989 by Tim Berners-Lee and others at CERN (Conseil Europeen pour la Recherche Nucleaire, now called European Laboratory for Particle Physics). The CERN scientists needed access to information available on a variety of computer systems. Berners-Lee came up with the idea of a universal approach that would allow anyone to read any piece of information online. Scientists involved in the Web's early development agreed that there should be no central control. They believed the Web would work because people would adhere to basic guidelines. As part of this Web ethic, anyone could publish and anyone authorized could read information.*

More Nuts and Bolts Resources

We've only brushed the surface of covering how the Internet works and what's involved in making sure everyone stays connected. Visit the following sites to get more details:

Basic Internet Terms for Newbies (just about any Internet-related word you can think of is listed and explained here)
http://www.jworkman.com/

FIGURE 3.2: Find an ISP is one of several sites with a searchable database of ISPs.

CIO—An Overview of the World Wide Web (how the Internet works and hints on how to use the Web)
http://www.cio.com/WebMaster/sem2_home.html

Discover How the Internet Really Works (an interactive series that covers e-mail, security, search engines, streaming media, and more)
http://www.learnthenet.com/english/animate/animate.htm

CNET—20 Questions: How the Net Works
http://coverage.cnet.com/Content/Features/Techno/Networks/

The Core Rules of Netiquette (the do's and don'ts of online communication)
http://www.albion.com/netiquette/corerules.html

Google Web Directory—Internet Help and Tutorials
http://directory.google.com/Top/Computers/Education/Internet/Help_and_Tutorials/

Stay on Top of Internet Developments

Nothing stands still for long in cyberspace, and that's why it's vitally important that you stay informed on changing issues and developments in the online world. One of the best ways to keep sharp is to regularly do your homework by visiting Internet news sources such as the following:

Yahoo! Internet Life (provides lots of info on interesting Web sites and trends)
http://www.zdnet.com/yil/

Internet News (covering Internet-related business news, advertising, and stock market issues)
http://www.internetnews.com/

The Standard (the online version of *The Industry Standard*, an e-commerce news source)
http://www.thestandard.net/

ZDNet (Internet and technology news, software reviews, and more)
http://www.zdnet.com/

***Pick and Choose Your News**—Just because you read about new trends or emerging markets on a news site doesn't mean you have to jump on every new gadget or Web strategy that comes down the pike. Honestly, I find it difficult to relate to most of the coverage given to multimillion dollar mergers, acquisitions, and IPOs, but it does help to be aware of the big Internet picture. As long as you know where your strengths lie and stay within your means, you can use your knowledge of new developments to your advantage.*

Internet World Online (described as "the essential business tool for Internet decision-making")
http://www.internetworld.com/

Traffic (follows Web portal trends)
http://www.traffick.com/

Yahoo! Internet and World Wide Web News
http://dailynews.yahoo.com/fc/Tech/Internet_and_World_Wide_Web/

Also, as you explore the Web, you'll discover a number of sites that cover news in your field. Add these industry-specific sites to your list of favorites and visit them often for the latest developments in your area of interest.

---

*Create Custom News by E-mail—In addition to searching the Web for the latest news and events related to your field, you can also have it delivered by e-mail. A number of sites offer a customized news delivery service. You indicate what topics or keywords you're interested in and the service scours news sites and e-mails you a list of results on a regular basis. Three such sites are **Crayon** at* http://crayon.net/, **InfoBeat** at http://www.infobeat.com/, *and **Individual.com** NewsPage at* http://www.individual.com/.

Choosing Your Brand Name

So far in this chapter, we've covered the basics of choosing a computer, getting Internet access, and becoming knowledgeable about Internet trends. Now we turn our attention to putting those tools to use in branding yourself. A recent *Business Week* magazine article commented, "With nothing to pick up or touch and hundreds of similar-sounding sites to choose from, online consumers have little to go on besides a familiar name." That observation sums up the heart of this section. To have the best chance of success online, you need to give potential customers and fans a name to remember—one they can use to find you with ease.

There are two types of names you must choose before embarking on your branding campaign:

- The name you use to promote yourself
- Your domain name (Web address)

Let's examine each one, starting with the name you use to promote yourself. Remember, on the Internet there are no tangible landmarks to help people remember where to find you. In the physical world, if you have a favorite Chinese restaurant, you don't have to know the name of the place to get to it. As long as you know the restaurant is located at the corner of Main Street and

Fifth Avenue, you'll always be able to find it. On the Internet, though, the name is everything. If you don't recall the name of the person, business, or Web address, you'll have a tough time tracking it down. Here are some of the options you have when choosing a brand name:

Use your real name—This is the most direct approach. If you're sold on the underlying premise of this book, it's a no-brainer to make your name the brand name. For example, one high-profile fashion company isn't called Cool Clothes Inc.; it's called Tommy Hilfiger. One popular TV program isn't titled *The Late-Afternoon Inspiration Hour Geared Primarily to Women*; it's called *Oprah*. The best way to establish yourself as an expert or to be widely recognized in your field is to use your real name as your brand name.

Use a stage name—Perhaps you have tons of personality, a pleasing visual appeal, and Internet techno savvy out the wazoo. The only thing holding you back is a user-*un*friendly name like Maude Cromwinkle-Swartz or Archibald K. Schraumboltenhofer. Fair enough. Even I'll admit that tongue-twisting names can pose problems for online brand-builders. If that's your situation, consider altering your name and using a cyberstage name instead. Film legend Kirk Douglas might have had a tough time gaining recognition if he had stuck with his real name, Isadore Demsky. The same principle applies to names that might confuse people or trigger unwanted associations. For instance, actor Albert Brooks decided not to use his real name, Albert Einstein, for good reason. Also, if you're going to use an assumed name, make sure it stands out. For example, have you ever heard of Eileen Twain? Probably not, but I'll bet you've heard of country music superstar Shania Twain, who successfully uses the unique stage name she chose for herself.

Use a company name—This is listed as your third option for a good reason: It's the least attractive of the three. Sure, many company brand names have made enormous waves on the Internet (America Online, Netscape, Napster, Amazon, etc.), which might cause you to consider coming up with a cool business moniker of your own. Brothers David and Tom Gardner did that when they created **The Motley Fool**, a series of books and a Web site (http://www.fool.com/) that cover personal finance and investing. Using a company name is an option to consider, but your personal branding goals will be met more forcefully if you use a human name instead of the name of an intangible business entity.

Choosing Your Domain Name

While you're mulling over the three types of brand names discussed in the preceding section, you must also consider how that name will work in tandem with a domain name—a particular Web site address that you register and own for as long as you want it. We cover the specifics of how to register a domain name and set up your own Web site in Chapter 5, "Creating Your Personal Brand Web Site." But for the purposes of the current chapter, we discuss the importance of choosing a domain name that complements your brand name.

If a friend tells you about a great new Web site or if you read about a site you can't wait to visit, what happens the next time you sit down at your computer? You type in the Web address, the same way your fans will when they start hearing and reading about you. Therefore, your domain name should have the following two qualities:

• It should be easy for people to hear and know immediately how to spell.

• It should be easy for people to remember after seeing it in print or on a computer screen.

Those qualities may seem simple, but they're not. Australian Charles Cave has an excellent, highly regarded site devoted to creative thinking skills called **Creativity Web**. The site's only drawback is its Web address: http://www.ozemail.com.au/~caveman/Creative/. No matter how much someone encouraged you to visit his site, what are the odds you'd remember (or even accurately write down) the full URL? Sure, you could probably remember "Creativity Web" and enter those words at a search engine and most likely find it; but why put your prospective fans through so much work? Make your domain simple, easy to remember, and simple enough to type accurately into a Web browser.

*Is Your Favorite Name Available?—If you're wondering whether the domain name you have in mind is available, surf to **Network Solutions** at http://networksolutions.com/. Enter the name you're considering and the site will let you know immediately whether the name is available as a .com, .net, or .org. In Chapter 5, we take a closer look at how to register a domain name and direct it to your Web site.*

Here are two types of domain names to consider:

Your exact name or business name—If your name is Carla Hall, the ideal Web address for you would be http://www.carlahall.com/ (shown in Figure 3.3). In fact, that was the domain name registered by singer-songwriter

FIGURE 3.3: Carla Hall's Web site promotes her career as a singer-songwriter and an author.

Carla Hall to promote her career. As I mentioned earlier, my music-marketing newsletter is called *The Buzz Factor*. It's an ideal phrase to describe the promotional "buzz" I help musicians create over their music. Therefore, I registered http://www.thebuzzfactor.com/. My readers are already familiar with the term, so it was easy for them to remember my Web site address and find me.

Your slightly altered name or business name—You may find that the domain name you want is already registered, or perhaps the brand name you've chosen doesn't lend itself to being a memorable Web address. For instance, even though David and Tom Gardner have registered http://www.motleyfool.com/, the URL they aggressively promote is the shorter http://www.fool.com/ (shown in Figure 3.4). There are just too many ways to misspell motley to rely on motleyfool alone. When I first looked into registering my name, I found that http://www.bobbaker.com/ was already being used by a Chevrolet dealer. However, http://www.bob-baker.com/ (with a hyphen separating the first and last name) was available, so I grabbed it.

You should also think about the way that brand names stick in people's minds before making final brand and domain name decisions. One mistake Internet

FIGURE 3.4: The Motley Fool is a good example of a site that wisely uses a shorter, simpler URL, http://www.fool.com, to make it easy for customers to remember and find the site.

entrepreneurs make is choosing a generic name that reflects the entire category, such as QualityLandscaper.com. The problem is that all people who specialize in this field promote themselves as quality landscapers. Nothing about that name stands out and triggers a distinct mental association.

Look at some of the more established Internet brands. The most recognized search directory isn't SearchDirectory.com; it's Yahoo.com. The most popular online bookstore isn't OnlineBookstore.com; it's Amazon.com. The most established job site isn't BigJobSite.com; it's Monster.com. There's no denying these sites have used advertising and publicity to etch their brand names into the public consciousness, but their wise choice of brand names did half of the marketing work.

What do Yahoo!, Amazon, and Monster have in common? They are simple, familiar words that are applied out of context to an online presence. It appears to defy logic, but using an obvious category reference in a name usually doesn't work as well as a name that's simple, clever, and unexpected. Here's the bottom line: Use your own name as a first choice, but if you must use a separate company name, stay away from generic phrases.

Don't Become a Name Stretcher —*Many people who experience success at establishing their brand name become overly confident and think they can expand what their name stands for. For example, Blockbuster did an excellent job of capturing the video rental market by establishing a retail presence in most major U.S. cities. Then the company extended its brand identity to music CD sales and created a massive chain of Blockbuster Music stores. The problem was, consumers associated Blockbuster with video, not music, and the business suffered as a result. Blockbuster Music locations were later transformed into Wherehouse Music, a separate brand identity that stands for music only. If you have another passion or side of your personality that's dying to get out, don't dilute your core brand name with an inflated message. Instead, establish a separate name, newsletter, and Web site for your other interests.*

Developing Your Brand-Building Game Plan

Promoting your brand online involves more than just assembling computer equipment, learning about the Internet, and choosing a name. To be successful, you must also upgrade your frame of mind. Every day presents a new opportunity to increase your notoriety, and you will build your brand name faster if you aim for specific goals. Here are the primary activities you must focus on:

Communicate using e-mail—If you're not an e-mail junkie yet, you will be soon; but you won't be sending joke messages or virus warnings to all your friends. You will be using e-mail to communicate with online media people and other movers and shakers in your field. You'll use e-mail to answer individual questions, carry on a personal dialog, and establish meaningful relationships with your fans. You'll turn your e-mail program into one of your most valuable communication tools.

Build and update your Web site—As important as e-mail is, you still need a place where your fans can go and get to know you in a more visually appealing and interactive environment. Your Web site satisfies that need. Once you build this inviting online gathering place, you must spend time regularly updating your Web site so that your fans have plenty of reasons to return often.

Publish your own e-mail newsletter—This falls under the e-mail umbrella, but I list it separately to emphasize the importance of creating an electronic publication. Start sending regular e-mail messages to your legion of fans to keep them abreast of your latest ideas and activities. No matter what other promotional avenues you pursue, make time for an e-mail newsletter.

Network through a variety of sources—You enjoy making new friends, don't you? If not, you better learn to enjoy it, because branding yourself online involves meeting lots of people. But these won't be awkward introductions, since you'll be connecting with folks who share a passion for your specialty. The Internet may seem cold and impersonal, but your new commitment to networking will make being online more lively than happy hour at your favorite local pub.

Seek out and generate publicity—While you're making all those new connections, you'll also develop an instinct for generating newsworthy ideas. Newsletter editors, Webmasters, reviewers, and feature writers need fresh content to feed to their audiences. It's now your job to satisfy their hunger by regularly sending press releases and engaging in media-friendly activities.

Compiling Your Branding Database

Branding involves communicating with a lot of people on a consistent basis. The Internet is so vast with so many people playing influential roles, it's easy to get overwhelmed and not know where to turn next. The solution is to create a database of the various people you'll be communicating with. I frequently get e-mails from readers who ask me for suggestions about whom they should contact to promote their music, art, design skills, or other special talent. Unfortunately, I can rarely give them a quick answer. Each individual has a different set of contacts that is ideal for his or her situation. There are not many generic, catchall marketing resources online, which means you'll be spending a good amount of time doing research to uncover Internet sources that are perfectly suited to your identity.

Before you start compiling this database, make sure you understand what type of contacts you'll be hunting for. As you search, be on the lookout for resources that may potentially help you in any of the following ways:

- Give you editorial mentions or write full articles about you (newsletter editors, content managers, journalists)
- Allow you to post information about yourself (link directories, message boards, classified ad pages, mailing lists)
- Write a review of your product (reviewers, Web site guides)
- Recommend you to visitors or readers (recognized experts in your field, authors, columnists)
- Exchange links and ads with you (Webmasters, newsletter publishers)
- Allow you to interact with like-minded people and demonstrate your knowledge (chat rooms, online communities and clubs, discussion groups)

Searching for industry-specific contacts is not a chore you do for a week or two and then stop. It's a process that will continue throughout your career, since the amount of online information is growing all the time. To keep track of it all, you need to store your resource data. I recommend using contact-management software that will allow you to enter details into separate fields. Contact-management software also gives you the ability to categorize each entry and easily find certain contacts by searching your entire database for them. Here are a few contact-management software applications to consider:

ACT
http://www.act.com/

FileMaker
http://www.filemaker.com/

MySoftware
http://www.mysoftware.com/

GoldMine
http://www.goldmine.com/

Maximizer
http://www.multiactive.com/smbiz/maximizer/

Playing the Fields—Most contact-management software applications allow you to create your own template into which you enter information. You can also determine what fields you include in your template. Keep it simple. Your primary fields should be Web site name, Web site URL, contact name, contact e-mail, and a description of the site. It's also helpful to either create a drop-down menu or come up with a code for categorizing each entry. That way, you can indicate whether an entry is a media outlet, newsletter, link directory, etc. Having clearly and consistently marked fields allows you to search your database and find certain types of resources quickly.

Where to Search

The Internet has often been referred to as the world's largest reference library. You can find information on practically every imaginable topic, so it won't take long to track down sources through which you can promote your brand. To help you find these sites even faster, I recommend you start by using the resources listed in the sections that follow.

Web Directories

There are a lot of similarities between Web directories (covered in this section) and portals and search engines (covered in later sections). Web directories feature categorized listings of Web sites, often compiled by human editors who evaluate thousands of sites and determine which ones are worthy of being added to the directory. A Web directory home page usually starts with a listing of about a dozen broad topics. Every click on a category takes you to a deeper level of subcategories until you get to the specific topic you're seeking. For a lengthy list of Web directories, check out the **Google Web Directories** page at http://directory.google.com/Top/Computers/Internet/WWW/Searching_the_Web/Directories/. Here are eight of the more notable Web directories:

Google Directory
http://directory.google.com/

Magellan
http://magellan.excite.com/

LookSmart
http://www.looksmart.com/

Starting Page—Best of the Web
http://www.startingpage.com/

Rough Guides Internet: Web Directory
http://www.roughguides.com/internet/directory/

The Argus Clearinghouse
http://www.clearinghouse.net/

Jayde.com
http://www.jayde.com/

Scout Report Signpost
http://www.signpost.org/signpost/

Do You Need Great References?—*It's not exactly a directory, a portal site, or a search engine, but I find **Refdesk.com**, at* http://www.refdesk.com/, *to be one of the more useful sites for hunting down information. Need to look up an acronym? How about Canadian postal rates? Want to know more about human anatomy? Or what about currency exchange rates? The thousands of links on this site can help you do research and find resources to add to your database.*

As you conduct your research on the Web, you'll soon come across directories dedicated to your specific topic. These sites offer a gold mine of links. Here are three examples of subject-specific directories:

Fitness Find
http://www.fitnessfind.com/

HumorLinks
http://humorlinks.com/

PetsHub.com (shown in Figure 3.5)
http://www.petshub.com/

Web Portals

Although they may also offer directory and search features, Web portals are sites that also have topic-specific sections with articles, recommendations, and message boards, as well as related links. Portals act as a gateway to other Internet resources on the subject at hand. For a big list of portals, take a look at the **Google Web Portals** page at http://directory.google.com/Top/Computers/ Internet/WWW/Web_Portals/. Here are some of the more popular portal sites:

About—The Human Internet
http://www.about.com/

NBCi
http://www.nbci.com/

Yahoo!
http://www.yahoo.com/

MSN.com
http://www.msn.com/

FIGURE 3.5: PetsHub.com is one of many Web directory sites dedicated to a specific topic.

Links Pages

As a service to visitors, many personal and business Web sites feature a page of interesting links. In particular, you should investigate these pages. Every new site you uncover will often lead to several more sites that, in turn, will point you to even more. It's a never-ending cycle. Here are examples of links pages from a variety of niche sites:

Natural Health World—Links Page
http://www.naturalhealthworld.com/links/index.html

Oscar Wilde Sites on the World Wide Web
http://www.showgate.com/tots/gross/wildeweb.html

Changing Course Links (for people who jump career paths)
http://www.changingcourse.com/links.htm

TAXI: Links to Bands, Artists, Songwriters, Musicians
http://www.taxi.com/members/links-featured.html

Web Rings

Some smart person years ago realized there was a better way for similar Web sites to work together than simply offering links pages. A Web ring is a collection of sites linked together via a navigation box located on every participating site's home page. Visitors are encouraged to click through to the other sites in the ring. If you find Web rings that cater to your niche, you'll find a solid list of sites you'll want to add to your database. A site called **WebRing.org** used to be the premier place that set up and kept tabs on Web rings. The site has since changed hands and is now **Yahoo! Web Ring**, located at http://dir.webring.yahoo.com/rw/. Here are three other sites that catalog Web rings:

The Rail
http://therail.com/cgi/station/

RingSurf
http://www.ringsurf.com/

Bomis
http://www.bomis.com/

E-zine and Mailing List Directories

Getting your name out through e-zines and mailing lists can help you reach a lot of people in a short period of time. E-zines are typically electronic newsletters sent by an individual or an organization to a list of subscribers. Mailing lists, though, are open forums that generally allow anyone who subscribes to the list to post messages that are sent by e-mail to every other subscriber. Either way, getting an appropriate message to appear in an e-zine or mailing list is an important element in branding yourself online. Here are four of the better places to find e-zines and mailing lists that cover your field:

Yahoo! Groups
http://www.yahoogroups.com/

Topica
http://www.topica.com/

Liszt—The Mailing List Directory
http://www.liszt.com/

PAML—Lists by Subject and Name
http://paml.net/indexes.html

Usenet or Newsgroup Directories

The words Usenet and newsgroup are practically synonymous. Both are similar to a mailing list, only the posted messages aren't sent by e-mail; they're logged onto a newsgroup message board. Readers must use newsgroup reader software to view the posts. Think of them as online bulletin boards. There are newsgroups for every topic imaginable, so you need to search for the ones that address your industry. Here are three good places to look:

Liszt's Usenet Newsgroups Directory
http://www.liszt.com/news/

CyberFiber Newsgroups Directory and Search
http://www.cyberfiber.com/

Deja.com's Usenet Discussion Service
http://www.deja.com/usenet/

Search Engines

Search engines are the first thing people usually think of when they need to hunt for information online, but for our purposes, they are the least effective. You're better off beginning with the more focused directories, portals, links pages, and so on listed in the preceding sections than in the wide open, free-for-all world of search engines, which often require you to wade through hundreds of unrelated search results. However, search engines do provide another option for uncovering sources you need to add to your database. Here are some of the better-known search engines:

Alta Vista
http://www.altavista.com/

Direct Hit
http://www.directhit.com/

Lycos
http://www.lycos.com/

Northern Light
http://www.northernlight.com/

Google Web Directory—Search Engines (a directory listing of search engines)
http://directory.google.com/Top/Computers/Internet/WWW/Searching_the_Web/
Search_Engines/

Metasearch sites will take your keywords and give you results from several different search engines in one fell swoop. Here are some good metasearch sites:

Ask Jeeves
http://www.ask.com/

Dogpile
http://www.dogpile.com/

MetaCrawler
http://www.metacrawler.com/

Mamma (shown in Figure 3.6)
http://www.mamma.com/

Your search endeavors will be far more productive if you apply some tricks that can increase the odds of finding relevant search results. First, stay away from entering simple generic terms. Let's say you're looking for sites that cover dog trainers specializing in animal behavior problems. If you only enter the word *dog* (as I did on the Google search site), it returns more than seven million results—a few too many to browse through even on the laziest Sunday afternoon. The phrase *dog training* returned a mere 364,000 results. That's better, but not good enough. Entering the four words *dog training bad behavior* knocked the total number of results down to 33,900. Now we're getting somewhere.

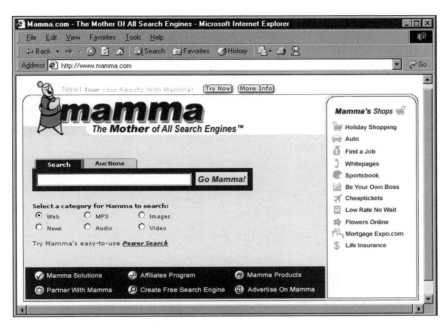

FIGURE 3.6: Metasearch sites, such as Mamma, give search results from several different search engines at one time.

When you enter keywords into a search engine, it looks for Web pages that include those words anywhere on the page. However, if you put quotation marks around a set of search words, the results will only contain pages that have those words grouped together in that exact manner. When I used *"dog training" "bad behavior"* the search engine returned only 282 results.

Know Your ANDs, ORs, and NOTs—*The 19th century mathematician George Boole had no idea his name would later be used in reference to Internet search engines, but the term Boolean logic is alive and well and thriving in cyberspace. Boolean refers to using the words AND, OR, and NOT (always in all caps) with keyword searches. For instance, if you enter* Beatles AND Ringo, *you'll get pages that include both names. If you search for a topic that's commonly referred to using multiple words, you might enter* Country OR Western, *which would yield pages containing either word. If you want details on singer Elvis Costello, but not Elvis Presley, you might enter* Elvis NOT Presley. *For more information on Boolean searches, check out* **ADAM: Boolean Search Tips** *at* http://adam.ac.uk/info/boolean.html.

If you still need a few more tips on Internet research or using search engines, take a look at these resources:

How an Internet Search Engine Works
http://www.howstuffworks.com/search-engine.htm

Finding Information on the Internet (an online tutorial from the University of California at Berkeley)
http://www.lib.berkeley.edu/TeachingLib/Guides/Internet/FindInfo.html

Guide to Effective Searching on the Internet (covers 48 topics for beginning to intermediate Web users)
http://www.completeplanet.com/Tutorials/Search/

Search Engine Guide (a guide to search engines, portals, and directories)
http://www.searchengineguide.com/

Google Web Directory—Searching the Web
http://directory.google.com/Top/Computers/Internet/WWW/Searching_the_Web/Help_and_Tutorials/

What to Do with Your Database

If you're going to go through all the trouble of compiling a list of Web sites, media outlets, e-mail newsletters, message boards, and more, you better believe you're going to put it to good use. Your plan of attack is simple: One by one, go through each of the resources in your database and either contact the Webmaster, post an appropriate message, or send a press release. In other words, one at a time, *do something* with each contact.

That was the grassroots approach taken by musician John Taglieri when he started promoting a new CD of his original songs. Taglieri is a pop-rock songwriter, so he searched the Web for sites that catered to his type of music. Whenever he found a site that met his criteria, he would contact the site owner and ask about submitting his CD for review. He did the same thing with dozens of similar sites. Progress was slow at first, but within a few months, he started making headway.

*Remind Yourself to Reconnect—Once you start communicating with the people in your database, it's important to follow up with the more responsive contacts at least once every couple of months, even if it's just to say hello. However, it's easy to get sidetracked. If you're a forgetful type, use a free service to send you an e-mail reminder message at certain intervals. Two services to consider are **Memo to Me** at* http://www.memotome.com/ *and **LifeMinders** at* http://www.lifeminders.com/ *(shown in Figure 3.7).*

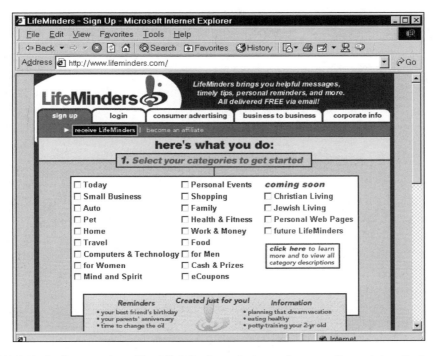

FIGURE 3.7: Online services like LifeMinders alert you by e-mail on dates that you preselect--a good option for reminding yourself to engage in promotional activities.

The first few positive reviews Taglieri earned opened the door to other sites that were reluctant to cover him. He spent more than six hours a day marketing himself on the Internet. Over a 12-month period, he racked up more than 50 reviews. He attributes his success to putting in the time, being pleasantly persistent, and having patience and determination.

Taglieri also brings a service attitude to his promotional efforts and believes you should treat everyone you come in contact with as a customer. "You want to be treated well for the things you do," he says, "and so do the Webmasters of the sites we all beg and expect reviews from." He also makes it a point to stay in touch with the people in his database. Every month or so he sends an e-mail to everyone who's ever reviewed his music. "This serves two purposes," he says. "First, it lets them know I'm thinking about them and stopping by their sites. Second, it keeps me in their minds, which can lead to more promotion." I've long advocated Taglieri's personal, one-on-one approach. Even against the backdrop of today's quick-fix era, this time-honored philosophy still pays dividends.

So, did all of Taglieri's effort pay off? Because of the notoriety he created for himself, he sold more than 2,000 copies of his CD, performed at major music conferences, landed a sponsorship deal with a guitar manufacturer, and signed a recording contract with a small record label. He also has investors paying for his next album and upcoming tour (plus he now has exposure in this book). Branding yourself online does work, as long as you have a plan and work it consistently.

The Goal: Critical-Mass Exposure

When you first start making connections with the sources in your database, it may feel like you're pulling teeth trying to get the reviews, media mentions, and recommendations you want. Your progress ebbs and flows. One month filled with successes is followed by another month during which no one seems to be listening. Even getting prime exposure on a heavily traveled Web site doesn't mean a tidal wave of traffic is heading your way. Newsletter subscribers, orders, and inquiries seem to trickle in.

This early stage of the online branding game is the most challenging to get through. It's like the first six months of learning to play the piano or other musical instrument. You stumble along, awkwardly learning the basics, taking a few steps forward and a few steps back, until finally, something clicks and you get it. When promoting your identity online, though, not only do you get it, your target audience gets it, too. Your early marketing efforts appear to go unnoticed, but in reality, you are laying the foundation for your future activities. It's the accumulation of branding messages you plant that finally causes them to break through and have an impact.

It's been said that people need to hear or see an advertising message seven to ten times before they act on it. For your potential fans to make that all-important connection between who you are and what you stand for, they must see your name and branding message often and from a variety of sources. Your ultimate goal is to achieve critical-mass exposure. Ideally, within the course of a month, people who make up your target audience will see your name pop up in some or all of the following ways:

- As the expert who writes an article in their favorite e-mail newsletter
- In a review on a Web site that caters to your industry
- Among a list of recommended links on a Web site
- In a message posted on a discussion list
- During a conversation with a friend at a party

- In an article in a print magazine that covers your field

When your brand identity reaches this critical mass of exposure, you have indeed established yourself as a celebrity or expert in your field. But you must have the stamina to stick with it before you get to that enviable position.

———————

In the next chapter, we talk about the best way to use (and not abuse) e-mail to exploit the branding database we've discussed in this chapter.

CHAPTER FOUR

Maximizing E-mail for Brand Delivery

The World Wide Web may draw most of the attention among Internet activities, but e-mail is the true workhorse of the online world. Long before the first Web browser was created, e-mail flourished. Even today, believe it or not, there are people with Internet access who don't spend a lot of time Web surfing. But you can bet they probably spend time reading and sending e-mail. In fact, in America alone, more than 80 million people send more than nine billion e-mail messages each day.

The lure of e-mail is intoxicating. There are no printing or postage costs and no long-distance expenses. You can shoot off a note to your next-door neighbor as easily as you can send one to someone half way around the globe. Used properly, e-mail can be one of your greatest online marketing tools; used improperly, it can rub people the wrong way and give you a bad reputation. To help you make the most of e-mail's potential, in this chapter, we cover the following topics:

- Various options for setting up an e-mail account
- Tips to help you effectively use signature files, subject lines, and body text to establish your brand image
- Pitfalls to avoid when communicating by e-mail
- Autoresponders and how to put them to work for you

Before long, you'll be an e-mail pro. You'll send electronic messages that are opened immediately, that people look forward to receiving, that inspire people to take action, and that cement your brand identity in the minds of the masses. Let's get started.

Let There Be E-mail—*The first e-mail was reportedly sent in 1971, when an engineer named Ray Tomlinson sent a text message from one computer machine to another using the now-familiar @ sign. Little did Tomlinson know what he had started.*

Your E-mail Options

With so many Web sites and Internet companies offering free or low-cost e-mail services, it's easy to become overwhelmed by the choices. First, let's look at what most of these options have in common. Regardless of what service you use, the only way you can send and receive e-mail is to use what's called an e-mail client—a geeky word for the type of software needed for e-mail. All e-mail clients allow you to log on and view a list of your incoming e-mail messages. You can see who sent each message and what subject heading the sender used, if any. In addition to being able to open and read your incoming messages, you can also reply to messages, write new outgoing e-mails, send attachments, save old messages to your hard drive, etc.

The following sections discuss the three most common ways of getting an e-mail account along with the advantages and drawbacks of each.

ISP E-mail

Just about all Internet service providers (ISPs) offer e-mail as part of their Internet access package. The more prominent names in this category are America Online (AOL), Prodigy, EarthLink/MindSpring, and CompuServe. When you use an e-mail account supplied by your ISP, your e-mail address will always include the ISP's domain name, such as yourname@aol.com.

Advantages: ISP e-mail accounts are generally quick and easy to set up. They're convenient, because you don't have to open another program or surf to a different Web site to start sending and receiving messages.

Drawbacks: To effectively brand yourself online you must give people predictable channels through which they can contact you. If you ever need to change your ISP (and people do often), you'll lose your e-mail address, which means you'll cut off communication with anyone who tries to use your old, defunct address—not a good thing to do if you want to create a favorable impression online.

Free Web-Based E-mail

A growing number of sites offer free Web-based e-mail. Some of the big players in this category are Yahoo!, Excite, MSN Hotmail, and Juno. These free e-mail services can be accessed no matter which company you use as your ISP. Even though they're free, they usually come with all the features of e-mail provided by your ISP. (Remember, though, you still need an ISP to access the Internet and get to your free Web-based e-mail account.)

Advantages: Yahoo! advertises its e-mail service as "free e-mail for life." Since you can indefinitely use the same yourname@yahoo.com or yourname@hotmail.com address, regardless of how you connect to the Internet, it does make Web-based e-mail more attractive than the ISP option.

Drawbacks: First, free Web-based e-mail addresses carry a stigma of not being professional. Since they are so easy to get, free e-mail services are often used by hobbyists, which isn't the image you want to project. Second, you should ideally be using an e-mail address that's consistent with your Web domain name. You may not have a domain registered yet, but if you follow the advice in this book, you will soon—and your e-mail address should reflect that.

Fast Forward—*Another option to consider is using an e-mail forwarding service that gives you an array of domain names to choose from, such as yourname@artlover.com, yourname@doctor.com, or yourname@theoffice.net. E-mail sent to you using these addresses is forwarded to the e-mail account you specify. This is a step up from the commonly used free e-mail services, because you can tailor the domain name to your identity. Two sites that offer free e-mail forwarding are* **Mail.com** *at* http://www.mail.com/ *and* **NetForward** *at* http://www.netforward.com/.

Domain Name E-mail Address

Your best bet is to have a business identity, Web site URL, and e-mail address that use the same name. For instance, the publisher of this book is Top Floor Publishing. The company's Web site address is http://www.TopFloor.com/. To contact someone at the company you would use an e-mail address like someone@topfloor.com. It would seem odd for the company to use an *@aol.com* or *@yahoo.com* e-mail address to reach any of the main people who work there. Similarly, my name is Bob Baker, one of my domain names is http://www.bob-baker.com/, and—yes, indeed—you can reach me by e-mail at bob@bob-baker.com. Your branding efforts are best served by using an e-mail address that matches your domain name.

In Chapter 5, "Creating Your Personal Brand Web Site," we discuss how to register a domain name and set up a Web site. For our purposes here, let's assume you already have your own domain name and a place to host your site. Now you have some options for having people use your new domain name to send you e-mail, as discussed in the following sections.

E-mail Forwarding

Most Web hosts offer e-mail forwarding, which means messages sent to your domain name can be forwarded to any e-mail address you specify. For instance, if you simply can't part with your Yahoo! or MSN e-mail system, you can instruct your Web host to redirect your messages so you can read them in the same way you always have. I had e-mail sent to an AOL account for quite a while after registering my own domain. It's a simple solution, but it does have drawbacks. For example, when I replied to e-mail messages, the recipient saw my AOL return address, not my domain address, which can confuse people. Some free e-mail providers, like Yahoo!, provide options for manipulating the From and Reply-To fields, so you may be able to work around this drawback.

Don't Mix Business with Pleasure—*It's a good idea to have separate e-mail addresses for business mail and personal messages. You'd also be smart to use your domain name e-mail for business while still having another e-mail account through your ISP or one of the free Web-based services. That way, if one server ever goes down, you have the other e-mail option to communicate. Plus, having a separate e-mail account on another system allows you to send test messages to check formatting and other compatibility issues.*

POP Account

All of the e-mail options we've discussed so far involve using the e-mail client that comes with an ISP or Web site offering e-mail service. The best solution, though, may be to use your own e-mail client. Before getting into more detail, let's discuss how e-mail works.

For an e-mail client to send and receive e-mail, it must communicate with a Web server. Let's suppose that jan@boogie.com is sending an e-mail to chris@birdhouse.net. Jan writes her message and hits the Send button. Jan's e-mail client communicates with something called the Simple Mail Transfer Protocol (SMTP) port at the boogie.com Web server. The SMTP software then connects to a computer called a domain name server (DNS) and asks where it can find birdhouse.net. After getting its bearings, the boogie.com server connects with the SMTP port at the birdhouse.net server. Once it recognizes that the incoming message is for Chris, the birdhouse.net SMTP server transfers the message to Post Office Protocol (POP) software designated for Chris. All incoming e-mail messages are stored in a file within the POP server. New messages are added to the end of the file. When Chris logs on and checks her messages, her e-mail client connects to the POP port at the birdhouse.net Web server and pulls all the new messages into her e-mail client, which transforms them into a scrolling list of new e-mail messages. It sounds like a long, strange trip, but it often takes place in only seconds.

IMAP Account

Internet Message Access Protocol (IMAP) is another method of accessing e-mail stored on a Web server. It works in much the same way as a POP account, only IMAP has advanced features that are particularly helpful when you have multiple users or are using more than one computer to access your e-mail. Either option may be adequate for now, but given a choice, IMAP is preferable, provided that your e-mail client supports it.

Many e-mail software packages, once you enter a few setup configurations, can communicate with your Web server directly. However, you can only take this route if your Web server offers a POP or IMAP e-mail account. Even some of the free e-mail services allow you to use your own e-mail client. For instance, Yahoo! offers a POP option with its free service, but AOL doesn't.

Here are some of the more common e-mail client options:

Eudora—One of the oldest personal e-mail packages on the Internet, Eudora comes in three versions, from a free Light version to a full-featured Pro version. http://www.eudora.com/

Microsoft Outlook—Many PCs these days come with a free version of Outlook Express. Like Eudora, it's functional but doesn't provide the full features of the for-sale version Microsoft Outlook (shown in Figure 4.1). The good thing about Outlook is that it integrates well with other Microsoft applications. http://www.microsoft.com/office/outlook/

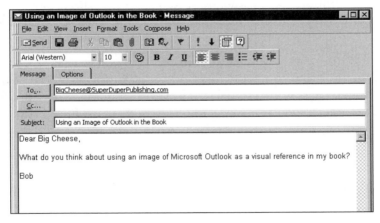

FIGURE 4.1: Microsoft Outlook is one of several good e-mail programs you can use in conjunction with a POP e-mail account.

Dozens of e-mail applications are available. For a long list of software choices, see the **Yahoo!–Software/Email** page at http://dir.yahoo.com/Business_and_Economy/ Business_to_Business/Computers/Communications_and_Networking/Software/Email/. For more general information on using e-mail, check out **E-mail Help and Tips** at http://everythingemail.net/email_help_tips.html.

Get Unlimited E-mail Addresses—Another big benefit that comes with having your own domain name is the ability to have an unlimited number of e-mail addresses. For instance, you can have messages sent to info@yourdomain.com, sales@yourdomain.com, bigcheese@yourdomain.com, and more. You can also set your server and e-mail client to filter different e-mail addresses into different folders or have some forwarded to an employee's personal e-mail system. Additionally, make sure your Web host offers something called unlimited aliasing, *which causes unrecognized e-mail to be dropped into a primary POP or IMAP box. If someone sends a message to odor@yourdomain.com instead of order@yourdomain.com, you still want to receive the message. Without unlimited aliasing, bad addresses are returned to the sender.*

Using E-mail to Reinforce Your Brand

Just because e-mail is quick and easy, don't take it lightly. You will be using e-mail extensively in your ongoing efforts to spread your brand identity to the masses. This useful electronic tool gives you the power to reach countless people in all corners of the planet, which is exactly why so many people run headlong into spitting out e-mail messages like a lawn sprinkler shoots out water. Those same people also desperately hope that some of their far-flung e-mail will stick to something. Don't blindly send e-mail out into the world without a purpose. Think before you hit the Send button. The following pages reveal a few e-mail guidelines.

Signature Files

The primary goal of branding is to indelibly link your name with what you do and how you approach your specialty. However, making that valuable mental connection is wasted if you don't also give customers and fans a way to connect with you. A signature file (or sig file, as it's commonly called) is simply a few lines of text that you add to the end of every e-mail message you send. It's similar to the details you find on a letterhead, only the information is included at the end instead of at the top of the letter. An e-mail message with a sig file might look something like this fictitious example:

Nancy,
Thanks for your kind words regarding my latest article. I'm glad you enjoyed it.
Jo

Josephine Beckler
Diet tips for women over 40
For a free newsletter, visit:
http://www.womenover40.com/
jb@womenover40.com
(555) 361-3322

Notice how Jo's sig file serves the function of a subtle advertisement. It includes her full name, immediately followed by the phrase "Diet tips for women over 40"—which serves as her Brand Identity Statement (BIS), discussed in Chapter 2, "Crafting Your Best Brand Identity." She then not only includes her Web site URL, but also supplies the lure of a free newsletter subscription to inspire people to pay a visit. Jo's e-mail address and phone number are included as additional contact options and to demonstrate she's not hiding in the shadows. Make sure every branding message you project—whether it's an e-mail, Web page, newsletter, or printed brochure—not only carries your BIS, but also includes complete contact information. Never assume that people will automatically know how to contact you. Don't make their lives more difficult by forcing potential fans to hunt down your e-mail or Web address. Make it easy for people to get in touch with you.

It's also a good idea to tailor your sig file to the person who will be receiving your message. As an example, when I send e-mail to a musician or anyone contacting me about a music business–related issue, I use this sig file:

THE BUZZ FACTOR
http://www.thebuzzfactor.com/
Resources, tips, and tools that will change the way
you promote your independent band or record label.
FREE newsletter subscription:
00-BuzzFactor-subscribe@egroups.com

However, I have a separate Web site that caters to creative people of all types, so when I respond to a message from an artist or writer, I use this sig file:

Quick Tips for Creative People
http://www.bob-baker.com/qt/
Inspiration and low-cost marketing ideas for artists,
writers, crafters, musicians, performing artists,
and others pursuing a creative passion.
FREE newsletter subscription:
00-CreativeQuickTips-subscribe@egroups.com

You may notice that all of these sig file examples do three things:

- Combine a name with a specific identity
- Promote a free newsletter
- Encourage readers to visit a Web site

These three tactics will pop up again and again as we travel along the road to personal branding success. Make them your steady companions and they will serve you well.

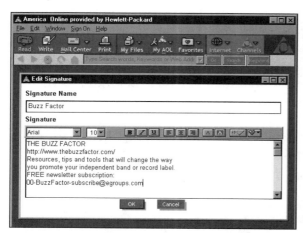

Store Your Sig Files—Most e-mail programs (including AOL's e-mail system, shown in Figure 4.2) allow you to store sig files and quickly insert one in your message with a simple click. Save a number of sig files with slight variations based on the type of people you communicate with. Each one should stress a benefit tailored to the recipient. Give each sig file a descriptive name so that you can easily find it and select it from the sig file menu.

FIGURE 4.2: AOL's e-mail system, like many e-mail programs, allows you to edit and store a variety of sig files that you can insert into your e-mail to reinforce your brand identity.

Subject Lines

A few years ago, using e-mail got a tremendous response. It was new and cutting-edge. You could send unsolicited ads for snowshoes to people in Florida and your messages would be eagerly read. Those glory days are over. Today, everyone is bombarded with e-mail. When people go online to read their messages, they want to take care of business and move on quickly. It's bad enough that more than half of the e-mail we receive these days is total junk. When you add ambiguous subject headings into the mix, it's a wonder people continue to use e-mail at all.

Think about it. When you log on and check your new incoming messages, how do you determine what's worth reading? Of course, by looking at the words the sender has typed into the subject field. Based on those descriptions, you open the most important e-mails first. The rest you either delete or save to read later. If you're like me, later usually never comes. Subject fields are important. Make better use of them and you'll find your online branding efforts having a lot more impact. Let's take a look at some examples of good and bad subject lines:

Hello

How many times have you seen this one? Is it from someone you know or someone trying to trick you into opening an unsolicited ad?

Question

I get this subject line a lot. Sometimes, it ends up being a fan asking for a suggestion on how to do something. Other times, it's someone wanting to know about an order they placed. Sometimes, though, it's a trick from somebody wanting to sell something. Until I open it (if I open it), I have no clue. Don't make your subject fields so generic. The more specific you are, the better. If you think you're being clever by adding a little mystery to your subject lines, think again. You're better off giving people as many specifics as you can squeeze into several words.

Any Ideas?

This is another example of a teaser type of message. It's also a subject line that frustrates more than it helps.

Thought of you

Okay, this one is either from a secret admirer, a pitch for a pornography site, or someone who really has something useful for me. But I'm so confused by the obscurity of the subject line, I may never open it to find out.

(no subject)

This is the worst crime of all. Never send an e-mail without a subject line. Period.

May I Reprint Your 'Digital Music' Article?

This is more like it! The subject line contains a specific question about a specific thing. I know why the person is contacting me, and I know exactly which article he or she is inquiring about—and all this before I've even opened the e-mail. Your goal with subject lines is not to see how tricky you can be to get people to open your e-mail. Instead, tell people up front what your message is about.

Bob, I've Added a Link to Your Music Site

Here's another subject line that grabs my attention. First, it has my name in it, which means it's most likely a personal message (although there are programs that can customize subject lines with bulk e-mail). Second, the line includes a direct benefit to me. Being a diligent brand marketer, I like it when other sites link to mine. I'll open this e-mail to find out what site is doing me a favor and to reply with a thank you note. Sure, this e-mail could have been sent with the subject line "Your Link," but that would have been too vague. Make sure your subject lines are specific so that your recipients know instantly what your messages are about, and always try to include a benefit that relates to your brand identity.

Address Lines

Let's quickly cover some basics concerning fields you may fill out before sending e-mail messages. I'm not including information on the To: line since you should already know that's where you place the e-mail address of the person to whom you're sending a message. However, there are a couple things worth noting on some of the other fields.

From:—Some e-mail programs allow you to customize the From: line, the field that shows your recipients who your e-mail came from. If you don't adjust the From: line setting, the people receiving your messages will see your e-mail address. That's fine, but your branding efforts will be better served if the From: line simply lists your name or whatever you've chosen as a brand name. For instance, your e-mails can appear to be coming from "Gilligan" instead of "gilligan@threehourtour.com."

Cc:—This line refers to *carbon copy*. With traditional paper letters, you may see a list of names on the bottom that are Cc'd, meaning those people also received a copy of the letter. You can do the same thing with e-mail and, on the Cc: line, enter the e-mail addresses of other people who should be in the loop regarding your message. You can also Cc: yourself if you want to retain a copy of messages you send.

Bcc:—This is the field that has a lot of e-mail newcomers confused. The Bcc: line stands for *blind carbon copy*. Like the Cc: line, it sends copies of your message to the e-mail addresses you enter. The beauty of the Bcc: line, though, is that recipients only see e-mail addresses entered in the To: and Cc: lines, not other addresses in the Bcc: line. What this allows you to do is send the same message to up to a hundred or more people at the same time without everybody seeing a list of all the other people who received the message. Some confused folks mistakenly enter countless e-mail addresses into the Cc: line and don't realize they're forcing recipients to scroll through all those addresses (see Figure 4.3 for an example of what this looks like). The thing is, most people won't scroll and will immediately delete such e-mail.

Reply to:—When people reply to e-mail you send, their return message will be directed to the e-mail address from which it was sent—the address you indicate in the From: field. However, you may be able to adjust your e-mail program to send replies to a different address, perhaps one you have specifically set up to receive e-mail replies.

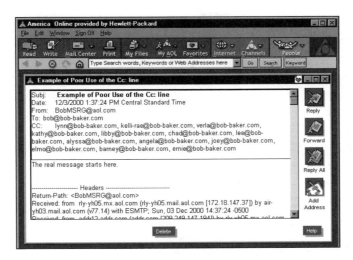

FIGURE 4.3: Everyone sees a list of everyone else who received the message when you use the Cc: line instead of the Bcc: line to send an e-mail to multiple addresses. Unless your recipients know each other, it's best to keep identities confidential by including your own e-mail address in the To: line and everyone else's in the Bcc: line.

Attachments: The Good, Bad, and Ugly—*Most e-mail programs allow you to attach files to outgoing e-mail. The recipient can download the file to his or her hard drive or, depending on the type of file, open it without downloading. The attachment feature is useful for sending .pdf files, Word documents, and other files you need to share with others while engaging in your branding activities. However, use them sparingly. Some e-mail services don't accept file attachments at all. Also, don't send attached files to anyone who isn't expecting it, and never, ever open an attached file sent to you that you didn't ask for—even if it's from someone you know. E-mail viruses often send infected attachments out to everyone in their victims' address books, so beware.*

Always Check for Grammatical Errors

This should go without saying, but I include it to emphasize the importance of being thorough with the e-mail messages you send. Compared to writing and printing a letter, looking it over, stuffing it into an envelope, finding a stamp, and searching for a mail box, shooting off an e-mail is a breeze. E-mail is quick, spontaneous, and convenient, which makes it ripe for abuse.

Granted, not everyone you send an e-mail message to will be a Hemingway or a college English professor, but a good portion of people who have Internet access are educated and sharp enough to recognize sloppy work when they see it. Don't turn off potential fans with poor grammar and typos before you've even had a chance to introduce your brand identity.

If your e-mail program has a spell-check feature, use it. But don't hit the Send button until you've used your eyeballs to look over your letter one more time. Spell-check is great for pointing out words that don't exist in the dictionary, but it's not very effective for recognizing words that may be spelled right but used incorrectly. For instance, there are no incorrectly spelled words in the following sentence: "If your looking far a way too improve you're productive, I can help." However, there are five grammatical errors that most e-mail spell-check features would never catch. Always scrutinize the accuracy of your writing and search your text for errors before sending e-mail. Your brand reputation depends on it.

Body Text Length and Style

I opened up an e-mail recently and was greeted with this message:

Hey, you should check out our site. It rocks! Have a good one. —Stu

What purpose did this e-mail accomplish, except to exercise Stu's fingers on his keyboard? It certainly did nothing to clarify his identity and give me warm, fuzzy feelings about him. Stu's message only let me know that he's clueless and enjoys wasting my time. Because there are so many Stu's in the world, it won't take a lot of effort for you to stand out and be recognized as someone who respects people's time and knows how to communicate effectively. Here are some tips to keep in mind as you craft your e-mail messages:

Keep messages short—People's attention spans are short-lived, especially on the Internet. Potential fans, no matter how compelling you are, won't want to curl up with a computer screen and read your life's story. Get to the point, establish your brand identity, and then get out of the way. That doesn't mean you should be as quick and ambiguous as our friend Stu above, but don't try to squeeze in every detail in a single e-mail message. The great thing about online communication is that you can give people links to Web pages that contain more information or ask them to contact you if they want more details on a particular topic.

Be conversational—The world is filled with stuffy business people who feel they have to show they mean business by putting on airs. If I read one more "As was stated in our prior communication" or "Per our conversation of the 26th" I'm going to strangle someone. Let this be your new mantra: Write the way you talk. If you wouldn't say something in a pompous manner to someone face to face, don't write it that way in an e-mail message. Let your personality and brand image shine through as you write. Be warm and engaging, perhaps even funny, as long as you don't force cleverness. Also, don't try to sound overly professional and bombard people with jargon. Above all, don't be dull.

Include the original message in a reply—When you hit the Reply button in most e-mail programs you have the option of including the sender's original message in your response. Use this feature. I've lost track of the number of times I've received a return e-mail from someone who wrote, "Great idea! Let's do it." Huh? I send and reply to a lot of e-mail, so it's quite possible that I may forget the idea I proposed to this person. If he or she includes my original note with the reply, it assures that I'm not left guessing. When you use this feature, though, only include the portion of the original message that's relevant to your response.

Use emoticons sparingly—Emoticons are those cute expressions you can create using various keyboard characters. For instance, you might use ;-) to indicate a wink and smile. Since body language and voice inflections don't accompany e-mail text messages, emoticons are often used to indicate sarcasm and other verbal subtleties. Emoticons have a place, but use them in moderation. I've read messages in which every other sentence ends with "LOL," which stands for "laugh out loud." Please. Going overboard with these cute characters and abbreviations will brand you as an amateur quicker than you can say cheese ball. LOL!

Watch the special characters—If you copy text from a word processing program and paste it into the body of an e-mail, you run the risk of creating an odd-looking message. Special characters such as curly quotation marks (sometimes called smart quotes), bullet points, and em dashes don't translate to e-mail text messages. Instead, they end up looking like comic strip curse words: "#%!@$?" To make certain your messages don't contain these visual speed bumps, send an e-mail message to yourself or to a secondary e-mail address on another server. That should reveal any problems.

10 Writing Tips for E-mail Branding Power

There are good ways and bad ways to use e-mail to convey your brand identity. Your goal is to string together words, sentences, and paragraphs that grab attention, and inspire and motivate people to act. Above all, you must accomplish all these things while communicating your brand message in ways that the busiest, most distracted reader will comprehend. Here are 10 writing tips to help you get your e-mail branding point across:

1. **Use the person's name in the salutation.** "Dear Bob" gets my attention far more than "Dear Sirs," which is politically incorrect on top of being boring. It's okay to send an anonymous e-mail to find the name of the person you need to contact or when sending a generic note to tech support. Otherwise, always send e-mail to a specific person and use his or her name in the

salutation, especially when marketing your brand. It's common these days to use a person's first name, even when contacting someone for the first time, but use your own judgment regarding when it's appropriate to be formal or informal.

2. **Have a great opening.** First impressions are important. When you meet someone face to face, the way you dress and groom yourself has a great impact. With e-mail, your first one or two sentences dictate whether your message gets read or deleted. Make your opening words count. Don't write lines such as "This is really important, so please read this" or "The best way to explain who I am is by starting from the beginning." Get to the point, be specific and indicate a benefit, as in "I just visited your Web site and loved your dog grooming articles so much I'd like to plug them in the next issue of my e-zine." Once you have the person's attention, you can spend a few more sentences explaining who you are and what you might like in return.

3. **Use short sentences and simple words.** For ten years I published a music magazine. Having seen hundreds of submissions from freelance writers, I know there are countless writers hell-bent on impressing people with their command of the English language. These wordsmiths bob and weave their way through longwinded sentences and hundred-dollar words. Don't engage in this nonsense. Keep your e-mail messages simple and focused on your brand message. Your identity will cut through the clutter more quickly if you do.

Hey You! Look at Me!—No matter how excited you are about your vocation, people will never be as interested in you as you are. To get people to absorb information about your brand image, you must first get their attention. The best way to perk up people's ears (or eyes, in the case of e-mail) is to praise them or offer a specific goodie that can help them accomplish their own goals.

---

4. **Focus on the recipient's self-interests.** With this topic, we encounter the yin and yang of branding and benefits. On one hand, you must communicate your name, what you do, and how you do it. On the other hand, you must cater to the self-interests and egos of the people to whom you send e-mail. Here's the best rule to follow: Lead with benefits, follow up with details on your brand identity. For example, don't write, "I am a great photographer with an excellent online gallery of my work. Please review my photos!" Instead, write something like, "My customers have been encouraging me to visit your photography site for months. I finally did and I'm sorry I waited so long. What a wonderful resource you've put together. I can also tell you enjoy exposing cutting-edge photography from up-and-coming artists. When you have a chance, please visit my online

exhibition of sports photography. I believe your visitors would appreciate knowing about this collection."

5. **Repeat your Brand Identity Statement (BIS) in different ways.** You already know the importance of having a BIS. The obvious place to use your BIS in an e-mail is to make it a part of your sig file. But don't rely on that one reference alone to get your message across. Repetition is the mother of learning, so paraphrase and repeat the essence of your identity throughout your message.

6. **Use pain and pleasure hot buttons.** As we discussed in Chapter 2, "Crafting the Best Brand Identity for You," you must find a way to position your brand image as providing a solution to your fans' problems. Be sure to make references to those problems in your e-mail messages, such as "Thanks for inquiring about my press release writing services. Having worked as an editor for over a decade, I can tell you that more than 90 percent of all press materials are poorly written and end up going straight into the trash can. I'd love to help keep your press release out of the 'round file.'" Don't go overboard with this idea and write a cheesy "If you don't act now, you'll be homeless and destitute" message, but do find ways to remind people of the pain you can alleviate and the pleasure you can help your fans attain.

7. **Have a purpose with every communication.** Don't just send e-mail for the heck of it. While it's true that you must take action to promote your brand, that doesn't mean any action will do. Before you send e-mail, ask yourself two questions:

   • What do I want to accomplish with this message?
   • What do I want the recipient to do?

   Use your answers to those questions to craft a better message. I often get "hey, check out my site" notes or vague requests to "help each other," which lead me to ask, "How?" and "Why?" Here's an example of how to be clearer in an e-mail: "I'm contacting you to see if you'd like to swap line ads in each other's newsletters. If interested, please send me your ad." Make a specific proposal in each e-mail and give the reader precise instructions on what step to take next.

8. **Add a sense of urgency.** It's one thing to make people aware of you, it's quite another to get them to take action to promote you or place an order. People are often lethargic and hesitant to move quickly, even toward things they are genuinely interested in. One way to battle this sluggishness is to create incentives: a deadline, a limited quantity, a free premium, and so on. You don't want to sound like an infomercial in an e-mail and write "Act

now while supplies last." However, you can inspire action with a simple offer like "I'll give you a free copy of my special report on fly fishing when you order my book, but I need to hear from you by 5:00 p.m. on Friday."

9. **Use endorsements and testimonials.** Even if people know and trust you, they'll still be slow to believe everything you say about yourself. The best way to overcome this skepticism is to use objective, third-party endorsements. For instance, if you're making a pitch to a Webmaster to review your hair-coloring Web site, it would help to include something like "*New 'Do* magazine described our site as 'the coolest place in cyberspace to learn about hair color.'" Include the URLs to any online reviews to back up your endorsement claims. If you're promoting a product, you can also include a "Here's what some recent customers had to say about ..." section. Anytime you get a positive comment from a fan or favorable review in the media, use it to get even more exposure for your brand.

10. **Walk the fine line between modesty and hype.** One thing that has become apparent with online commerce is the overwhelming attitude that advertising and hype is a turn-off. Over the decades, people have become tolerant of intrusive ads and marketing messages, but that acceptance is wearing thin. Knowing this, write your e-mail messages so that your brand identity is unmistakable and the benefit you offer is clear, but present them in a soft-sell manner. Instead of writing "My amazing software program will erase your bill-paying worries overnight. Call now. Operators are standing by," write something more casual like "I used to dread paying bills. It was such a pain. Then I developed my own software program to make the process easier. Now I'd like to share this program with you."

Using Form Letters and Mail Merge

As you get down to the nitty-gritty of your online branding activities, you'll soon discover reoccurring questions and topics coming up in the e-mail you receive from fans and curious onlookers. You'll also find yourself sending similar-sounding messages to Webmasters and media people as you seek exposure opportunities. At first, you may write these messages from scratch, but before long you'll see the benefit of having prepared form letters. The next time someone expresses an interest in hiring you, you'll pull up your saved list of services, add a personal note or two, and off it'll go. When you come across a new Web site dedicated to your craft, you'll open your introduction letter, customize it a bit, and fire it off. The branding life gets easier when you use form letters.

There are a few different ways to save and file away these pre-written messages. Eudora, for example, allows you to save various boilerplate letters as stationery. Outlook lets you save e-mail messages as templates. At the very least, you can simply save form letters in a text file, and then copy and paste the one you need into a new e-mail. Always customize a form letter before you send it. At the very least, add the person's name to the salutation. You should also include some personal comments at the beginning and end, if possible.

Before we leave the form letter topic, let's talk about mail merge. Let's say you have a couple dozen or more Webmasters to whom you'd like to send an introductory letter or cross-promotion proposal. Using a mail merge function, you can send a form letter e-mail and customize each one with the Webmaster's name and URL. It's a nice feature to have when you have to contact a lot of people with the same message at the same time. Although you can often use your favorite word processing program to help you send mail-merge e-mail, you might also consider some of these stand-alone mail-merge programs:

WorldMerge (an easy, user-friendly program)
http://www.coloradosoft.com/

Campaign (a program with great features, but difficult to use)
http://www.arialsoftware.com/

eMerge (for the Mac)
http://www.galleon.com/

WWMail
http://wizardware.com/wwmail.htm

Text Versus HTML—*A growing number of e-mail programs can display HTML e-mail, which means e-mail messages that are graphically formatted using the same code used to design Web pages. True, HTML-based e-mail looks prettier than plain text-based e-mail. However, not everyone has the e-mail software needed to view it accurately—if at all. A more practical approach is to send your e-mail as plain text and provide URLs to Web pages that feature a more visually appealing presentation of your information.*

Using Autoresponders

In the previous section we talked about form letters and how easy it is to pull up a template and respond to a request for information. Well, there's an even easier way—so easy you can send e-mail responses while you sleep, literally. I'm talking about autoresponders, a tool that allows you to send a return message to anyone who sends an e-mail to a specific address. For instance, if someone wants a complete list of the music marketing products and services I offer, all he or she has to do is send an e-mail to orderform@bob-baker.com. In less than a minute, he or she gets an e-mail containing details on all of my stuff and instructions on how to order. It doesn't matter if I'm at home, stuck in traffic, or on vacation in Toledo; people interested in that information can get it right away. This single-message e-mail response is sometimes called a *one-to-one autoresponder*.

The best way to create an autoresponder is to set it up through the server at your Web host. That way, the e-mail address will contain your domain name, like my orderform@bob-baker.com does. Having your domain name appear in your autoresponder addresses further imprints your brand name. Hopefully, your Web hosting company has a simple way for you to designate that certain incoming e-mail addresses will trigger automatic return messages (see a sample of a basic interface in Figure 4.4). You then load up the text that will be sent.

If your Web host isn't autoresponder-friendly or if you don't have a Web host at all yet, there are several free and paid options. The free services offer autoresponders at no charge in exchange for placing a text ad in all of your outgoing messages, though most of them have fee-based options without ads. The following sites can help you set up an autoresponder:

> **GetResponse.com**
> http://www.getresponse.com/

FIGURE 4.4: Many Web hosting services offer a simple control panel that allows you to enter the text for autoresponder messages and indicate what e-mail address will trigger a response. Autoresponders provide a great way to communicate your brand message around the clock.

FastFacts.net
http://www.fastfacts.net/

Send Free
http://www.sendfree.com/

Autoresponders.com
http://www.autoresponders.com/

Some of these sites also allow you to set up *follow-up autoresponders*. These gems send a series of messages over the course of days or weeks to the person who requested information. This is particularly useful for branding. Repetition is a key factor in winning over potential fans. The more you present your brand name and BIS to interested parties, the more likely they are to embrace you.

I successfully marketed a music PR service using autoresponders. I listed a description of the service on my Web site along with the retail rates. I also offered a two-for-the-price-of-one discount to anyone who sent an e-mail to an autoresponder address. Over the next 30 days, people who acted on it were sent six follow-up e-mails filled with tips on getting more out of the service, testimonials from satisfied customers, warnings of an upcoming discount deadline, and more. Sales took a noticeable jump after I started using the autoresponder to promote the service. I'm sure the recognition of my brand identity improved as well.

Use follow-up autoresponders responsibly, though. Make sure people know they will receive a series of mailings beforehand; don't surprise them with follow-ups. Also, give people instructions in every message on how to get off the train if they decide they're no longer interested in your offer.

You may be thinking, "Instead of using an autoresponder, why not just send people to a Web page with the information?" There are two reasons: First, many people, particularly those in emerging countries, have e-mail capability but not Web access. Don't cut off these good folks from receiving your information. Second, some people just won't want to visit your Web site and will prefer to get the specific information they need by e-mail. Whether you set up a one-to-one or a follow-up autoresponder, there are many ways to use one. In addition to a product list and order form, you can send the following:

- Articles you have written
- Frequently asked questions (FAQs) on your area of expertise
- A list of recommended resources related to your field
- The latest issue of your newsletter
- Your one- or two-page biography (for the media) that stresses your brand identity

Spam: The Ultimate Pet Peeve

As you probably know, spam is not just a meat product or the subject of a Monty Python skit. With the expansion of the Internet, the term has become widely known to mean something else altogether. Here's my best definition of spam:

Electronic messages that are sent indiscriminately to people who have not requested the information.

Spam originally referred to unwanted postings to scores of Internet newsgroups, but the term has since been applied to uninvited messages sent via mail-list discussion groups and e-mail. You've no doubt opened your e-mail inbox and have rummaged through advertising pitches for online casinos, search engine submission services, college girls who are supposedly awaiting your arrival, and more. Who are these people and how did they get your e-mail address?

The ease and low-cost of e-mail makes it highly susceptible to abuse. Unscrupulous marketers learned early on in the Internet's development that they could scour cyberspace and collect e-mail addresses from newsgroup postings, online directories, and so on. Some of these programs can even worm their way through Internet chat rooms and record only the e-mail addresses of people who talk about certain topics or key words. These so-called "marketers" either rent or sell their acquired lists to advertisers, or send their own e-mail announcements to unsuspecting people.

Why do these desperados engage in this unethical practice when it is so hated? They do it because it can be profitable. If you know your way around Internet technology, you can send an e-mail message to a million people for little or no cost. If only one tenth of one percent of those people convert to buyers, you'll have 1,000 paying customers. It's enough to make anyone's head spin. *Warning*: From a standpoint of branding yourself online, stay as far away from these spamming techniques as you can!

Remember, your goal is to positively link your brand name with what you do and how you do it. The last thing you want to do is have your name associated with spam. While it's not necessary for everyone to love what you do, there aren't many people who will appreciate you for your widespread use of unsolicited e-mail. Not only are most people irritated by spam, some hard-core anti-spam advocates will go to great lengths to make life difficult for you. They'll report you to your Web host, who may cut off your service; they'll use a special program to bombard you with so much e-mail, your server will shut down; they'll post messages to the Web community about how mean and nasty you are; and much more. The risks of spam far outweigh the rewards, so don't be tempted by the lure of a mass-marketing quick fix. Building your brand name slowly but surely is the best route to take.

Unsolicited E-mail Exceptions—*Some people define spam as any message that's sent unsolicited. That view is a bit restricting. There are exceptions. For instance, when online journalists or reviewers make their e-mail addresses available at the beginning or end of their articles, that's an open invitation to contact them, regardless of whether they've asked you for it. Anytime a Web site has a* Contact Us *page that lists e-mail addresses, that gives you a green light to send a message. If a potential fan sends an e-mail to you to ask a question or make a comment, it's appropriate to later send a follow-up message. If a friend recommends you contact someone he or she knows, you'd be correct in sending an introductory note and dropping your mutual friend's name. As with everything, common sense is the best gauge when it comes to spam.*

Now that you have a full understanding of effective e-mail principles, it's time to add the next piece of the branding puzzle: your own Web site. In the next chapter, we discuss how to register a domain name, how to design an effective site, and where to put it so that thousands of fans can visit and find out more about you and the great things you have to offer.

CHAPTER FIVE

Creating Your Personal Brand Web Site

If you're going to be active in branding yourself in the online world, you're going to need a Web site. Having your own site will do wonders in establishing your brand identity, attracting fans, and allowing you to interact and connect with customers. There are many reasons to have a Web site. Here are just some of the things you can do with your own piece of Internet real estate:

- Provide personal and company information
- Express your ideas
- Promote a product, service, or event
- Sell a product or service
- Display images of your work or yourself
- Provide useful information on your area of expertise

In this chapter, we'll cover the fundamentals of creating a Web site. We'll discuss the common ways of making Web pages and where to store them so they appear online. We'll talk about how to register a unique domain name and how to put your Web pages on the radar screens of the major search engines and directories. After you've completed this chapter, you'll be ready to design and finely tune your site—a topic we'll cover in-depth in Chapter 6, "Designing Your Web Site for Brand Impact."

Where to Put Your Web Site

After you have a good handle on your brand identity and a head full of ideas, you'll be ready to start using them on your own Web site. The first step is deciding where your Web site will reside. As we discussed in Chapter 3, "Developing Your Online Branding Arsenal," the files of a Web site are stored on a Web server, which is maintained by a company called a Web host. The physical location of a Web host isn't necessarily important, but you should be concerned about the type of Web host you use. What follows are the five most common Web hosting options.

Your ISP's Web Space

The ISP is the Web-hosting method that many Internet newcomers use to get their feet wet. Since an ISP is the company that provides access to the Internet, many folks naturally use the Web space options that come with the service. I started dabbling with my own Web site years ago by using AOL's free personal home page space. However, there were a few drawbacks, including the following:

- I ended up having a URL that looked something like http://members.aol.com/screen-name/, which is not exactly a user-friendly, easy-to-remember address.
- An obvious ISP Web address isn't perceived as the epitome of stability and professionalism, and many search engines and directories don't list such Web sites for those reasons.
- What happens if you want to change your ISP? You switch and lose the Web address you've worked so hard to market, or you stick with an ISP you don't like just to keep the URL you started with.

Web space provided by your ISP may be a good place to experiment and learn the ropes, but it's not your best option for online branding.

A Free Web-Hosting Service

You can't surf far on the Internet without running into countless offers for free Web space. Why? Everyone wants to own a Web site these days—not just businesses or people wanting to brand themselves, but everyday folks wanting to post pictures of their kids or details about their favorite band or hobby. We're in a digital age of self-expression and people are expressing themselves through Web sites in droves.

Free Web-hosting sites make money selling banner ads and other ad-related services. The more eyeballs they attract, the more the sites can charge for ads, which explains why they're so anxious to give away space to anyone who wants it. But there's a catch: Your free site almost always comes with a pop-up window ad or a banner ad at the top of each page you build. Not only are these ads annoying, you also have no control over what these banners advertise. Uncomplementary ads may confuse visitors and make your brand identity appear to be out of focus. Also, as with the ISP Web space option, your URL will be long and unprofessional looking, as in http://www.FreeWebHost.com/hobbies/yourname/.

Still, if you're tight on cash, free sites are an option. Another good thing about free hosting sites is that you can keep the Web address as long as the site is in business. Here are a few of the higher profile free Web-hosting services:

Angelfire
http://www.angelfire.com/

Tripod
http://www.tripod.com/

Geocities
http://www.geocities.com/

FreeWebspace.net (searchable index of more than 400 free Web space providers)
http://www.freewebspace.net/

ClickHereFree.com
http://www.clickherefree.com/

A Cybermall, Web Store, or E-commerce Service

The free Web-hosting services attract anyone who wants a Web site, but some Web services are set up specifically for people who want to conduct business on the Internet. They come in many flavors, and while some offer free space, many of these business-related sites charge a fee. Here are the three main types of sites in this category:

Cybermalls—These services set up Web pages for businesses in a wide range of categories. Like a real-world mall, you'll find a variety of product and service sites under one roof. The promoters of these sites lead you to believe that they generate a lot of traffic. All those curious shoppers browsing around, the cybermall owners reason, improve your chances of being discovered by a paying customer. Two examples in this category are **ExciteStores** (http://www.excitestores.com/) and **Big Step** (http://www.bigstep.com/), both geared toward small businesses. As convenient as these services may be, for branding purposes, they aren't a good move. Your goal is to have a brand identity that stands on its own, not a brand watered down amid a cluster of other business sites. Still, if you'd like to see a lengthy list of more cybermall sites, check out the **Google Web Directory—Web Hosting—Business** at http://directory.google.com/Top/Computers/Internet/ Commercial_Services/Web_Hosting/Free/Business/.

Niche Web stores—This type of service is a step up from the cybermalls because Web stores feature a group of sites that share a common theme. For instance, **BookZone** (http://www.bookzone.com/), shown in Figure 5.1, specializes only in authors and small publishing companies that produce their own books. **ITheo.com** (http://www.itheo.com/) offers Web space to fine artists only. Even though a niche Web store gives you a site that's mixed in with many other sites, it does at least have a focus—an important element in online branding. There are drawbacks, though. First, Web stores often have limited features; for example, many restrict the number of pages you can build, which means what you can do with your site is limited. Second, the URL assigned to you will be a directory of the Web store's domain name, as in http://www.webstore.com/mypage/. That means you'll lose your Web address if you ever decide to host your site elsewhere.

FIGURE 5.1: BookZone is a Web store that specializes in one type of merchant: authors and small book publishing companies.

E-commerce services—While similar to Web stores and cybermalls, e-commerce services also allow you to process secure credit card transactions online, sometimes without having to set up your own merchant account. If you sell products related to your brand image, this may be an attractive option. However, many e-commerce sites don't offer the flexibility to add important nonproduct information pages that are crucial to your online branding efforts. **Yahoo! Store** (http://store.yahoo.com/) is a big player in this category, with rates starting at $100 per month to sell up to 50 items. Other examples include **CD Street** (http://www.cdstreet.com/), which processes credit card orders for unsigned bands and small record labels.

Read This Book—*Choosing a Web host, creating Web pages, registering a domain name, and submitting to search engines are topics we merely touch on in this chapter. These subjects deserve a complete book to fully cover them. In fact, one book you should strongly consider reading is* Poor Richard's Web Site: Geek-Free, Commonsense Advice on Building a Low-Cost Web Site, *by Peter Kent, Top Floor Publishing. It's one of the most widely reviewed books on the topic. For more details, visit* http://topfloor.com/pr/website2/index.htm.

A Web-Hosting Company

Think of a Web server as a big apartment complex. The landlord, your Web host, rents one of the apartments to you. Even though the landlord rents apartments to many other tenants, the apartment you pay for has a separate address and is yours to do with as you please. As long as you don't do anything illegal with your little piece of real estate, you're free to arrange the furniture and decorate any way you want.

Web-hosting companies operate the same way. You rent so many megabytes of space on a Web host's server. Within reason, you can upload and display any documents you want in any manner you see fit. You're not restrained by the templates and limited design features of many cybermalls, Web stores, and so on. Web hosting is by far your best choice for a brand-building Web site, because it gives you complete freedom about how you position yourself and present who you are to the world.

However, as with apartments, you often get what you pay for. You may get a cramped studio apartment version of Web space through your host, or you may choose to pay more and get a spacious townhouse with extra features. Keeping with the low-cost Poor Richard's theme of this book, though, you can usually find all the features you need at a fairly low cost. I have never spent more than $9.95 a month for a Web host. Here are three good sources to help you find Web-hosting companies:

BudgetWeb.com
http://www.budgetweb.com/budgetweb/

TopHosts.com
http://www.tophosts.com/

Compare Web Hosts
http://www.comparewebhosts.com/

Before making a final decision about a Web host, you'll want to look carefully through each company's list of services and FAQ pages. Here are some things to keep in mind: If you use Microsoft FrontPage to design your pages, make sure the server has FrontPage extensions installed. Try to go with a site with no set-up fee that lets you pay one month at a time; however, you can often get a better rate by prepaying for a year in advance. If your Web site grows, find out how much it will cost to add more disk space, transfer more data, create more e-mail accounts, and so on. This section only scratches the surface of how to evaluate a potential Web host. For more details, read this excerpt from Peter Kent's *Poor Richard's Web Site* book: **20 Questions to Ask a Web Hosting Company** at http://www.topfloor.com/pr/freeinfo/20q.htm.

Should You Serve Yourself?—*Another Web site option is to host your pages on your own server. Using the apartment-complex comparison in the accompanying section, this would be like buying your own house instead of renting an apartment. It's expensive to purchase the necessary computer equipment and takes a lot of know-how to set up your own server. That puts this option out of reach for most people interested in branding themselves online.*

How to Create Web Pages

Now that you know the various options about how to host your Web site, you must create the brand-building pages to put there. How do you do that? The first step is learning the language of Web browsers. No, you won't have to take a semester of Geekspeak 101 or become fluent in Techno Mumbo-Jumbo, but you must become familiar with HyperText Markup Language (HTML). The next time you display a Web page in your browser, place the cursor over the page and right-click your mouse. A small window opens. Select the View Source option. A new window that appears to be filled with Egyptian hieroglyphics opens. That's what an HTML file looks like (see Figure 5.2). HTML files include the text that appears on the Web page along with a series of tags enclosed in angled brackets. These tags tell the browser how to display the page: the size and style of the text, where images appear, how design elements are aligned, and so on.

At first sight, the code used to create HTML documents seems intimidating. Your early attempts to figure out what the tags mean will have you cocking your head like a German Shepherd hearing a high-pitched squeal. But I implore you to take time to learn at least the basics of

FIGURE 5.2: Selecting the View Source option allows you to see the HTML code behind any Web page.

HTML. Doing so will be helpful, even if you end up using one of the easy HTML editors we discuss in the next section. If you get the hang of HTML, you may even be able to design your own Web pages from scratch. If you go the do-it-yourself route, all you'll need is a simple text program, such as WordPad (Windows) or SimpleText (Mac). Many people don't realize that HTML files are merely text files that are given an .html or .htm file extension name.

Tag, You're It—*Learning the nitty-gritty of HTML tags takes a little effort, but it's well worth your time. At the very least, have some fun writing your own HTML code and designing some simple practice pages. It will give you a much better understanding of how Web browsers browse. Here are four sites that do a good job of explaining how HTML works and how to use this tag-filled language to create your own Web pages:*

HowStuffWorks, http://www.howstuffworks.com/web-page.htm

HTML Goodies—Beginning HTML, http://htmlgoodies.earthweb.com/

Dave's Site—HTML, http://www.davesite.com/webstation/html/

HTML Primer, http://htmlprimer.com/

Another way to create your pages is to use the design tool that may be provided by your Web host. Many free Web-hosting sites, cybermalls, and Web stores offer this feature. However, as mentioned in the previous section, these interfaces frequently give you templates with limited design options. The last thing you want to do is introduce yourself to a new crop of potential fans using a Web site that looks hastily thrown together.

An additional method for creating Web pages is by using a simple HTML converter. The most common types of converters are word-processing programs, such as Microsoft Word, that allow you to save documents as HTML files. When these programs convert, they automatically add the appropriate HTML tags. The problem is, converter programs often add unnecessary tags and what they can do is limited. However, they are good options if you need to convert lots of Word files to Web pages and don't need them to look fancy. The following sections give you still more choices about how to create Web pages.

Using HTML Authoring Tools

The best way to design a nice-looking Web site using the least amount of time and effort is to use what's called an authoring tool, also known as an HTML editor. *Authoring tools* are programs that create HTML code for you based on the design elements you want. Here are the two main types of authoring tools:

HTML editors—If you like clicking a button to get a desired result, HTML editors are for you. Instead of having to memorize specific HTML tags, these editors allow you to select text and simply click an appropriate icon to make it bold, turn it into a headline, make it an active hyperlink, and so on. HTML editors automatically insert the code required to duplicate the look or function you want. More sophisticated HTML editors also allow you to view what your Web page looks like as you design it, which lets you make minor corrections as you go. Some HTML editors to consider include **SiteAid** (http://www.siteaid.com/), **HomeSite** (http://www.allaire.com/products/homesite/), **CoffeeCup** (http://www.coffeecup.com/), and **BBEdit** for the Mac (http://www.barebones.com/).

WYSIWYG HTML editors—WYSIWYG stands for *What You See Is What You Get*. These HTML editors work from a visual perspective and don't concern you with HTML tags at all. You design your Web pages in much the same way you do a paper-based layout in a desktop-publishing program. You indicate the links and other interactive features you want on the page, and the WYSIWYG editor generates all the HTML code needed to produce the design you see on your computer screen. **Microsoft FrontPage** (http://www.microsoft.com/frontpage/) is one of the leading programs in this category. Other WYSIWYG editors include **Adobe GoLive** (http://www.adobe.com/products/golive/), **HomePage** (http://www.filemaker.com/products/hp_home.html), **WebExpress** (http://www.mvd.com/webexpress/), and **Dreamweaver** (http://www.macromedia.com/software/dreamweaver/).

Hiring a Web Designer

Perhaps all this talk of tags and code and HTML editors has your head spinning. If you just don't feel up to learning all the details, hiring someone else to create your pages may be the way to go. Many Web-hosting companies offer design services for an extra fee. You might also choose to hire a freelance Web designer to help you produce your pages. If you go the freelancer route, you might try finding one through **AAADesignList.com** at http://www.aaadesignlist.com/. You can also find sites you think have an appealing look and feel and contact the owners to find out who they used to design their sites.

Before you hire a Web designer, ask for references and to see samples of his or her work. Hopefully, the designer can show you active online sites, as opposed to speculative offline experiments. You want to see how the designer's site navigation and loading speeds operate on a live, working site. Design fees are all over the map. A novice or someone doing you a favor may charge only $25 per page, while a more experienced Web design pro can bill you a couple thousand dollars or more to do your entire site. For information on finding and choosing a Web designer, check out these two helpful articles:

Building a Better Web Site—Hiring a Web Designer
http://romance-central.com/Workshops/website6.html

Intuitive.com—How to Pick a Web Designer
http://www.intuitive.com/articles/web-designer.html

Once you select a designer, make sure you have a good idea of what you want ahead of time. Use the steps outlined in Chapter 6, "Designing Your Web Site for Brand Impact," to determine the sections to include in your Web site and how to present them. Show the designer other sites that appeal to you and sketch out some crude layouts. You certainly want to ask the Web designer for suggestions, but remember, your Web site needs to be a reflection of you. It must ooze your personality and style. It has to establish your brand identity in no uncertain terms. Therefore, you must clearly communicate your image to the designer and make sure the final look of your site effectively gets across your message.

What's File Transfer Protocol?—Web pages are designed on a personal computer's hard drive. To be seen by the masses online, those HTML files need to be transferred to your host's Web server. Unfortunately, you can't have Scotty beam them up. Some Web hosts offer an interface that allows you to use your browser to select files from your hard drive and upload them, but the most common way is to use a File Transfer Protocol (FTP) client. FTP clients are programs that communicate with Web servers and allow you to upload, download, rename, arrange, delete files, and so on. Most FTP programs are available as freeware or in full-featured demo versions, including **WS FTP** *(http://www.ipswitch.com/Products/WS_FTP/),* **CuteFTP** *(http://www.cuteftp.com/),* **AceFTP** *(http://www.visicommedia.com/aceftp/), and* **Fetch** *for Mac users (http://www.dartmouth.edu/pages/softdev/fetch.html).*

Your Web Site URL

Once you've designed attractive, easy-to-use Web pages and have arranged to store them on a Web host's server, you need to register a domain name for fans to use to find your site. Registering a Web address is a lot like setting up an 800 number with a long-distance provider. You might come up with the great idea of promoting your fine art business with a toll-free number that spells out 800-FINEART. First, though, you have to find out whether that number is available. If it's already taken, you must come up with alternate choices that do an equally good job of getting your brand identity across.

Know Your Levels—*A top-level domain is the part of a Web address that comes after the dot: com, net, org, and edu are all top-level domain names. The part that comes before the dot is the second-level domain: yahoo, amazon, monster, and NBCi are all second-level domain names. When you register a Web site address, you're registering a specific combination of top-level and second-level domain names.*

Similarly, you should come up with a list of domain name possibilities and see whether they're available. Use the tips we discussed in Chapter 3, "Developing Your Online Branding Arsenal," to come up with the most powerful Web address possibilities. Whatever domain name you choose, keep in mind that it must be unique and easy to remember, spell, and type into a Web browser. The words that make up the address must also be directly related to your brand name and image. Hundreds of sites will allow you to perform domain-name searches. One of the better-known places to check is **Network Solutions** at http://www.networksolutions.com/. If you go there and type a name, the site lets you know if it's available in a .com, .net, or .org version.

For instance, you might be interested in registering JanesSilkStockings.com and discover it's only available as JanesSilkStockings.net. Some domain-name search sites also give you a long list of other possibilities based on the words you entered, such as Janes-Silk-Stockings.com or JanesSilkStockingsOnline.com. Then you'll have a choice to make: Take the .net name; go with one of the suggested derivative names, or continue looking for a more favorable option as a .com. The general consensus is that a .com top-level domain is better than .net. The .org domain is usually used for associations and nonprofit organizations; .edu is reserved for educational institutions and .gov for government agencies.

There have been a lot of changes in the domain registration end of the Web in recent years. By the time you read this, it may be possible to register Web addresses with the following top-level domains:

.biz (specifically for businesses)

.info (for any site)

.name (for personal Web sites)

.pro (available only to professionals in the medical, legal, and accounting fields)

.museum (for accredited museums worldwide)

.aero (for airlines and related organizations)

.coop (for business cooperatives, such as credit unions and rural electric coops)

Some of these new top-level domains are expensive propositions. For instance, .biz domains cost $2,000 to register and $150 a year to maintain. The reason for the hefty fees is to limit the use of the .biz address to serious business entities. As it is now, .com domains can be registered as easily by an international conglomerate as by the frat boy down the street who threw up a Web site to display his beer-bottle collection.

The good news is registering a meat-and-potatoes, top-level domain is less expensive than it's ever been. To explain this, I need to give a quick history lesson. For years, an organization called InterNIC was solely responsible for issuing and cataloging .com, .net, .org, .edu, and .gov Web addresses. InterNIC is run by Network Solutions (whose site I suggested you use to search for a domain name). Network Solutions recently changed its name to VeriSign Global Registry. Are you with me so far? The company, whatever name it's going by, has settled into a fee structure that includes $70 to register a domain name for two years, with a $35 annual renewal fee after the second year.

In 1999, an organization of Internet experts with the awe-inspiring name Internet Corporation for Assigned Names and Numbers (ICANN) made a smart decision to deregulate the domain registration industry. VeriSign still compiles and stores the Web addresses, but a long list of other companies has been authorized to register domain names. That old $70-for-two-years fee is still the price you hear reported frequently as the going rate for domain-name registration. However, it simply isn't true. I registered both my domain names for $15 a year, with a one-year minimum. Why such a low price? Because deregulation did away with fixed prices and opened the market to competition. Authorized domain name registrars pay VeriSign just $9 for every domain they register. Any amount charged above that is profit. As a result, domain-name registration prices have dropped dramatically. These days, why pay $35 a year when you can pay $15 or less? Here is a short list of domain-name registrars with discount prices:

ImperialRegistrar.com ($13)
http://imperialregistrar.com/registration/

DirectNIC ($15)
http://www.directnic.com/ (shown in Figure 5.3)

EyeOnDomain.com ($15)
http://www.eyeondomain.com/

Low Cost Domains ($24)
http://www.lowcostdomains.com/

Top-level domain names are also available for many countries, such as .uk for United Kingdom, .ca for Canada, .au for Australia, and so on. Unless you're conducting business exclusively in one of these countries (or need to make it

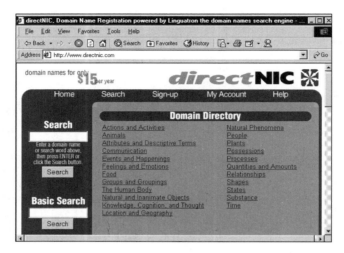

FIGURE 5.3: DirectNIC is one of many authorized registration services that offer domain names at reduced prices.

appear that you are), it's better to have the international appearance of a .com or .net. Some companies have done creative things with more obscure country domains. The country of Tuvalu, for example, was issued a top-level domain of .tv, which has prompted many businesses to snatch up URLs such as www.free.tv or www.web.tv. I discovered that St. Tome and Principe was issued .st as a domain, which quickly led to visions of www.easy.st or www.main.st. However, when I entered those URLs into my browser, it couldn't find the pages. Proceed cautiously before registering a foreign domain, but it is something to think about, especially if the letters spell out something that reinforces your brand identity. For more information on international domains, check out **Alldomains.com** at http://www.alldomains.com/.

*Taking a URL Shortcut—In 1997, a company called **V3—The Internet Identity Company** (http://www.v3.com/) registered dozens of second-level domain names using the top-level domain of Tonga, which uses .to. V3 ended up owning URLs, such as go.to, come.to, welcome.to, and more. Instead of selling these domain names, the company gives away subdirectories of these domains and markets them as shortcut URLs. For instance, to reach my music business site, you can use* http://go.to/buzzfactor; *to reach my site for artists, use* http://go.to/quicktips. *What these shortened Web addresses do is redirect you to whatever site the owner specifies. Like most free services online, the redirection is accompanied by either a pop-up ad banner or an ad in the browser's window. A registered domain name is still your best bet, but shortcut URLs do provide another option to consider.*

When you register a domain name, you basically own it. It's yours for life, as long as you continue paying the annual fee the registrar charges.

Search Engine Tips and Tricks

For years, there's been a lot of hype on the Internet regarding search engine placement. Lots of companies charge lots of money to help Web site owners get a higher ranking in search engine results. I've never been swept up in this search hysteria, and I suggest you steer clear of it, too. If you do a good job of branding yourself online, you'll have far more people finding you through means other than stumbling upon you through search engine results. WebSideStory's StatMarket, an Internet usage research firm, reports that search sites account for a little more than 7 percent of global referrals. Direct navigation and bookmarks (meaning people who already know where they want to go) account for the largest percentage with over 46 percent. Internet links, which include link directories, banner ads, and affiliate programs, account for 45 percent.

Search engines will never be your biggest source of new fans and customers, so don't get too sidetracked trying to improve your placement when you can use far more effective tactics to get noticed online. Still, you can do some simple things to improve your chances of popping up in search results based on keywords related to your brand.

There are many different types of search engines and directories. Some search sites use so-called *bots* that visit Web sites and automatically evaluate the HTML documents for relevance based on the words that appear on the page. Other sites, particularly directories, use human editors to visit sites and determine whether they deserve to be added to the directory's database. There's also something called eXtensible Markup Language (XML), which uses a Document Type Declaration (DTD) to specify the organization that issued the XML document; some search engines use XML and DTD to limit the number of sites found in search results. Volumes have been written on how various search engines work and how people can trick the systems into ranking a particular site higher in results. We won't delve into that nonsense, but I'd like to cover a few practical steps you can take to make your Web site more search-friendly.

Page Titles, Meta Tags, and Keywords

When someone types search terms at a search site and presses Enter, the engine gets busy looking for Web pages that are most relevant to the terms. If you entered *fried fish*, the results would display pages with fried fish recipes, commentary, and other kinds of content. Many search engines use certain sections of a Web page's HTML code to determine relevancy. Those sections include the <TITLE> tags, which determine the title that appears in the upper-left corner of your browser. Another important section is the area that includes <META> tags for the page's description and keywords. <META> tags are invisible to people viewing your Web page, but search engines often use them to help clarify what your page is about.

Most HTML editors include features for inserting these tags and their related content into your Web pages. In other cases, you may have to insert the information manually with a plain-text editor, such as the Windows' Notepad. Following is an example of <TITLE> and <META> tag HTML code in action:

```
<HTML>
<HEAD>
<TITLE>Fried Fish Tips—recipes and advice on fried fish
preparation and cooking at home</TITLE>
<META NAME="description" content="Low-cost recipes and tips on
how to fry fish in your own kitchen">
<META NAME="keywords" content="fish, fried, fry, recipes,
cooking, kitchen, pan, battered, fillets">
</HEAD>
```

Notice how the words between the <TITLE> and </TITLE> tags not only give the page its title, but also include a little extra description to further clarify what content is on the page. This helps your standing in some search results, especially when someone uses one of the words in your title as a search term. The "description" <META> tag is simply a short description of the page's content. Some search engines display this text under the page's name, while others merely use the description to home in on the page's true content. Some search engines use the <META> *keywords* tag to match search terms.

Put ALT Text to Work—ALT *text is an attribute used on Web pages to describe hyperlinks and images. With most newer browsers, if you leave the mouse pointer on an image or link for a few seconds, a small text message appears that explains what the image or link is. Some search engines consider* ALT *text descriptions when evaluating search-term matches. It would be smart to use* ALT *attributes in your HTML code and make sure the text reinforces your primary keywords.*

To make the best use of these tags, it's important to know the words and phrases that potential fans use to search for information on your specialized field. Think of your ideal customers. Put yourself in their shoes and make a list of the words they would use to hunt down a resource, such as the one you offer. Make sure those words are listed somewhere in your <META> and <TITLE> tags. It can also help if your most defining keywords are repeated throughout these tags and within the body of text that appears on your page. Don't get lured into hiding invisible keywords that are repeated dozens of times in an attempt to trick the search engines. Most search functions these days are wise to this method and summarily toss out any sites that use this technique. Just make sensible use of the primary words that define your brand and what you offer.

Submitting to Search Engines and Directories

A number of online services will submit your Web pages to search engines. Some promise to present your site information to thousands of search engines for a fee. Others submit your site to a limited number of engines for free. Some of the freebie services include the following:

Add Me
http://www.addme.com/

Submit Express
http://submitexpress.com/

Submitco
http://www.submitco.com/5engines.html

While there's nothing wrong with using these services for some of the secondary search engines, your branding efforts will be better served by submitting individually to the dozen or so top search engines. Read each site's submission policy carefully. Some require you to enter only your Web address; however most require a lot of information. Some want only the main home page submitted, and others welcome the submission of individual pages. To speed this process along, create a text file with the following things: your page's title and full URL; your name and e-mail address; a 10-word, 20-word, and 50-word description of your site; a keyword list of up to 25 phrases, with the most important words first; and your physical address and phone number. With this information ready to go ahead of time, you'll be able to copy and paste the required information quickly. Here's a list of the top sites where you should submit your Web pages individually:

Yahoo! (Spend some time looking through Yahoo!'s directory categories. Find the category that best suits your brand identity and your page. Click the Suggest a Site link on the bottom of that page and follow the instructions.)
http://www.yahoo.com/

Open Directory (This is a directory compiled by human editors. Many search sites use Open Directory listings when providing search results. Get listed here and you'll automatically have a shot at being listed on many search engines.)
http://dmoz.org/

Google (Yahoo! uses Google, shown in Figure 5.4, to power its search function, which makes it a good place to get listed.)
http://www.google.com/

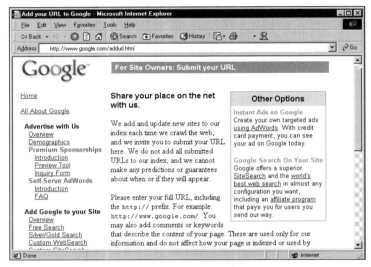

FIGURE 5.4: This URL submission page at Google is an example of the type of instructions to submit your Web pages individually to the major search sites.

MSN (This is the highly traveled Microsoft Network's search engine.)
http://www.msn.com/

Go.com
http://www.go.com/

Alta Vista
http://www.altavista.com/

Excite
http://www.excite.com/

Hotbot
http://hotbot.lycos.com/

Lycos
http://www.lycos.com/

Northern Light
http://www.northernlight.com/

Fast Search
http://www.alltheweb.com/

whatUseek
http://www.whatuseek.com/

Many search-engine submission pages offer you an express service to speed along your site's inclusion. Of course, this service comes with a fee, often in the $199 range. Some people feel it's worth it. I've never paid a dime for any search engine submission. Considering the small percentage of Web sites that are found via search results, I don't consider this the first priority for my hard-earned money. Stick with the basic free submission options.

Go to **Google** (http://www.google.com/), the search engine that supplies Yahoo! with its search results, and type *Bob Baker music*. What comes up in the results are many Web pages on my own site as well as pages that contain articles written by or about me on other Web sites. I didn't get that kind of prime placement by spending hundreds or thousands of dollars on search engine ranking services or by engaging in underhanded schemes to take advantage of search technology loopholes. I did it by using the simple steps described in this chapter and being active enough online to be included in the search results of other sites that write about me or link to my site. You should do the same.

———————

Now that we've covered the basics of creating your Web pages and making them readily available online, it's time to design your Web site for maximum brand impact. In the next chapter, we discuss the most important elements of your Web site and how to present them to attract the kind of fans who will make you a cyberspace celebrity.

CHAPTER SIX

Designing Your Web Site for Brand Impact

In Chapter 5, "Creating Your Personal Brand Web Site," we discussed the mechanics of setting up Web pages. In this chapter, we talk about the particulars of effective online presentation. If you've spent any amount of time surfing the Web, you've already developed a feel for the types of sites you like, don't like, and find confusing. When you visit a Web site for the first time, you most likely know within seconds whether you're going to spend time there or move on quickly.

Your goal is to design a Web site that, within seconds, lets people know what topic your site covers, who you are, and why you're the best person to do what you do. Designed correctly, your Web site will draw in people who make up your target audience and inspire them to stick around and return often. The best Web sites feature a combination of these three powerful elements:

- **Content**—Content refers to the words that appear on your Web site, along with the various pages and sections that are presented within it. Good content immediately conveys your personality, flair, and attitude, while also being clear, direct, and informative.
- **Design**—The look and feel of your Web site should complement and reinforce the site's content and your brand image. A well-designed Web site communicates the site owner's character and attitude, and sets a tone that's carried throughout the site.
- **Interactivity**—The best Web sites usually give visitors the option of doing something while they're there. Whether it's posting an opinion, taking a self-test, or submitting their sites to a link directory, offer your fans some form of interactivity.

Over the next several pages, we'll focus on the three key areas in the previous list. By the time you finish this chapter, you'll have a clear vision of how to design your site so that it grabs the attention of the people most likely to embrace your message and brand image.

Content Is Not Only King, It's the Entire Kingdom

Graphic designer Roger Black, author of *Web Sites That Work*, once wrote, "The problem with most Web sites isn't technical. It's that they don't have anything worthwhile to share with other people." Take Black's comment to heart. You must give visitors a reason to not only surf to your Web site, but to stay put long enough to get to know you. The glue that makes visitors stick is content.

The best type of content is useful and amusing information. Whether you offer free how-to articles, opinions, industry trend predictions, jokes, or recommendations, you should load up your Web site with content that entertains, helps people reach their goals, or solves problems.

To brand yourself online, your Web site must demonstrate your in-depth knowledge of your field and why you're a top resource in your area of expertise. Good content helps you do just that.

A Few Words About Words

Go to a favorite Web site and look at it. Now imagine you have to strip away all the technological flash. Take away the logos, the cool graphics, the dancing icons, even the basic color palette and font-sizing options. What are you left with? That's right, words.

Of all the elements that make up a successful Web site, words are the most important aspect. Sure, I may be biased because I'm a writer, but I believe the heart and soul of your Web site is imparted through the words you use in it. The manner in which you use language reveals your attitude, your confidence level, your knowledge of your specialty, your personality, and a lot more. No amount of flashy animation or dazzling special effects will ever overcome the drawbacks of lackluster verbiage and ho-hum prose. Your brand is what you write about it, so make sure the words that appear on your Web site are power-packed.

The founding fathers and mothers of the Web created HTML simply to make text documents readily available online. They had few notions of streaming media, mind-boggling JavaScript code, and so on. It was all about words. And it still is. When people venture onto the Web, it's usually because they're in search of specific information—in other words, words. Rarely do people search for cool pictures or neat graphics alone.

Spend time thinking about and crafting the words that will represent you on your Web site. What personality and mood do you want to greet your potential fans when they visit your site? If your brand identity is lighthearted, be sure to use humor and levity. If your approach has a spiritual slant, make certain your words reflect that perspective. Are you a serious, straight-talking person? Great. Write that way on your Web site. Whatever slice of your personality you've decided to emphasize as part of your brand image, make sure it shines through on every page of your site.

Respect the Language—*When you visit a site for the first time and find it riddled with typos and grade-school level sentence structures, how do you react? Yes, you probably write off the site as a feeble attempt at e-commerce by a sloppy person. Don't let your visitors say that about you. Always spell-check your text and, if at all possible, have two or three grammatically inclined people look over your words before committing them to the Web.*

Deciding What Pages and Sections to Include

Once you have a Web host, HTML editing software, and some ideas for the words that will appear, you're ready to start creating pages. At this point, you may have the same feeling that an artist has when staring at a blank canvas. Where do you start? Your options are endless. The sky's the limit. You could create a site with 10 pages, 50 pages, or 347 pages. Before you start cranking out pages for every whim that strikes you, ask yourself these three questions:

- Who are my ideal fans?
- What do they want that's related to my brand identity?
- How can I give that to them in the quickest, clearest way possible?

Internet technology gives you the ability to do practically anything with your Web pages, but that doesn't mean you should strive to do everything. Your two goals at this point should be to keep things simple and to provide the content that will most directly help visitors grasp who you are, what you do, and how it benefits them. What follows are some of the most common and effective Web pages you should consider putting on your site.

The All-Important Home Page

When people visit your site, most of them will see your home page first. Your potential fans will form an initial impression of you and your Web site within seconds. As much as we like to think people take time to absorb the many intricacies of what we do, in reality, people form opinions quickly after merely skimming over our finely crafted prose. That means your home page carries the awesome responsibility of having to connect with visitors instantly. Don't make potential fans work too hard to figure out what your site is about, unless you want them to leave as quickly as they came.

Though it may seem contradictory to your online branding philosophy, don't make your name or company logo the primary element on your home page. Yes, branding is all about making a mental connection between your name, what you do, and how you do it. But branding is also about stressing customer benefits to your current and future fans. Right off the bat, your home page should tell visitors what you have that benefits them and why they should care.

For instance, instead of splashing the top half of a home page with *Arnold Jackson, Illustrator,* an artist could use something such as *Lively Spot Art to Spice Up Your Web Pages.* Which of these might entice visitors more: *The Janet Ziffle Group* or *Online PR Services for Small Businesses on a Budget?* As Marcia Yudkin, author of *Internet Marketing for Less than $500/Year,* says, "In most cases, you'll do better leading with what you do rather than with who you are." If you do a good job of drawing people into your site by stressing benefits on your home page, it won't take long to make that important branding connection between what you do and who you are. Amy Gahran's home page, **Contentious** at http://www.contentious.com/ (shown in Figure 6.1), does a nice job of telling visitors what her site is about.

Your home page should also include instructions on how to subscribe to your free e-mail newsletter. In the next chapter, "Publishing an E-mail Newsletter," we'll discuss the details of setting up your own electronic newsletter. For now, just know that a newsletter is something you absolutely must publish and that you

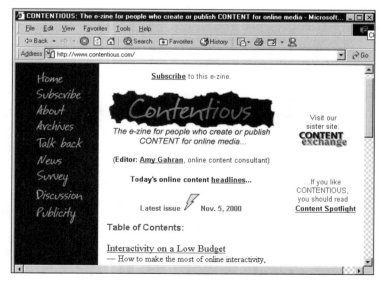

FIGURE 6.1: Content consultant Amy Gahran uses three important elements on her *Contentious* home page: a clear description of what she does, an invitation to subscribe to her newsletter, and a plainly labeled navigation menu.

have to go out of your way to make visitors aware of it. Somewhere near the top of your home page, provide a clear invitation to subscribe.

Also, every good home page on the Web must offer a plainly visible, clearly labeled navigation menu. Think of your home page as a simple introduction to what you do and who you are. Don't try to cram in too many details on this first page. A navigation menu lets people know where else on your site they can go to get more details. On these individual pages, you'll be able to go into more specifics on whatever each page covers.

Add a Search Feature to Your Home Page—*If your Web site grows to the point where it contains dozens of pages with lots of information, you might consider adding a search feature to help visitors find what they want more quickly. Major search engines are set up to search for keywords across the entire Web. However, services that allow visitors to search for words located on your site only are available. Four free search services are* **FreeFind.com** *(http://www.freefind.com/),* **IndexMySite4Free** *(http://www.indexmysite4free.com/),* **PicoSearch.com** *(http://www.picosearch.com/), and* **Atomz** *(http://www.atomz.com/).*

About Page

If you're the type of person who feels you have enough to offer to brand yourself online, you undoubtedly have a rich personal history that your growing legion of fans will want to know about. In addition, you most likely have some passionate ideas regarding why you have a Web presence and what you hope to accomplish online. You may be tempted to express these thoughts on your home page, but your best bet would be to keep your main page clutter-free and move these background details to a separate page.

On your *About* page, you can fully explain who you are, how you got involved with your area of expertise, why visitors should care about the information on your site, how you can help your fans accomplish their goals, and more. If you're selling a product or service, you shouldn't necessarily use this page to push for a sale. The primary purpose of an *About* page is to shed light on the person, people, or company behind the Web site. You may also use this informational page to describe the kinds of content visitors will find throughout your site.

A couple examples of effective *About* pages can be found at **Lean Bodies** at http://www.leanbodies.net/aboutlean.html and **Jeremy Wilkey's MX-TECH** at http://www.mx-tech.com/aboutus.htm.

Articles and Other Informational Content

To connect with people online, you have to provide content that either helps or entertains them. People who do the best job of branding themselves online position themselves as valuable resources with a wealth of information available on their core topics. Some people mistakenly believe that you should only offer free articles on your Web site if you sell information products, such as books, courses, audiotapes, and so on. Nothing could be further from the truth.

Let's say you sell unicorn-themed knick-knacks, posters, and greeting cards. You could simply display an online catalog to take orders, but doing that alone wouldn't take advantage of your full potential to generate interest in your unicorn niche on the Web. A far better approach would be to set up your site as a one-stop destination for all things unicorn-related. You could provide articles on the history of unicorns, how unicorn lore has evolved over the centuries, and perhaps personal stories from customers who have been touched by their unicorn possessions. The idea is to make your site a place where people can get in touch with your area of expertise.

The home page of **Hot Air Ballooning** (http://launch.net/) illustrates how a site can use this tactic:

We're all about balloons. If you've been looking for detailed information about hot air balloons, you've found the right place!

If you want to find out how balloons fly or what it's like to fly in one, you'll want to read The Basics and our Ballooning Q&A. Interested in going for a ride? Our section on Balloon Rides offers the most complete list of ride companies found anywhere. Our Festivals Directory contains a worldwide list of balloon festivals sorted by region.

If you've decided you want to become a balloon pilot, our Pilots Corner has lots of great information to guide you. You'll also want to check out the books available in the Balloonist's Pilot Shop.

Beware that you shouldn't take this aspect of your Web site lightly. Don't just throw up any content you can muster to fill up pages and convince yourself that you're providing content. People can smell fluff a hundred miles away. Your content must be thoughtful, useful, and preferably the type of information not readily found elsewhere. Most importantly, it should radiate an attitude that reflects you and your brand identity. Here are several types of written content you might include on your site:

How-to articles—This kind of article has a timeless appeal. Anyone interested in your area of expertise will want to know how to do something related to it or how to do that something better. If you can provide the step-by-step details your fans crave, and if you can go beyond simply covering the basics, you will soon find yourself embraced by a legion of appreciative fans.

Interviews and Q&As—Target prominent people in your industry and contact them about featuring them in an interview on your site. Talk to them on the phone, or better yet, use e-mail to send a set of questions that your interviewees can answer at their convenience. People love to read about others in their industry.

Success stories—Similar to a Q&A, a success story is a short piece that reveals how one of your fans is accomplishing success with some aspect of his or her activities. These small features can be written by you or by the successful people themselves. Every issue of Angela Adair-Hoy's *Writer's Weekly* newsletter contains a success story from a freelance writer. It's one of the first sections I read. Personal success stories can be very inspiring. Use them.

Ask the expert—Invite visitors to submit their questions to you. Pick out the best ones and write brief responses. These features are not only popular, they also do an excellent job of demonstrating your knowledge of your field.

Current news roundups—This is an especially appealing type of content if you don't consider yourself a polished writer, but it's something you may want to include even if you do have a way with words. Every week or so, visit some of your favorite news Web sites and do a search using keywords related to your niche. When you find a current news story that would be of interest to your visitors—one that's clearly focused on your brand image—write a short blurb about it and provide a link to the page that contains the full story. If you compile them on a regular basis, your fans will view your site as a clearinghouse of information on your chosen field.

Reviews and opinions—As you begin to establish yourself as an expert online, you'll slowly become a mover and shaker whose opinions matter. People will be interested in getting your take on the latest books, Web sites, gadgets, and trends in your industry. Don't be shy. Get over your fear of rubbing people the wrong way. Give your honest opinion on the things that matter to the people who are attracted to your brand. Your fans will reward you with tons of respect.

Humor columns—Any field could benefit from a little jocularity. Scott Adams' Dilbert cartoon has become an institution among people who work away their lives in the cubicle trenches. If you can shine some lighthearted light on your well-defined brand niche, you may find yourself with throngs of laughing fans.

You can do a few helpful things on your article pages that will not only help your visitors absorb the information, but will also help spread the word of your brand. If your articles are displayed on pages that also contain banner ads, navigation bars, and other non-article design elements, you may want to offer print-friendly pages as well. This can be accomplished by simply including a Print This Article link that takes the visitor to the same article on a Web page with a very basic layout. Many people don't read at length while online, but they will print to read laterarticles that interest them. Make it easy for your visitors to print your articles.

I provide an autoresponder option for each article on my music-marketing site. If visitors want the article they're reading e-mailed to them, they just click a mailto: link that sends an e-mail to the appropriate autoresponder address. By doing this, they get the article in a text-only, printer-friendly form; they're more apt to read the article since it'll be sitting in their e-mail inbox, and they'll be able to share the article easily with others by forwarding it via e-mail.

Spice Up Your Online Articles—*Many Web sites offer helpful article features, such as* E-mail this article to a friend, Comment on this article, *or* Rate this article. *These functions usually require that some type of CGI or JavaScript be inserted into the HTML of each page. Two good places to check for these interactive scripts are* **Free Scripts** *at* http://www.freescripts.com/scripts/ *and* **Matt's Script Archive** *at* http://www.worldwidemart.com/scripts/.

Online Portfolio

Regardless of your brand identity, you most likely will benefit from including Web pages that show samples of your work. Some of the more obvious categories include fine artists, cartoonists, designers, and photographers. What better way to demonstrate a mastery of their craft than to display specific examples of what they do? Dan Knudson's photography site, **Dan Knudson Photography** at http://www.danknudson.com/ (shown in Figure 6.2), displays his talents well. If you sell physical products via mail order, images of the items on your site would no doubt help sales. Freelance writers often make a collection of their previous work available online to show editors what they can do.

Watch Your Image Download Time: Use Thumbnails—*If your brand identity is best served by displaying images of your work, consider using thumbnail graphics. Particularly if you need to show a lot of images on a single page, don't make people wait for several large graphic elements to load before they can proceed. Instead, create small thumbnail versions of each image and allow visitors to click the images they want to see in larger versions. Use real thumbnails, which are smaller graphic files created from larger ones. If you simply change the* `Height=` *and* `Width=` *attributes but still reference the larger image files, you won't save any download time.*

There are other, less obvious ways to display a portfolio of your skills. If your brand identity involves helping people change something (their weight, hairstyle, or wardrobe, for example), you'd do well to show before and after

FIGURE 6.2: Photographer Dan Knudson makes good use of displaying images and establishing an identity on his promotional Web site.

pictures. Your skill may be in landscaping, sculpture, architecture, antiques, or auto detailing; such specialties deserve visual representation on your Web site. Even though written information may be the cornerstone of Web content, don't overlook ways to reinforce your brand image using the visual capabilities of the Internet.

Links Page

To be considered a comprehensive resource on your area of expertise, your site should include a page of links to useful sites closely related to your topic. Many people shy away from providing links that take visitors away because they fear they'll lose potential fans before visitors have a chance to warm up to their site. This view is shortsighted. To be effective on the Internet, you can't operate in a vacuum. Recommending other sites to your visitors can pay off in many ways, including the following:

- Helps you further establish yourself as a true resource in your field
- Allows you to get reciprocal links back from the sites you include on your links page
- Gives you credibility by demonstrating you're not afraid to share your knowledge and send your fans to other sites

By having the confidence to reveal other online resources related to your field, you create more value for your brand, which inspires people to return to your site often to get more of your unselfish advice.

Other Pages That Help Build Your Brand

Here are several more sections you should consider adding to your Web site:

Discussion forum—If you have a lot of people with similar interests visiting your site, you may as well give them a chance to communicate with each other. Include a discussion forum page where people can post their own messages and respond to others' messages. A forum provides another reason for people to visit and spend time on your site.

What's New page—Web users are impatient for information. They'd prefer not to spend time figuring out what you've added since the last time they stopped by your site. Your fans may appreciate having one page that lists your latest additions.

Weblog—Informational content isn't limited to full-length articles. In fact, the most widely read type of prose on the Internet comes in the form of short, concise nuggets of information. It may take you a week to write an article; but a quick idea, tip, or recommendation can be hammered out in minutes. Weblogs are like online notebooks where you can post these brief thoughts as they come to you. If you use a free service like **Blogger** (http://www.blogger.com/), your weblog can be updated and uploaded instantly.

Resume, brochure, or product pages—If you sell products or services online, you absolutely must include Web pages on your site that spell out benefits, features, and ordering instructions. If you're asking people for money, you need to provide pages that fully explain each thing you're selling and why customers should fork over their cash to get it.

Order form—Once you've sold visitors with your brochure or product pages, you should direct them to a secure online ordering page. Even if people can purchase directly from each item's page, you should also supply a general order page that lists everything available for sale.

Press releases—Some companies post press releases they send to the media in special sections of their sites. A press release archive acts as a What's New page for media people, while it also makes casual visitors aware of the Web site's activities.

Testimonials—Nothing sells a product or service like a rousing endorsement from an objective third party. It doesn't hurt to sprinkle a positive testimonial or two on each page of your site. Quotes from the media or satisfied customers lend reinforcement to claims you make about your worthiness. In addition to splashing some well-placed testimonials on various pages, you may want to feature a full collection of them on one *Here's what people are saying about...* page.

Contact page—You've probably noticed that many sites offer a page that includes a variety of communication options: e-mail, physical address, and phone and fax numbers. The best advice is to put this basic contact information in the same spot on every page of your site. That way, people won't have to go far to send you an e-mail, find out what city you operate out of, and so on. If you're a one-person operation with minimal contact details, you may not need a separate contact page. However, if you have five different people who handle different functions and get messages at different e-mail addresses, a contact page makes sense.

Web Content Style Tips

First things first: When it comes to your Web content, keep the reader's perspective in mind. Always speak to your visitors as if they're standing right in front of you. Write like you're having a personal conversation. Some text on the Web is so formal and stiff, it's more exciting to read every name and address in the White Pages. Don't write something dry, such as *Individuals who visit this site will benefit from the wealth of kangaroo information they will access while perusing our articles.* Instead, phrase that thought this way: *If you like kangaroos, you'll love the wealth of information we have for you on those lovable, hopping creatures from Down Under.*

Research has consistently shown that people are far more eager to read when the writing style is conversational and informal, as opposed to stuffy and overly business-oriented. These reader preferences have been true in the offline world for decades, but hordes of people regularly ignore this reality and continue to write more like machines than human beings. It's no surprise, then, that this lifeless writing trend continues on the Internet. Don't fall into this trap. When you write the text for your Web site, be warm, real, friendly, and approachable.

While you're being so amiable, make plentiful use of the word *you*. Using that one word repeatedly is the best way to make your visitors feel you are speaking directly to them. Go through your text and look for distant, third-person references, such as *user, visitor, customer, they, their,* and so on. Whenever possible, rewrite your sentences so that they reflect the more personal, second-person point of view.

Avoid puffery at all costs. Many people despise disguised advertising or anything that reeks of hype online. People may feel that way because hype and disguised advertising run rampant on the Internet. Separate yourself from this hyperbole by ridding your prose of inflated adjectives, such as *amazing*, *unbelievable*, *best*, and *biggest*. The best way to convince people that you're the best is to confidently demonstrate your knowledge or skills and let people draw their own conclusions about how cool you are.

Unlike their print-based counterparts, words on the Web are consumed briskly and in quick doses. To keep readers reading, you need to get to the point fast. Most surfers won't wade through an ambiguous opening paragraph without knowing exactly where your words are leading them. Present summaries and conclusions up front and then follow up with meaty details and related tangents. Unless you're appealing to fans of poetry, people simply won't sit through wandering introductions or verbiage that teases more than it informs.

Another important fact revealed through usability research is that people rarely read online. Instead, they scan, searching for something that catches their eye and their interest. Long, scrolling pages of plain text are a turnoff for scanners. Print editors refer to pages filled with lots of text as *gray*, meaning bland and uninviting. Don't create gray Web pages. The best way to overcome the gray demon is to write short and break up your text into lively nuggets of information. Here are a few elements and concepts you can use to create more inviting text pages:

Use headings and subheads—Let readers know what topic each section covers by using headings. You can further break down each section with a series of subheads under the more general heading. You see examples of this concept in action throughout this book. Headings should not only pinpoint the topic being discussed, they should also offer people a reason to read the text that follows. For instance, instead of using the plain heading *Winter Car Maintenance Tips*, you might use a more benefit-oriented version, such as *Five Ways to Keep Your Car from Breaking Down This Winter*.

Use bullets and lists—By far, the best way to create content that people who scan text online will devour is to use bullet points and similar types of lists. Consider the list you're reading right now. I've taken four Web writing suggestions and have presented them in a quickly digestible format. Since I've put each point's primary idea in bold text, you could scan this list and know in seconds what my advice covers. Since this topic interests you, you read further for more details. Give your Web site visitors the same treatment. Raleigh Pinskey uses a bullet-point technique well on her home page, **Raleigh Pinskey** at http://www.promoteyourself.com/ (shown in Figure 6.3).

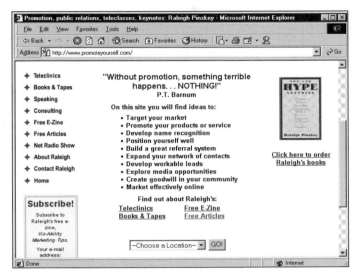

FIGURE 6.3: Notice the effective use of bullet points on Raleigh Pinskey's home page. How easy would these points have been to read if they'd been strung together in one long paragraph?

Bold, italicize, and highlight key words and phrases—Emphasizing key words isn't limited to lists. Even within normal paragraphs, you can use bold, italics, or a colored highlight to draw attention to your most important ideas.

Present one idea per paragraph—Words are wonderful things, but you shouldn't expect too much of them. Before you write anything, determine the main point you want to make. Stick to that point as you write. Each paragraph should support your main point with a single idea. Don't litter your paragraphs by trying to cover too many angles.

Before we move on to Web site design tips, let's cover a couple word-related navigation issues. Many experts rightly recommend not using terms that refer to the mechanics of the Web. The rampant use of *click here* is usually cited as the biggest offender. Whenever possible, avoid the use of *click* or *go here* and instead turn the obvious verb or noun into a hyperlink. For instance, don't write, *For more information on bird seed, click here.* Opt for something such as, *Our bird seed page shows you everything you need to know about food for finches* and hyperlink the words *bird seed page*. The result is the same, but you haven't distracted people by reminding them what they should do with their mouse.

Finally, be careful about the words you use for your navigation links. Some sites try to be clever and use fun phrases to label the various link options within the site. The best advice is to stick with clear directions, such as Home, Subscribe, About, Contact, Tips, Samples. Which do you think is clearer? *Recommended Links* or *Surf-O-Rama*? *Testimonials* or *Mouthing Off*? As tempting as the cute references might be, it's probably better to stick with navigational road maps people will understand quickly and use.

Use It or Lose It—*Jakob Nielsen is considered by many to be the guru of Web content and usability. His books and research studies are often quoted and highly regarded, primarily because his advice is based on observing real people interacting with real Web sites. Visit his site,* **useit.com** *at* http://www.useit.com/, *and you'll find lots of content-related information. His presentation is a bit academic, but the lessons he reveals will come in handy as you design your branding site.*

---

21 Rules for Better Web Site Design

Content may be king, but without an effective Web design in place, your precious words could easily go unread because visitors don't like the way your site looks or operates. Consider this scenario: You want to purchase a book online and decide to check out the selection at Amazon.com. You type the URL into your browser and go. It takes several seconds for the page to load. Eventually, you slowly start to see a Flash animation of a large river of books flowing across your computer screen; meanwhile, a cheesy electronic keyboard version of "Take Me to the River" starts to play over your speakers. The animation sputters on until it finally fades into the regular home page.

Of course, this is a fictitious account, but what would you think if Amazon really did that with its home page? Most likely, you, like millions of other Web surfers, would start looking for other places to buy books online. Amazon doesn't use these distracting special effects. Neither does Yahoo!, America Online, nor the Microsoft Network. Those companies could certainly afford to add all sorts of groovy design elements, but they don't. Why? Time-consuming Web theatrics chase far more people away than they attract.

Why, then, do so many so-called Web marketers bombard visitors with these visual and audio displays? Why do they use garish color schemes? Why do their pages leave so many visitors scratching their heads, wondering how to get to a desired page? The answer is they haven't mastered the key elements of effective Web site design. Read the following collection of design tips; use them, and you'll find yourself far ahead of the pack.

1. **Make sure the visual elements reinforce your brand identity.** The essence of your brand can most likely be summarized using words, but your identity is also accompanied by many intangible qualities. Brands are as much about attitudes, feelings, and emotions as they are about factual

information. The overall look of your Web site must support these defining factors. Is your brand identity best served by hard edges or softer, rounded shapes? Do primary colors capture your personality or would earth tones be a better match? Experiment and find the right fit before settling on a design scheme.

2. **Forget cool, think useful.** This phrase is borrowed from Peter Kent's book, *Poor Richard's Web Site.* No matter how much your Web designer or your computer geek friends encourage you to use the latest online gadget, don't add a new effect unless it reinforces your brand or provides something truly useful to your visitors.

3. **Lead visitors where you want them to go.** Earlier in this chapter, in the section "Deciding What Pages and Sections to Include," I encouraged you to keep your fans in mind by filling your site with the information they want. But you have needs too. While your content may fulfill the needs of your visitors, your site design should guide them naturally to the places you want them to go. For instance, before fans can download a sample chapter of a writer's book, they might be shown a page that makes them aware of the full-length version and how to order it. Determine your goals and find a way to deliver value to your visitors while also getting what you want.

4. **Offer clear, limited choices.** Some Web sites are so cluttered with navigation bars, banner ads, links, promotional blurbs, image maps, and the like, it's difficult to choose what to do first. Make it too hard for your visitors and they may decide to go elsewhere. Decide what information is most important for your visitors, particularly on your home page, and resist the urge to add more information.

5. **Let visitors know what your site is about.** The worst thing you can do is promote your Web site, get curious people to take a first look, and confuse the heck out of them when they arrive. View your home page through the eyes of a new visitor. Does it spell out exactly what you offer and what your brand stands for? If not, redesign it so it does. Also, remember that many people will arrive at your site through a secondary page, especially if they hear about it through a search engine or recommendation. Therefore, every page needs to explain what your site is about.

6. **Avoid long, scrolling pages.** Sites overdo page length on both sides of the issue. Some sites make visitors scroll through endless reams of announcements, news items, articles, and more—all on a single page. The solution is to break things up. As a general rule, design with one item or concept per page. Provide a menu to related pages. On the other hand, don't break things up too much. Some experts contend that Web pages shouldn't be any longer than one screen length. As a result, many Web sites

force readers to hit a Next button and wait for a new page to load before they can continue reading a relatively short article. If the content on a single page takes up only two or three screens, it's easier to do a little scrolling than to keep hyperlinking to more pages.

7. **Use simple, clean layouts.** Basic is better when it comes to Web site design. That doesn't mean your site has to be boring. Your goal is to keep your pages clutter free, using lots of white space to allow visual breathing room. Have fun with your page layout, but make sure every design choice you make helps you communicate your brand identity.

8. **Keep a consistent theme throughout.** Most designers start by creating the home page, since that's the page most people see first. That's a smart move as long as you carry the home page's look and feel throughout the rest of your site. Wherever the navigation menu is positioned on your home page, make sure the menu is in that same spot on every other page. If you use a fuchsia-colored border under the logo on one page, use fuchsia on all pages. Got it?

9. **Think big—type, that is.** Along with creating a simple, clean design, you also want a site that is easy to read. Don't make surfers squint to absorb your brand-building information. Make it as easy as possible for people to get the details they want. Avoid putting small text on colored or busy backgrounds. Also, some fonts look better as HTML font size 2; others read better at 3. When in doubt, go with the larger size. (Many HTML editing programs specify fonts in points rather than using the older HTML font size designations. Ten-point type may be a good size for your needs.)

10. **Use color tastefully and sparingly.** Color is a funny thing. Used properly, color can create a mood and help establish your brand image. Used irresponsibly, it can look ugly, scream "amateur site, run for your life," and cause thousands to get queasy instantly. Make sure your Web site color choices lean more toward the former.

11. **Provide navigation along the top, left side, and bottom.** When people surf the Web, they love to slip and slide from site to site and page to page. Make sure each of your pages has easy-to-find navigation options along the top and bottom of the page. When visitors come to the end of an article, don't make them scroll all the way back up to the top to get to their next destination. Most well-designed pages also have menu options in a left column. In this column, you can either duplicate the navigation options you offer at the top and bottom or create a separate set of links to pages directly related to the content on that page. Take a look at the **Huge Magazine** site at http://www.hugemagazine.com/ (shown in Figure 6.4) for an example of using a menu in the left column.

FIGURE 6.4: Huge Magazine's art page not only displays images of paintings and drawings, it also provide visitors with a handy navigation menu along the left side of the page.

12. **Adhere to the three-click rule.** Many experts advise that any piece of information on your site should be no further than three clicks away from your home page. I suggest you go further and limit the rule to two clicks. Think of your home page as the first level. All pages you provide a link to from the home page would be considered the second level. Any additional pages you direct people to from the second level would be considered the third level. Third-level pages are two clicks away from the home page. Don't create pages that go any deeper than the third level, if you can help it.

Avoid Getting Framed—*If Frankenstein's monster were a Web geek, he'd probably grunt, "Frames. Bad." A site designed with frames divides the screen into segments that have their own frame and scroll bar. Some browsers don't display them properly. Pages with frames are difficult to bookmark. If you're considering using frames in your design, my advice is to run the other way. Basic is better.*

13. **Stay away from autoplay sounds.** For some reason, many Web site owners love heaping musical ditties on visitors the minute they arrive. It may seem like a good idea, but do your potential fans a favor and get over this misguided notion. Autoplay sounds take extra time to load. They can also come blaring out of someone's speakers when he or she least expects it, for example, at work near the boss's office or at home when the baby is sleeping. These predicaments will not help your brand exposure one bit.

If you want people to hear your music, give them the option of being subjected to it.

14. **Check for browser compatibility.** The most common Web browsers display pages in pretty much the same way, but there are variations. The last time I checked statistics, close to 80 percent of Internet users listed Microsoft's Internet Explorer as their browser of choice. You definitely want to make sure your site is designed to accommodate Bill Gates' favorite browser. However, Netscape Navigator is still used by a significant number of people, as are many other, lesser-known browsers. Try to view your Web pages using different browsers to make sure everything displays correctly. Three sites that can help you determine the browser-friendliness of your pages are **Net Mechanic** (http://www.netmechanic.com/maintain.htm), **Web Site Garage** (http://websitegarage.netscape.com/), and **AnyBrowser.com** (http://www.anybrowser.com/).

15. **Update your site often.** While your goal should be to make your site appealing to first-time visitors, you also need to give visitors good reasons to return and soak up more of your brand-specific offerings. Keep your site fresh by adding new content on a regular basis. That doesn't mean you should make radical changes to your design all the time, but you can add new articles, products, giveaways, and so on.

16. **Check regularly for link rot.** There's nothing more disappointing than reading a cool description of a link, clicking it, and getting an error page. This situation is most common on pages that feature lots of links to recommended sites. Eventually, many of those sites go out of business or switch URLs, and you'll end up with a bad case of link rot. The best cure is to go through your links to external sites at regular intervals and double-check that they're still working. Some online services can perform this function for you. Two that offer free trials are **SEVENtwentyfour** (http://www.seventwentyfour.com/) and **LinkAlarm** (http://www.linkalarm.com/welcome/). And never, ever provide a link to a page on your own site that leads to an error or a page that's under construction. When you delete a page from your site, or when a page isn't quite ready for public consumption, remove all links to it.

17. **Go easy on the gizmos.** Though the free-enterprise system is trying hard to make it one, the Web is *not* currently set up to be a multimedia entertainment center. I once heard morning radio jock Howard Stern joke about how he waited an hour to download a movie clip that eventually played in a grainy frame about two-inches wide. He suddenly realized that in the next room was a life-size TV hooked up to 120 clear-channel cable stations. Why do people continue to squeeze basketball-size media files

through a connection the size of a garden hose? Your visitors will reward you if you chill out on the special effects and don't force them to download dozens of plug-ins to view your pages.

18. **Make good use of page titles.** This is a simple but often-overlooked design tip. The words you put between the `<Title>` and `</Title>` tags show up at the top of your visitor's browser. Those words are also indexed by many search engines. Make sure they describe the specific page, your name, and some reference to your brand image. Commercial HTML editing programs generally provide an easy way to insert page titles.

19. **Stick with standard link colors.** Certain standards have developed on the Web. One of those standards concerns the colors given to various types of hyperlinks. Blue is used for unvisited links, red for an active link as it is being clicked, and purple for links that have been recently visited. With all the skepticism that exists on the Internet, your brand will benefit by providing your visitors with some surfing standards they can count on.

20. **Use hyperlinks, especially within your site.** One of the most appealing aspects of the Web is its interconnectivity. Some of the best sites encourage visitors to bounce around from page to page within the site—or even section to section on the same page. One article can reference a topic covered in another article. Instead of plainly stating, *You'll find more information on Labradors in my FAQ on hunting dogs*, make the words *FAQ on hunting dogs* an active hyperlink that takes the reader straight to that page.

The Dating Game—*One nice touch you can add to make your home page appear fresh is to display the current date near the top of the page. There are simple JavaScript codes available that you can copy and paste into your HTML file that automatically show the current month, date, and year. Two sites that offer these scripts are* **Internet Related Technologies** *at* http://www.developer.irt.org/script/34.htm *and* **JavaScript World** *at* http://www.jsworld.com/scripts/clocks/.

---

21. **Conduct informal usability research.** Once you've come up with a site design plan you're happy with, invite a few friends over who know little about your planned site. Have them visit your home page. Ask them to tell you what the site is about; then ask them to browse around and click what interests them. Observe the pages they go to and which navigation links they use to get there. Next, give them specific tasks: Place an order, subscribe to the newsletter, and so on. Note which steps come easily and which reveal obstacles. This isn't rocket science, but this kind of casual research will help you find your site's strengths and weaknesses quickly. A book on this subject you might want to check out is *Don't Make Me Think! A Common Sense Approach to Web Usability* by Steve Krug.

Adding Interactivity

Have you ever received a direct mail advertisement for a magazine subscription that asked you to peel off a Yes or No sticker and place it on a reply card? Have you ever been given a scratch-off discount ticket at a fast food restaurant or department store? Companies use these hands-on techniques because interactive devices get potential customers involved with their products, not only on a mental level, but a physical one as well. The more involved people are with an item or an idea, the more likely they are to connect with it.

The same goes for Web sites. You may not be able to offer peel-and-stick or scratch-off pages (not yet, anyway), but you can provide several ways for people to interact with you and your brand image. Here are some of the best ways to get your visitors more involved:

Polls and surveys—People love to express their opinions. Offering surveys and polls on your site allows your visitors to use their heads and make choices. This serves two purposes. First, polls inspire people to expend more mental energy and concentration while at your site. Make sure your survey topics or questions are firmly focused on your brand. If you run a tap-dancing Web site, don't ask visitors what their favorite sitcoms are. Ask them to vote for their favorite tap dancer or tap-dancing technique. Persuade people to zero in on your area of expertise. Second, by asking the right questions, you can gather valuable information about your fans' likes and dislikes, wants and needs, and so on. Many online polling services and scripts give you detailed stats on results, complete with graphs and charts. Share this information with your visitors and use it to your advantage as you craft the best site and image for your brand. One free online survey tool that looks promising is **Zommerang** at http://www.zoomerang.com/. **Uptilt**, at http://www.uptilt.com/, provides a fee-based polling application along with other interactive features.

Quizzes—Test your visitors' knowledge and you'll soon have a curious group of potential fans swarming around your site. With the success of trivia shows like *Who Wants to Be a Millionaire*, people seem to be hooked on multiple-choice questions. Reel in your visitors with a cleverly crafted set of questions and possible answers. To make the best use of quizzes, when you reveal the answers, point the visitor to a related article or resource on your site that provides more information on the subject. Marcia Yudkin's helpful article, **Become a Quiz Whiz** (http://www.yudkin.com/quizwhiz.htm), offers some good advice and a list of quiz-building URLs.

Discussion forums and message boards—It's good for your visitors to interact with you, but don't hog them all to yourself. Let people who visit your site interact with each other. Message boards and discussion forums are basically the same thing: a place on your site for visitors to post messages for all to see. Some forums are monitored and extremely topic-focused; on others, more wide-ranging content can be posted. Either way, forums offer a good way to get people to express themselves on the subject of your brand identity. Many sites can help you set up a free message board, including **CoolBoard** at http://www.coolboard.com/, **Inside the Web** at http://www.insidetheweb.com/, and **ezboard** at http://www.ezboard.com/.

Chat rooms—Similar to discussion forums, chat rooms allow visitors to post instant messages to each other in real time. With discussion forums, you at least have the option of approving messages before they are posted. Chat rooms, though, are complete free-for-alls. You should determine whether that type of open format would be good for your brand image before committing to a chat room.

Registration forms—Ask people to sign up for a free newsletter, special report, or access code to a special section of your site. Visitors fill out a simple form, you capture their information, and everybody's happy.

Privacy Protection—*Any time you ask visitors for their e-mail addresses or other personal information, let them know how you plan to use it. People are especially concerned about privacy and security issues on the Internet, so be honest about what types of messages they'll receive from you and who else you'll share their information with. The best bet is to let your fans know that their information is safe with you. Tell them that you won't sell, trade, rent, or give away their information to anyone. And stick to your promise!*

Feedback forms—Once again, give people plenty of opportunities to vent their feelings and let you know what's on their minds, especially if their ideas are related to your brand specialty. Feedback forms allow visitors to express themselves and give you the constructive criticism you'll need to improve your site.

Contests—One musical act ran a clever contest. The band made three of its songs available for digital download and asked fans to submit a written review of their favorite tune. The three most insightful reviewers won free CDs and band merchandise. This is a perfect brand-building strategy. The band members didn't mindlessly give away stuff. In essence, they forced their fans to listen closely to the music and get a better understanding of it. Perhaps you should do something similar.

Giveaways—People love free goodies. Write a special report or choose a sample of your product to give away. Make sure your freebie will cause people to connect with your brand when it is read or used. Also, ask people to do something—sign up for your newsletter, take a short survey, indicate their interests—before giving them your freebie.

Classified ads—Using one of the many free services or scripts available, you can quickly have your own free classified ad page up and running. If your visitors have something to sell or promote, this would be a good interactive feature to employ.

Links page—Like classified ads, a free links directory is another way to keep people busy on your site as they add their own Web site to your listings. When I added a free link directory to my music business site, **The Buzz Factor Music Directory** at http://www.bob-baker.com/buzz/directory.html (shown in Figure 6.5), it generated a lot of extra traffic. If transforming casual surfers into active participants is your goal—and it should be—a links page is a step in the right direction.

Electronic greeting cards—This feature is especially effective. Not only do electronic greeting cards get visitors more involved with your site, they also spread the word about you and your brand to people who have never been to your site. Greeting cards are particularly effective for visual artists since images are part of the greeting. However, greetings can work for nonartists, as well. Using clip art and clever slogans related to your brand image, you can easily come up with greetings your visitors will send on to friends with

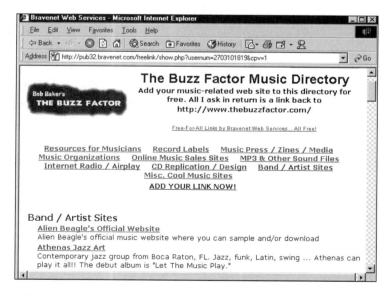

FIGURE 6.5: The free music business links page at The Buzz Factor site generates a lot of activity.

similar interests. Just make sure each greeting credits you and your Web site as the source.

Refer-a-friend forms—One of your goals should be getting happy visitors to recommend your site to their friends. Many sites offer a Recommend Us button that opens up a new window and allows someone to enter the e-mail address of a friend and a note explaining how cool your site is. A number of sites offer this refer-a-friend function for free. Beware, though; many of these free services make your visitors jump through hoops by filling out forms before sending the recommendation. The last thing you want to do is annoy a satisfied visitor who is just starting to connect with your brand.

---

*Free Interactive Resources—Most of the interactive features mentioned in this section are provided free by countless sources on the Web. Two good places to start looking are **Bravenet** at* http://www.bravenet.com/ *and **Free Internet Resources** at* http://www.idaboss.net/.

Once your Web site has useful content, a solid design, and lots of interactive features, it's time to add another powerful element to your brand-building arsenal: your own e-mail newsletter. We cover this tool in the next chapter.

CHAPTER SEVEN

Publishing an E-mail Newsletter

Of all the online tactics we discuss in this book, an e-mail newsletter is the most powerful tool to promote your brand identity. Using the tips in this chapter, you'll build a subscriber database of people who are interested in your specialty, and more importantly, interested in the unique spin you put on your area of expertise. Whether you send it daily, weekly, or monthly, an e-mail newsletter allows you to connect with a growing number of fans who come to know you and embrace what you stand for.

There are many things you can accomplish with an e-mail newsletter. Here are some of the ways to use one:

- Distribute articles you've written
- Provide links to online content by or about you
- Express your opinion regarding the state of your industry
- Announce new products and services
- Alert fans when new content has been added to your Web site
- Promote events
- Make money selling sponsorship line ads

In this chapter we'll talk about the many advantages of publishing an e-mail newsletter along with some of the challenges you'll face. We'll cover the various options you have for compiling a subscriber database and delivering your newsletter, as well as the best ways to handle your newsletter content, format, length, and frequency. Finally, we'll go over the many ways to promote your newsletter and attract subscribers.

Why Publish an E-mail Newsletter?

The main reason to publish an e-mail newsletter is because it is the most direct and cost-effective method to reach your target audience on a regular basis. Web sites are great, and your site will play a huge role in your branding efforts. But the success of a Web site relies on having lots of visitors who decide to view the pages that convey your brand—something you can work hard to influence but never completely control. An e-mail newsletter, though, puts you in the promotional driver's seat. You determine the frequency and type of messages visitors receive.

I've always thought of e-mail as the equivalent of direct mail in the physical world. Web sites, on the other hand, are similar to print ads in newspapers and magazines. Companies spend millions of dollars to run ads and then sit with their fingers crossed and hope that enough people notice their ads and act on them.

Marketing people discovered long ago that it was a smart idea to gather the names and addresses of people who expressed an interest in a particular product or service. Armed with those names and addresses, companies could send promotional messages directly to peoples' homes, instead of waiting for them to respond to ads. Direct mail puts the marketer in control of the promotional exchange. It's the difference between watching a football game from the sidelines and being the quarterback.

Your e-mail newsletter will not only put you in control of which messages are in front of your fans, it will also let you use the power of repetition. Raving fans are rarely enthusiastic right off the bat. They usually start with a mild interest that evolves over time. The more subscribers read focused messages about who you are and what benefits you provide, the more recognized you become. People who subscribe to your newsletter usually find out about you through a mention on another Web site, in another newsletter, or based on a recommendation from a friend. Subscribers start as blank slates, intrigued by the potential of what you have to offer them. The quality of what you consistently deliver over the coming weeks and months determines whether those slates get filled with admiration or disdain.

E-mail newsletters have a number of different names. They are frequently called e-zines. The *e* part, of course, stands for *electronic*. Most people assume the *zine* part is short for *magazine*. Many Internet purists, though, believe it stands for *fanzine*, a word that usually refers to a low-budget print publication that covers a defined topic put out by a hard-core fan or enthusiast. Regardless of what you call them, when done right, newsletters can grow a subscriber base quickly and direct a lot of attention to their publisher. Here are some examples of e-mail newsletter success stories:

DVD Talk—Geoffrey Kleinman started *DVD Talk* in January of 1999 because he couldn't find many discussion groups or Web sites that reviewed new DVD titles. His Web site, **DVD Talk** at http://www.dvdtalk.com/, and newsletter of the same name provide reviews, commentary, and online forums for all things DVD-related. Kleinman had more than 76,000 subscribers just two years after he started the newsletter.

A-CLUE.COM—Dana Blankenhorn has some strong opinions on e-commerce and the digital economy. Through his free newsletter and Web site, **A-CLUE.COM** at http://www.a-clue.com/, he's built up a lucrative career as a reporter, speaker, consultant, and writer.

This Is True—Colorado humorist Randy Cassingham reports on bizarre-but-true news items found in legitimate newspapers from around the world (never "tabloids," he insists). Each story ends with a comment from Randy—a tag line that is humorous, ironic, or opinionated. He started publishing a free weekly e-mail newsletter filled with these "stories of human weirdness" in 1994. Today, he has more than 150,000 subscribers and thousands of people who visit his site, **This Is True** at http://www.thisistrue.com/. In addition to a sign-up form on his home page, Cassingham has a "Why Subscribe?" page (Figure 7.1) that gives visitors extra incentives to subscribe. Cassingham has received widespread media exposure and has parlayed his notoriety into income-producing books and syndicated columns.

Writers Weekly—Angela Adair-Hoy publishes a newsletter for freelance writers. Each issue is filled with freelance job postings, tips for writers, success stories, and lots of plugs for the many electronic books written by her and other authors. Last time I looked, her number of subscribers was racing toward 50,000. *Time* and *Wired* magazines have written about her, and she reportedly pulls in more than $5,000 a month in book sales.

FIGURE 7.1: Randy Cassingham's "Why Subscribe?" page inspires visitors to subscribe to his *This Is True* newsletter.

Another great thing about e-mail newsletters is that, unlike traditional direct mail, there are no printing or postage costs. What's not to love? With all those great benefits, it's a wonder everyone isn't publishing e-mail newsletters.

Here's the bad news: Just about everyone is. There are tens of thousands of e-mail publications being flung all over the Internet. There are newsletters on music, gardening, diet tips, auto racing, you name it. There are tons of newsletters covering computer-related topics, marketing tips, and e-commerce. Heck, there are even dozens of e-mail newsletters about publishing e-mail newsletters.

How Specialized Is Your Niche?—Think your newsletter topic is out of the ordinary? Consider these real-life e-mail newsletters: Update from the North Pole *is a cheerful newsletter for children that provides the latest news from Santa's home town.* Horse-Sense *is Jessica Jahiel's weekly newsletter filled with sound advice for horse owners. The* KidzNSnow *newsletter is full of fun ideas for kids and parents looking for new games and outdoor winter activities.* Protective Strategies Self-Defense *is published by a police officer, detective, and former SWAT member.* Student Nurse Advisor *offers advice for those seeking a career in the medical profession. There's hardly a focus that's too narrow for an e-mail publication.*

If you're the least bit active online, you probably subscribe to a number of these electronic publications. Some people's e-mail boxes are flooded with them, which means a lot of these newsletters are ignored or deleted instead of opened. It's a busy world on the highways of cyberspace. People can't possibly read everything that's delivered to them. For your e-mail newsletter to be effective, it has to be read. That means you'll have to work to make your newsletters so tantalizing that your subscribers will make opening your messages a priority.

Here's the good news: The majority of your e-mail newsletter competition is just plain bad. Most electronic publications contain weak content and are hastily thrown together and overflowing with poor writing and grammatical errors. Some are filled with nothing but self-serving promotional hype; others are jam-packed with screen after screen of line ads; still more are entirely too long for most time-deficient humans to bear. With a little effort, your newsletter could easily rise above the great electronic junkyard and, like the newsletters mentioned earlier in this section, become a publication your subscribers look forward to receiving.

Newsletter Delivery Options

To publish an e-mail newsletter, you need a way to compile a database of subscribers and send your newsletter issues to readers. Here are four options to help you accomplish that task:

Your e-mail program—If you publish a newsletter with a small circulation, you can simply open a word processing file and enter the e-mail addresses of subscribers, separated by a comma and a space. When you send a newsletter to your list of subscribers, place your own e-mail address in the To: field and copy your entire list in the Bcc: field. You must send the list as a *blind carbon copy* to keep subscribers from seeing the e-mail addresses of all the other subscribers.

Using this bare-bones approach is time-consuming, because you have to manually add new subscribers and remove bad addresses and people who no longer want to receive your e-zine. Another drawback is that many ISPs (particularly AOL) won't allow you to send e-mail messages in bulk. ISPs have such policies to cut down on spam and may shut down your account if you send e-mail to hundreds of people at one time, even if your messages are legitimate.

Free mailing list host—Many online services will help you manage your newsletter for free. Using one of these mailing list hosts is far more convenient than managing your list manually. People can sign up for your newsletter by using e-mail or a sign-up page at the list site, all without any involvement from you. These services store and maintain your subscriber database. All you do is e-mail your newsletter to a unique list address, and the service distributes it to everyone on your list.

Free list hosts have drawbacks. For starters, every newsletter you send to your list includes a line ad. Selling ads is how the free services make money. Also, if you ever have a question and send an e-mail to technical support, you may wonder if a support staff even exists. If you use a free list host, be sure to regularly save your database of subscribers. If the host's server malfunctions, you may have no recourse to recover your database. Three of the better-known free list hosts are **Yahoo! Groups** (http://www.yahoogroups.com/), **Topica** (http://www.topica.com/, shown in Figure 7.2), and **ListBot** (http://www.listbot.com/).

Fee-based mailing list host—List hosts that charge you a fee do basically the same things as a free service, only they're supposed to do them better. You won't have any ads inserted into your messages, plus you should be able to get better customer support if problems arise. **Lyris** (http://www.lyris.com/) and **SparkLIST.com** (http://sparklist.com/) are two fee-based list hosts. For a full list of these services, visit **List-Business.com** at http://list-business.com/ list-service-providers/.

List server software—You can use many software packages on your Web server to manage your mailing list. This option may give you more control, but it will also take time and money to set up (although some free software packages are available). **Majordomo** (http://greatcircle.com/majordomo/) and **Listserv** (http://www.lsoft.com/) are common list-management applications. You'll find a comprehensive list of server-software options at **List-Business.com** (http://list-business.com/list-software/).

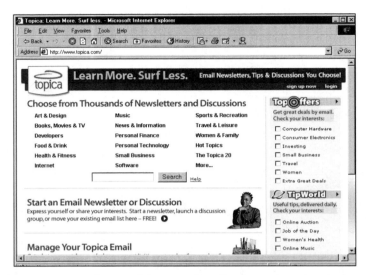

FIGURE 7.2: Topica is one of several free mailing list host sites that help you manage and deliver your e-mail newsletter.

Your Newsletter's Content

You have a lot of choices about what you'll send to your newsletter subscribers. The main thing to keep in mind is that your electronic publication is a powerful tool you'll use to cement your brand identity into the minds of readers. It should reflect your personality and the unique perspective you have of the world. And, like your Web site, it must be tightly focused on your laser-sharp online image. Since it won't cost you any more to send 2,000 words than it does to send 500, you may be tempted to fill your newsletters with interesting tidbits and whatever tangents strike your fancy. However, don't make the mistake of confusing readers by watering down your focus.

Remember your Brand Identity Statement (BIS)? We first discussed it in Chapter 2, "Crafting Your Best Brand Identity." Everything you do online should reinforce the identity you've chosen to promote. If your BIS is *Jim Taylor—Master of Aardvark Trivia*, you should fill your newsletter with fun facts about those ugly, long-nosed creatures. Tossing in Elvis trivia or commentary on the state of swimwear would only confuse your subscribers. They signed up to get aardvark trivia. They're looking forward to aardvark trivia and pray that you're the best darn aardvark trivia expert on the planet. Don't let them down.

Your Welcome Message

When new subscribers sign up to receive your newsletter, the first thing they should receive is a welcome message. This initial contact with new subscribers accomplishes the following things:

- Confirms that their subscription was successful
- Provides a warm greeting and thanks them for subscribing
- Gets them excited about what they can expect from upcoming issues
- Reinforces your name and brand image
- Reminds them about your Web site and some of the specific content on it

If a subscriber doesn't get a welcome message from you, he or she might think the subscription didn't take. Don't leave your new subscribers in the dark. The free and fee-based services make it easy to set up an introductory message. Whatever you do, don't send the generic default message offered by your list service. Tailor your welcome message to your brand. Let your new subscribers feel as if they have just joined a special club. Here's a welcome message you might get from the aardvark trivia expert mentioned in the previous section.

Welcome!

Thanks so much for subscribing to Jim Taylor's Aardvark Trivia Times. *Every Wednesday you'll receive a new issue filled with fun facts on those lovable anteaters. From folklore and fiction to movies and cartoons, I'll bring you aardvark trivia you won't find anywhere else. Guaranteed!*

USA Today *recently described the newsletter as "a fun-loving cornucopia of aardvark trivialities!"*

Can't wait for the next issue? Head to the Web site for some of my most popular pages, including:

10 Things You Probably Didn't Known About Aardvarks
http://www.aardvarktrivia.com/10things.htm

The Ugly Truth About Arthur the Aardvark
http://www.aardvarktrivia.com/arthur.htm

Remember, your information is safe with me. I'll never sell, rent, or give away your address to anyone. And if you ever no longer want to receive the newsletter, just send a blank e-mail to unsubscribe@aardvarktrivia.com.

Thanks again for subscribing. We'll talk about aardvark trivia and have some more fun this Wednesday. See you then!

Jim Taylor,
Editor

Your e-zine may not deal with aardvarks, but hopefully you can use the branding aspects of this welcome letter in your own message.

Great Source of E-zine Tips—*Five days a week,* ***Ezine-Tips.com*** *(http://www.ezine-tips.com/) sends out a newsletter filled with ... you guessed it, e-zine tips. The editors come up with fresh angles and recommendations to share with other e-zine editors. They pull it off by providing excellent advice on content, promotion, list management, ad revenue, formatting, and a lot more. I highly recommended it.*

The Two Es: Educate and Entertain

The best e-mail newsletters provide large doses of two key ingredients. For an e-zine to succeed, it must *educate* and *entertain*. Many popular newsletters do get away with doing one or the other really well. For instance, the *Joke of the Day* mailing list, which reaches about 175,000 subscribers, does a lot more entertaining than it does educating. On the other hand, well-read corporate and academic newsletters probably educate more than they entertain. The best newsletters, though, do both. If you can deliver truly useful information focused on your core brand identity and deliver that information with the natural wit and humor that radiate from your personality, you'll be well on your way to building a large and enthusiastic list of subscribers.

One of the best examples of a Web site and e-mail newsletter combination that educates and entertains is **Lockergnome** (http://www.lockergnome.com/). Published by Chris Pirillo, author of *Poor Richard's E-mail Publishing*, Lockergnome is one of the great newsletter success stories, with something like 150,000 subscribers. Pirillo specializes in Windows-related computer news, including reviews of the latest freeware, multimedia developments, tips and tricks, system updates, and more. They are all topics that, in lesser hands, could easily make for a dry read. But Pirillo adds zest and humor and makes his newsletters sing with personality. By educating *and* entertaining his audience, Pirillo has made Lockergnome a brand-name institution.

A Smorgasbord of Newsletter Features

To ensure that your newsletter educates and entertains, you must fill it with meaty content. That doesn't mean fill it to overflowing. You must respect your subscribers' time restraints and pick the elements that will most effectively give subscribers what they want while also hammering home your brand identity. Some e-mail publications stick with a set format; subscribers can count on every issue containing the same three or four features. Other newsletters have more flexible formats, depending on what the editor wants to impart with each issue.

My own e-zines, *The Buzz Factor* and *Quick Tips for Creative People*, have evolved over the years. I sometimes discover new directions I want to go and phase out older features while phasing in newer ones. In some issues, I may write a several-paragraph pep talk; in other issues I might offer a rundown of helpful Web sites. As long as you don't vary the content too drastically, and as long as you stay focused on your brand's theme, you'll be in good shape.

What follows is a list of editorial possibilities for your e-mail newsletter:

News story summaries—If your brand would benefit from helping your subscribers stay on top of developments in your field, you'd do well to regularly scour news sites for stories on your specialty area. Then write pithy summaries of the stories that are most likely to impact your subscribers. This feature is even more effective if you add your own comment or opinion to each news item. Always try to give readers something they won't find anywhere else—that something is usually your unique brand perspective.

Links to topic-related articles—Dan Poynter publishes a free e-zine for aspiring authors and self-publishers called *Publishing Poynters* (**Para Publishing** at http://www.parapub.com/). Somewhere in each issue, Poynter mentions at least two or three helpful online articles and resources he's discovered. He provides a brief description of each article and the URL where subscribers can go to read more. Your subscribers should think of your e-mail newsletter as a shortcut to the information they really need. To help you hunt down relevant articles, check out **MagPortal.com** (http://www.magportal.com/) and **InfoJump** (http://www.infojump.com/, shown in Figure 7.3), two nice magazine-article search engines that cover a variety of topics.

Survey results—People like to know what others in their industry are doing and thinking. Once a month, pose a question or offer a multiple-choice survey through your newsletter. Compile the results and reveal them in a future issue. Let subscribers know what issue the results will be featured in to build some excitement and anticipation.

Reader feedback—I've generated a lot of interest in my newsletters using the tactic of reader feedback. Even though I don't have a regular Letters to the Editor section, certain topics inspire my subscribers to express themselves. In my *Quick Tips for Creative People* e-zine, I once listed some of the books and tapes I consider my top sources of inspiration. At the end of the piece, I asked subscribers to offer their own inspiration sources. I was able to fill the next two issues with the many responses I received. You'll find that some topics illicit far more reader feedback than others will. You'll often be

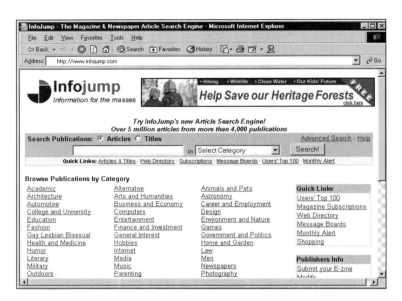

FIGURE 7.3: Using InfoJump's magazine-article search engine, newsletter editors can easily find topic-specific news stories to mention in their newsletters.

surprised by what gets subscribers' juices flowing, but these revelations will give you greater insight into what's important to your readers.

Articles by guest writers—To lighten your editorial load, you can solicit other experts in your field to contribute articles. Every issue of Jim Daniels' *BizWeb eGazette* features a new article by him followed by a short article written by someone else. It's okay to use other writers, as long as your brand image doesn't get lost in the shuffle. Remember, it's your opinions and recommendations that subscribers are really looking forward to, so make your guest writers' contributions icing on the cake, not the entire cake.

Inspiring quotations—Quotes are a good addition to any newsletter. I don't use them in my music-marketing e-zine, but every issue of *Quick Tips for Creative People* starts off with a *Creative Quick Quotes* section.

How-to columns—This is the type of content that really allows your brand to shine. Shed some light on how your subscribers can do something that directly relates to your identity. If you are a sushi expert, tell readers how to find sushi, prepare sushi, eat sushi, and impress their friends with … you got it, sushi.

Helpful tips—How-to articles may take several paragraphs or so to write, but helpful tips and tidbits of useful information can often be presented in two or three sentences. As you read books and articles on your specialty, stay on the lookout for little idea nuggets you can turn into tips. Your readers will love them.

Opinion pieces and editorials—Let subscribers know what you think of current happenings in your chosen field. Don't wimp out and take the middle road on important issues. Take a stand, get on a soapbox, and express yourself. You may rub some subscribers the wrong way, but you might find they'll respect you for not apologizing for your beliefs.

Promotional messages that plug your products or services—When planning your newsletter's editorial content, don't overlook your own needs. After all, you probably aren't just promoting your brand image for the sake of promoting it. Most likely, you have something to sell: a book, a consulting service, your public speaking abilities, an artistic craft, and so on. It's okay to make references to the stuff you sell in your other content, as long as it's tastefully done. For instance, in your how-to tip on cleaning your cat's teeth, note that you have an entire chapter devoted to the topic in your new book on cat hygiene. Also, don't be bashful about including special sections in your newsletter that blatantly hawk your wares. I sprinkle these plugs throughout both of my e-zines. Readers not interested in purchasing will happily tolerate them as long as the bulk of your content is meaningful. For those who are prone to buy from you, these plugs remind them of the goodies you have awaiting them, if only they place an order.

Still need a few more editorial content ideas? Here are several more features you might add to your e-mail newsletter:

- Interviews
- Jokes
- Trivia
- This day or week in history
- Book reviews
- Software reviews
- Web site reviews

How to Format Your Newsletter

When you deliver your e-mail newsletter to subscribers, it ideally should arrive in a format that's readable for every recipient. First off, don't compose your newsletter in a sophisticated word-processing program, such as Microsoft Word. These applications often turn quotation marks and apostrophes into more visually friendly, curly "smart quotes." That feature is great for printing words on paper, but as we discussed in Chapter 4, "Maximizing E-mail for Brand Delivery," those cute curly characters get turned into gibberish when sent by e-mail. Use a text editor such as WordPad or SimpleText when composing your newsletter.

The next big question: Should you send your newsletters as HTML-based e-mail or plain text? For years, the prevailing notion has been to play it safe and send plain text. As more e-mail programs become equipped to read HTML documents, the pressure to go with HTML has become stronger. Still, if you want to assure that everyone who subscribes can read your newsletters, stick with plain text e-mail for now. A number of publishers give potential subscribers the option of choosing which format they'd like to receive. Not a bad idea, if you don't mind the extra work of producing two separate versions of your e-zine.

What's the Best Line Length?—Another newsletter formatting issue you'll want to consider is line length. If you've ever received an e-mail in which the text seems choppy with new paragraphs seeming to form in mid-sentence, you know what funny things can happen with e-mail text. The best defense against having your newsletters appear in this butchered fashion is to set a maximum line length of about 65 characters. Use hard carriage returns—which simply means you press the Enter key—when you get to that line length. For more information on this topic, read Brian Alt's "Line Length is Critical" article on the **Ezine-Tips.com** site at http://www.ezine-tips.com/articles/format/19990520.shtml.

Text Characters Spice Up Your Design

If you wisely decide to send plain text e-mail newsletters, you can do some creative things to make them look more interesting. The basic keyboard offers lots of possibilities for creating interesting dividing lines, section headings, and so on. What follows are two versions of an excerpt from one of my recent e-zines. This first one demonstrates a lackluster use of text:

The Buzz Factor — Bob Baker's music marketing tip sheet
http://www.thebuzzfactor.com/

Buzz Factor Sponsors

Sell more CDs online!
Accept credit card orders. No setup fee. CD Street makes it all possible.
http://www.cdstreet.com/ - Tell them Bob Baker and the Buzz Factor sent you!

Two Tips for Better Online Bios

Carey Colvin has the right idea when it comes to presenting an online artist bio. In fact, she has two right ideas.

First, Colvin's site uses a dark green background color. To remain consistent, her main bio page properly carries this color theme. But the dark background looks garish when printed. That's why she also offers a print-friendly version. If your pages are similarly designed, start offering a printable option ...

The preceding example is pretty dull. Nothing stands out and catches your eye. Every element carries the same weight. Compare that to this treatment of the exact same text:

THE BUZZ FACTOR — Bob Baker's music marketing tip sheet
http://www.thebuzzfactor.com/

=================== Buzz Factor Sponsors ===================

SELL MORE CDs ONLINE!
Accept credit card orders. No setup fee. CD Street makes it all possible.
http://www.cdstreet.com/ - Tell them Bob Baker and the Buzz Factor sent you!

==

=> TWO TIPS FOR BETTER ONLINE ARTIST BIOS

Carey Colvin has the right idea when it comes to presenting an online artist bio. In fact, she has two right ideas.

First, Colvin's site uses a dark green background color. To remain consistent, her main bio page properly carries this color theme. But the dark background looks garish when printed. That's why she also offers a print-friendly version. If your pages are similarly designed, start offering a printable option ...

Which version do you think looks better?

The Long and Short of Newsletters

When is enough enough? How long is too long? These are the questions that e-mail newsletter editors ponder. You need to tailor the length of your newsletter to the tastes of your subscribers. Many successful e-zines keep it short and sweet while others appear to ramble on for an eternity without turning away subscribers. Here are some possible approaches to newsletter length:

Keep it short—Most readers are pressed for time. Many e-zine editors are sensitive to this time-crunch factor. Marcia Yudkin's *Marketing Minute* newsletter is aptly titled. It is designed to literally be read in one minute. Every week, she delivers on that one-minute promise. You may not want to be quite as terse with your e-zine, but there's something to be said for brevity. The last thing you want is to have subscribers saving your newsletters to be read later because they're so long; that usually means they won't get read at all.

Give readers the full enchilada—Some newsletters are so enthralling, they have subscribers scrolling and reading virtually every word. Angela Adair-Hoy's *Writers Weekly* is densely packed with tips and job leads for freelance writers. Based on the significant business she generates every month and her increasing number of subscribers, it appears this lengthy format works for her audience. It's your job to determine whether in-depth content will work for your readers, too. Keys to long newsletters are to make each section quickly stand out for readers who skim and to include a table of contents near the top of the newsletter for readers who want to decide which sections interest them.

Use an e-zine as your Web site's table of contents—Some e-zines are primarily published on a Web site. That's the case with Steve Outing's *Content Spotlight*, a resource for online content creators and publishers. Every week, Outing sends an e-mail newsletter highlighting the new articles and features added that week to his site, **Content-Exchange** at http://www.content-exchange.com/. The entire newsletter consists of brief descriptions of each article along with the URL where it appears. This format nicely bridges the gap between a short newsletter and lengthy content.

Create a hybrid—Another way to mix and match these formats is to publish a newsletter that offers, for example, an article, some tips, and a few quotes in an e-mail version and then directs readers to a Web site for other new content. This way, you give subscribers some immediate information to consume, but you also tease them to visit your site, where they can get a more visually appealing dose of your brand-focused advice.

How Often Should You Publish?—*Think long and hard about your publishing schedule before making a commitment to subscribers. For instance, if you promote a daily newsletter that only arrives three times a week, readers may view you as someone who can't be trusted. A daily newsletter works for some editors, since it gets their information in front of subscribers often and keeps the brand name top of mind. But the daily newsletter grind can be tough for publishers to keep up with, plus it can cause many subscribers to grow weary of too much of a good thing. A monthly schedule works well for publishers who want to connect with readers but need a little breathing room between issues. From a branding standpoint, weekly is your best bet, since it delivers your message often enough to make an impression without being as overwhelming as a daily. Your next best option would be publishing twice a month. Your newsletter's frequency will be best determined by balancing your available time with your subscribers' needs.*

---

12 Ways to Promote Your Newsletter

For an e-zine to be successful, it must be read by subscribers—preferably, a *lot* of subscribers. To inspire hordes of people to sign up for your newsletter, you'll need to promote it relentlessly. Luckily, there are at least a dozen solid ways to lure readers to your e-zine, including the following methods:

1. **Your personal contact list**—Start with the basics: your own circle of influence. Send an e-mail message to everyone in your address book who might be remotely interested in the subject matter of your newsletter. Also, if you have a customer database filled with physical addresses, mail a post card that announces your newsletter with instructions on how to subscribe. These mailings should be limited to inviting subscriptions—never subscribe someone without permission.

2. **Free subscription offers on every page of your site**—People who visit your Web site are curious about your area of expertise. Many of those visitors are hearing about you for the first time. Don't let them leave your site without subscribing to your newsletter. The best way to entice visitors to sign up is to remind them of your e-zine's existence repeatedly. And do so at the top of every page on your site.

3. **Pop-up windows**—Using JavaScript, many Web sites have their home pages set up to open a small pop-up window that encourages visitors to subscribe. Use this feature with caution. Webmasters claim that pop-up windows increase the number of subscribers, but these distracting windows may annoy many of your fans. You can find pop-up window scripts on some of the script sites mentioned in Chapter 6, "Designing Your Web Site for Brand Impact."

4. **Free premium for new subscribers**—Sometimes potential subscribers need a little something extra to motivate them. In addition to a compelling description of your newsletter, consider offering a free report or item people can get only if they subscribe. Jim Daniels offers a free copy of his e-book, *A Beginner's Guide to Starting a High-Income Business on the Internet*, to anyone who subscribes to his *BizWeb eGazette* (see Figure 7.4). This technique alone could significantly boost the percentage of Web site visitors who subscribe.

5. **Free sample issue by autoresponder**—Sometimes people need to sample even a free item before they commit to it. Make one of your best recent issues available via an e-mail autoresponder. Make sure to include complete instructions on how to subscribe in that sample issue.

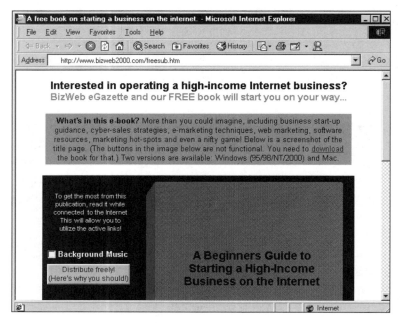

FIGURE 7.4: Jim Daniels' Web site offers a free e-book to entice visitors to subscribe to his e-mail newsletter.

6. **Newsletter forwarding**—Make the best use of the Internet's version of word-of-mouth advertising. Have your current subscribers forward their newsletter issues to friends. Invite readers to share your tips with others by including a prominent reminder to do so. In my *Buzz Factor* e-zine, I include a couple lines of text that read, "Forward this issue to your music biz pals and encourage them to subscribe. It's easy … and best of all, it's free!" Current fans are your single best resource to help you develop new fans.

7. **Newsletter ad swaps**—One of my more effective subscriber-building tactics has been trading line ads with other newsletter publishers. You should do the same. Make a list of e-zines that reach subscribers who would most likely be interested in your brand identity. Contact each editor and offer to exchange a free line ad, sometimes called a sponsorship, in each other's e-zine. To get the most from your efforts, go after e-zines that have at least as many subscribers as you have. **Ezine-swap.com** (http://www.ezine-swap.com/) is a site set up to connect swap-savvy publishers with one another.

8. **Joint ventures**—You have all sorts of creative ways to team up with like-minded Web sites and newsletters. Four Internet marketing sites joined forces to print four-color bookmarks that promoted all four sites. Each company included the bookmarks when fulfilling book orders. By

combining forces, they were able to reach four times as many people with their marketing messages. How might you hook up with other online forces in your field?

9. **E-mail signature files**—Whenever you send an e-mail message, make sure to include your signature file at the end. For more details, see the related discussion in Chapter 4, "Maximizing E-mail for Brand Delivery." In addition to your BIS and Web site address, make sure your sig file includes a plug for your free e-mail newsletter.

10. **Article byline blurbs**—As we'll discuss in Chapter 8, "Exploiting E-zines and Web Sites of Others," you'll soon be contributing articles to numerous online sources. Your articles will always include blurbs at the end that explain who you are and how to contact you. Like your e-mail sig files, these blurbs also promote your BIS, Web site, and free newsletter.

11. **Paid e-zine ads**—If you identify one or two e-zines that reach a large number of subscribers who fall into your target demographic, first offer the editors of those e-zines an ad swap or joint-venture arrangement. If that effort fails and you're sold that these subscribers would fall in love with your newsletter, consider running paid ads. Many publishers use this method successfully. However, don't rely on paid advertising to take the place of good, old-fashioned promotional work.

12. **Pay-per-subscriber sites**—Another fee-based method for attracting subscribers is to use one of the e-zine directories that charges publishers per each subscriber they sign up. These sites list your newsletter in the categories you determine, along with many other newsletters. Visitors select the e-zines they want and once a week, the site passes on your new subscribers' e-mail addresses to you. Two pay-per-subscriber sites are **Worldwidelists.com** (http://www.worldwidelists.com/) and **Ezine Central** (http://ezinecentral.com/). Visit **List-Resources.com** at http://www.list-resources.com/s/Promotion/Directories/Paid/ for a list of other subscriber-generating sites.

Another thing you'll want to do is submit your newsletter to many of the e-zine announcement sites and lists. The sources in the following list are all free, so start surfing and promoting your newsletter.

AAnnounce
http://www.egroups.com/community/Aannounce/

Ezine Announce
http://www.egroups.com/group/ezine_announce/

Ezines Today

http://www.egroups.com/group/ezinestoday/

Internet Scout Project

http://scout.cs.wisc.edu/

Mailman

http://www.topica.com/lists/mailman/

List of Lists

http://www.egroups.com/group/List_Of_Lists/

List Builder

http://www.topica.com/lists/List_Builder/

New-List.com

http://new-list.com/

Promote!

http://promotefree.com/promote.htm

---

*Get Reviewed at List-A-Day.com—Every weekday the year 'round, the dedicated editors at **List-A-Day.com** (http://list-a-day.com/) select an e-zine and give it a thoughtful review. The editors not only send out the review to the many subscribers of their own e-zine, they also archive the review at the List-A-Day site. My own newsletter,* Quick Tips for Creative People, *received a nice write-up. Check out the site and submit your own newsletter for possible review.*

Once you've hit all the e-zine announcement sites and mailing lists, it's time to turn your attention to the countless e-zine directories and search engines on the Internet. Here are some of the better ones at which to submit your e-zine:

BestEzines.com

http://www.bestezines.com/

eScribe

http://www.escribe.com/

eZINE Search

http://www.ezinesearch.com/

EzineSeek

http://ezineseek.com/

Ezine-Universe.com

http://ezine-universe.com/

EzinesPlus.com
http://ezinesplus.com/

E-Zines Today
http://www.ezinestoday.com/freesubs/

E-ZineZ
http://www.e-zinez.com/

DIY Search
http://www.diysearch.com/

Free Directory of Ezines
http://www.freezineweb.com/

Inkspot's Zine Scene
http://inkspot.com/zines/

List of Lists
http://catalog.com/vivian/interest-group-search.html

Liszt
http://www.liszt.com/

Newsletter Access (shown in Figure 7.5)
http://www.newsletteraccess.com/

Published.com
http://www.published.com/add/

'ZinewOrld
http://void.oblivion.net/zineworld/

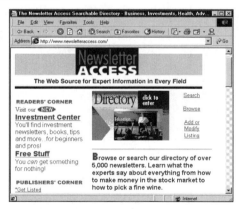

FIGURE 7.5: Newsletter Access is one of many free e-zine directories and search engines.

For a comprehensive list of e-zine directories, look at http://list-resources.com/s/Promotion/Directories/ on the **List-Resources.com** site.

Dealing with E-zine Rejection

The journey to online branding success is filled with various forms of rejection. No matter how well you craft an image and design an e-mail newsletter that any guru would be proud of, some people still won't buy what your selling—both literally and figuratively. Readers will disagree with you, get angry with you, and never want to hear from you again. When this happens, keep these two things in mind:

- First, make it easy for newsletter subscribers to leave. If people want off your e-zine train, give them a clear and easy way to exit. Every issue of your newsletter should include instructions about how to subscribe (for those who get your newsletter forwarded to them by a friend) and how to unsubscribe (for people who no longer want to receive your e-zine). Your choice of mailing-list service determines the various options you give readers to unsubscribe. Whatever you do, don't make them jump through hoops to get off the list. Providing a special e-mail address for unsubscribe requests is usually the best option.

- Second, don't let rejection get you down. You want to be open to suggestions from your readers. The feedback subscribers give you can be valuable, but the occasional gripe or mad rant from an irritated reader is par for the course. When you get negative messages, realize that the people who write them are either having a bad day and need to vent or they simply don't get what your brand is about. You're probably better off without those people on your list anyway.

You'll never please everybody all the time, so don't expect to. If you do a good job of establishing your brand image and have a well-defined niche, you will appeal to many people who are drawn to your specialized area. But that also means people who don't quite fit into your niche may be rubbed the wrong way or simply not understand what you're all about. That's fine. Your life will move on without them and vice versa, so don't sweat it. As long as you remain true to yourself and your brand identity, you'll be able to sleep soundly every night.

Throughout the last three chapters, we covered developing your own Web site and e-mail newsletter. Now it's time to leverage your brand image and market yourself through other people's Web sites and e-zines in the following chapter.

CHAPTER EIGHT

Exploiting E-zines and Web Sites of Others

When you promote your brand on the Internet, you don't operate in a vacuum. As unique as you feel your brand identity is, probably hundreds of Web sites and e-mail newsletters already cater to the same audience whose attention you hope to capture. Instead of worrying about the competition, you should be grateful that so many avenues exist to help promote your brand message directly to potential fans.

In this chapter, we discuss how to use those other online sources to your advantage in the following ways:

- To build up your number of newsletter subscribers and Web site visitors
- To help establish you as a recognized authority in your field
- To act as a vehicle to dispense your expert advice to the masses

By the time you finish reading this chapter, you'll know why Web sites and e-zines need good content, why it's worth your time and effort to give away free articles, and how to craft articles so that they draw readers to you and your brand identity. You'll also discover the importance of an author blurb and how to construct one, the ins and outs of self-syndication, and where to find sources that help you circulate and publicize your free articles. You'll also find out about ways to get paid for your writing and learn about sites that will bring you on as a resident expert. In short, if you're ready to help yourself while helping a lot of other Web site owners and e-zine editors, this chapter is for you.

Welcome to Your New Online Goals

Now that you have a focused brand identity, a Web site, and an e-mail newsletter, it's time to introduce you to your new online objectives. From now on, whenever you undertake a promotional activity on the Internet, your primary goals are to get people to subscribe to your free e-zine and visit your Web site. To venture onto the Web and not ask people to do one or both of these things is futile. Coca-Cola, Calvin Klein, and Bud Light might be able to invest millions in image advertising that does nothing more than get their names and images in front of the masses. But not you.

Your needs are best served by launching an online branding campaign that consists of free and low-cost tactics that slowly but surely increase your notoriety. To make that approach work, you have to market yourself in a way that goes beyond simply getting your name out there. You have to promote yourself in a manner that gets people to take action. The two actions you want people to take are subscribing to your e-zine and visiting your Web site. Inspiring these actions is so crucial, it's worth repeating. Make this phrase your mantra: My primary online objectives are to get people to subscribe to my free e-zine and visit my Web site.

Of the two, getting potential fans to subscribe to your e-zine is the more important. Once you have someone as a subscriber, you can follow up and repeatedly deliver your brand-focused message. If you do a good job of providing useful content in your newsletter, your subscribers will visit your Web site. However, if you only get people to visit your Web site and they don't subscribe to your e-zine, they can easily slip away and forget about you, never to return. A Web site visit alone is better than no interaction at all, but to achieve your ultimate goal of establishing yourself as a celebrity or expert in your chosen field, you'll need to attract large groups of people who visit your site *and* subscribe.

One of the best ways to attain your two new online objectives is to leverage the clout of other e-zines and Web sites, particularly those that reach your target audience. To get exposure through these other online sources, you'll need to give something of value in return. The rest of this chapter talks about one of the most effective ways of offering that value: your expertise.

Becoming a Recognized Online Expert

When I first went online in 1995, one of the first things I did was publish an e-mail newsletter to promote my reputation as a music-marketing author and consultant. I didn't set up my own Web site until a couple of years later, but I still managed to get a lot of Web exposure. Even though it was a primitive version of what it is today, my newsletter in those early days was filled with useful tips and short articles on how to promote a band or new CD release.

Within months of publishing my e-zine, I started receiving requests from music site Webmasters to reprint my articles on their sites. I enthusiastically gave all of them the green light to do so. One site owner even offered to dedicate an entire section of his site to my articles, products, and services. By doing so, he knew I would drive traffic to his site through plugs in my newsletter. That section with my articles also gave visitors to his main site a reason to stick around and soak up some good advice, since his site was also music promotion–related. It was a win-win situation.

It should be easy for you to position yourself as an expert whom other Webmasters and e-zine editors will want to expose to their audiences. If you've followed the suggestions in the chapters that make up Part II, *Gathering Your Branding Tools*, you should already be creating content for your own site and newsletter. While you may decide to make select portions of your content exclusively available through your own vehicles, most of your content should be freely shared with the world. I'm not talking about material you write that's sold in books and other formats; material from those projects should be reserved for paying customers. What we're addressing now are the many articles, columns, and tips you publish with the sole intent of spreading them far and wide.

***Recycle Your Written Content**—You may not have to write all your promotional articles from scratch. Smart online marketers learn to recycle and repackage the information they write. For instance, if your e-mail newsletter contains short tips that take up only one or two paragraphs, you may conclude this information isn't enough for an article. However, you could combine several of these tips into one article, as long as they're tied together with a common theme. Always think about ways to reuse your written material. Tips can be turned into articles, columns can be transformed into special reports, reports can be shaped into books, and so on.*

Why will Webmasters and e-zine editors be interested in the free content you have to offer? Here are some of the reasons:

- E-zines need quality content that inspires subscribers to open their e-mail and read it.
- Web sites need useful content to draw first-time visitors.
- Webmasters need to update their sites constantly to get return visitors.
- Good content is hard to find.
- Experts on specialized topics are even harder to find.
- Most marketers offering free content are turned down because they fill their articles with self-serving hype.

A lot of people who have identities to establish and products to sell are busily offering free articles and other content to anyone who will post them. But many of these self-promoters are pushing weak material that is poorly presented. With a little practice, you could be crafting and dispensing expert advice that hundreds of online sources will eagerly accept and share with tens of thousands of Internet users.

Starting today, begin viewing your written expertise as a valuable, in-demand commodity you can use to help others while meeting your own needs. In return for the use of your material, Webmasters and e-zine editors give you access to their audiences—the type of exposure that plants mental seeds that will soon sprout into full-blown recognition of you and your brand identity. When your articles, columns, and tips carry the right type of author attribution, this exposure will also motivate thousands of people to subscribe to your e-zine and visit your Web site.

Thousands of online resources are eager for good content. For example, during the week I was writing this chapter, I received the following message via e-mail:

We are looking for articles covering self-improvement and personal growth (health, fitness, spiritual enrichment, goal setting, and stress management). The articles help to enrich the content of our Web site and give you an opportunity for free exposure.

The potential for widespread notoriety is enormous. What are you waiting for?

***What If Your Brand Is Visually Oriented?**—There are circumstances in which your brand may not be best served by focusing only on writing expert advice. If you're a fine artist, illustrator, or cartoonist, you'll need to get images of your work shown on other people's Web sites, in addition to your own site. Like articles, visual representation of your work is valuable content that you can share with other Web sites. Set aside some of your artwork to be used as free clip art, editorial illustrations, or electronic greeting card art, as long as a credit and link to your Web site are included. And what if you're a fashion model? Do a few freebie photo shoots for high-profile sites in exchange for a link. Whatever your brand image, give away some of what you do to get exposure.*

---

10 Tips for Writing Attention-Getting Articles

A lot of entrepreneurs and freelancers think the only people who write articles to promote themselves are professional writers. Nothing could be further from the truth. I can't think of an area of expertise that wouldn't benefit from articles on the subject. If you're an experienced gardener, write tips on how to garden. If you're a tattoo artist, write articles on how to give and get a tattoo. If you're a choreographer, write pointers on dance and theatrical movement.

Perhaps you don't feel your specialized field lends itself to written advice. If Martha Stewart had been similarly less ambitious, years ago she might have thought, "All I'm good at is decorating my house and throwing parties. Who wants to learn about that?" Instead, she started dishing out helpful tips to a distinct segment of the population. Now her name is not only a brand, it's a media empire. All of us can benefit from writing about our passions. Use the following tips to help you craft the articles that will bring you fame and, hopefully, fortune.

1. **Craft a strong title**—The title you attach to an article can mean the difference between it being widely read and completely ignored. Often, your title is the only thing that appears in a list of available articles by you and other experts. Make sure your titles are so strong and appealing that readers will choose them over other articles on the list. Titles are so important, I recommend writing them before you write the articles. Starting with a strong title ensures that the content you write lives up to a title's promise. Which is more appealing to you: *Tax Tips for Individual Filers* or *Nine Things the IRS Doesn't Want You to Know*? What about *How to Have a Successful First Date* compared to *First-Date Maneuvers That Will Have Him Begging for More*?

   Scouring the magazine rack at your local bookstore should supply plenty of article title ideas. The following list may also help get your mental wheels turning. Just fill in the blanks with a word that relates to your area of expertise.

   > *Seven Things You Need to Know About _____*
   > *The 12 Biggest Mistakes Made by _____*
   > *Take the _____ Self-Test: How Well Do You Know _____?*
   > *Eight Questions Every Good _____ Should Ask*
   > *What Every _____ Needs to Know About _____*

   Damon G. Zahariades does a good job of writing tantalizing headlines on his **Web Business Today** site at http://www.webbusinesstoday.com/ (shown in Figure 8.1).

2. **Address problems and solutions**—Readers are attracted to articles that promise to help them reach a desired goal; but articles that tell people how to avoid or overcome a problem are even more in demand. Think about the people you want to draw to your brand image. What problems do they encounter that are directly related to your identity? What solutions can you provide to help them deal with these problems? Your answers to those questions hold the key to some of your best articles.

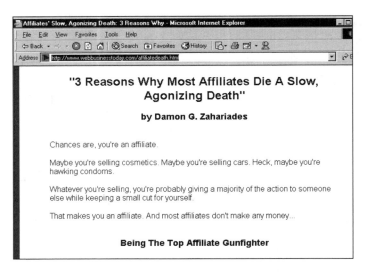

FIGURE 8.1: Damon G. Zahariades' online articles use attention-getting headlines to draw in readers.

3. **Provide ordered how-to steps**—How-to articles are one of the most popular formats. Hopefully, you'll write many columns that demonstrate your expertise by telling readers how to do something related to your brand. When you choose to go this route, make sure your articles cover all the bases. Ask yourself, *What's the first thing the reader must do to accomplish this?* Then ask, *What's the next logical step in the process?* Let readers know what procedure to take to get from point A to point B. If you promise a how-to article and skimp on the specifics, you'll disappoint the reader and lose a potential fan. You may have noticed that most of the sample titles earlier in this section suggest a numbered-list format, which is perfect for delivering a step-by-step, how-to article.

4. **Supply how-to details with your what-to-do advice**—Too many how-to articles tell readers what to do without telling them how to do it. For instance, a lot of PR articles suggest that one needs to "put together a professional media kit." Great, but what elements make a media kit professional? What does a media kit include? How do you put one together? You'll impress a lot more people with your articles if you go beyond simply telling them obvious, surface-level facts. Your true expertise will shine in the details you provide.

5. **Use concrete examples and quotes**—While dispensing helpful advice on your area of expertise, you'll get your points across more forcefully by providing examples to back them up. Regularly weave in a combination of personal anecdotes, stories of other people's experiences, and quotes from people who can validate the tips you offer. Consider this bare-bones, how-to paragraph:

Use four-color post cards to promote your business. Four-color printing costs are more than basic black and white, but you'll find the extra expense well worth it.

Now compare that to this version:

Four-color post cards get a better response than basic one- or two-color cards. When I switched to four-color cards to promote my latest book, sales doubled. Author Jane Doe had a similar experience when promoting her genealogy book. "As soon as I started using the more professional-looking post cards, my direct mail response rates jumped from two percent to more than five percent, which made it well worth the extra expense.

Anecdotes, examples, and quotes add meat to your articles.

Keep an Idea File—*One practice that will help you write good articles is to be constantly on the lookout for story ideas, examples, quotes, and so on. Designate a file folder into which you put newspaper clippings, printouts of relevant sites you've found on the Web, random ideas that strike you, and more. Refer to this idea file as you craft new articles that cover your specialty.*

---

6. **Include relevant links**—When writing your brand-building articles, don't forget about the interactive nature of the Internet. As you write each section of your article, ask yourself if there's a place you can send readers to get more information. You don't have to supply a link in every paragraph, but most articles you write should contain at least a couple of online resources. If you start to think that it's counterproductive to send people to Web sites other than your own, think again. Remember, your job is to establish yourself as an expert in your field. That means you need to share your knowledge and give people whatever they need to succeed. Your readers will appreciate your openness and your wisdom, and they'll reward you by visiting your site and subscribing to your newsletter so that they can get even more of your comprehensive guidance.

7. **Avoid jargon and twenty-dollar words**—The purpose of writing is to communicate. Too many beginning writers feel they need to write to impress. Don't make that same mistake. Potential fans who read your online tips and columns won't think you're more important because you "integrate paradigm shifts" or "facilitate automated processes." Using the latest buzzwords and over-inflated phrases won't help you brand yourself online. Write your articles in a conversational, straightforward manner. Don't use twenty-dollar words when a fifty-cent word will do just fine. If you clearly communicate your expertise and truly help your readers, they will be plenty impressed.

8. **Keep sentences short**—Another bad habit some writers, including me, have is to try to say too much at one time. I can tell you without hesitation that rambling on and on, attempting to cover every angle of the subject you want to discuss, can get you in trouble, because by the time your readers get to the end of your long and winding sentence, they've forgotten what you were talking about in the first place (very much like this sentence). Try to keep many of your sentences short. Sometimes, very short. Like this. Readers process your ideas more efficiently when you keep your sentences on a leash.

9. **Make it personal**—Speak directly to your fans through your articles. Have a personal conversation with them. Imagine you're standing face to face with each reader at a happy hour, your fingers smeared with sauce from the chicken wings both of you are munching. You're not reciting a thesis. You're chatting it up with someone who shares similar interests.

   Here's an example of how *not* to write:
   Landscapers wishing to attain a larger market share in their region should integrate direct mail into their promotional mix.

   Huh? Wouldn't you rather read the following more personal version?

   You run a landscaping company and you want to grow your business, right? To accomplish that goal you'll need to attract more customers. Great, but how? One tactic that might help is direct mail. I'm not talking about printing ultra-fancy catalogs filled with pictures of supermodels (although that's not a bad idea). I'm talking about using postcards to promote your business.

   When you write your promotional articles, you'll get more mileage from them if you relax, have some fun, and impart useful information in a conversational manner.

10. **Self-promote sensibly**—Obviously, the articles you write and use to demonstrate your expertise to the masses are self-promotion tools. The articles are supposed to shine a positive light on you and what you do. Therefore, while writing them, you may be tempted to work in a lot of references to how cool you are. When the urge strikes to pat yourself on the back in an article, proceed cautiously. You can talk about successes you've had, if mentioning them helps the reader learn something. However, too many experts gratuitously weave in awkward plugs for their products and services for no other reason than to promote themselves. Concentrate on giving your readers what they need to know. If your article's topic is focused on your area of expertise, readers will think you're cool even if you don't go out of your way to point it out.

The Three-Step Writing Formula—Here's a piece of advice that's often given regarding public speaking, but it applies equally to article writing. The formula for a good speech consists of three parts:
1. *Tell the audience what you're going to tell them.*
2. *Tell them.*
3. *Tell them what you told them.*

In other words, start out any article with a strong title and brief introduction that explains the problem or situation you're addressing. The introduction should also give a general overview of the solutions or recommendations you're about to make. The meat of your article is then made up of paragraphs that detail the steps readers need to take to achieve the promise made in the title. Your conclusion summarizes what you just covered and gives readers specific marching orders to get busy doing what you just recommended.

Online Resources to Hone Your Writing Skills

The more you write, the better your skills at it will become. Check out the following writing-related sites for inspiration and guidance:

Coffeehouse for Writers (online writing workshops, discussion lists, and critique groups)
http://www.coffeehouse4writers.com/

Inkspot (articles and tips on freelance writing, self-publishing, networking, and more)
http://www.inkspot.com/

SharpWriter.com (book reviews, grammar resources, copyright information, and job markets)
http://www.sharpwriter.com/

Writer Online (writing courses, publishing news, and tips for poets, fiction writers, and more)
http://www.novalearn.com/wol/

Writer's Digest (online home of the established print magazine, featuring the 101 best Web sites for writers, a freelance market of the day, online workshops, contest listings, and a book club)
http://www.writersdigest.com/

Writer's Resource Center (tips for landing freelance jobs, articles on writing better, and an extensive directory of publishing-related links)
http://www.poewar.com/

WritingNow.com (guidance on how to get published and paid, interviews with writers and editors, and more)
http://www.writingnow.com/

Your All-Important Author Blurb

Once you have a collection of solid, helpful articles on your special topic, you will be armed with valuable gifts you can offer to other Webmasters and e-zine editors. But your gift giving must come with strings attached. For anyone to use your articles for free, they must agree to run an author blurb somewhere on the page, usually at the end of your article. An author blurb serves the following four purposes:

- Acts as a short biography of the author
- Lets readers know how to contact the author
- Reinforces the author's brand identity
- Encourages readers to subscribe to the author's newsletter and visit his or her Web site

Without an accompanying author blurb, your articles would be getting only half the job done. The articles may provide useful information and establish you as someone who knows your subject area better than most; but without an author blurb, you and the reader move on without making a deeper connection. Make sure every article, tip, or column you give away includes this essential element.

Here's the author blurb I use at the end of my music-marketing articles:

Bob Baker is a musician, former music magazine publisher and author of "The Guerrilla Music Marketing Handbook" and "Ignite Your Creative Passion." Get a FREE subscription to Bob's weekly music marketing tip sheet, The Buzz Factor. Just visit http://www.thebuzzfactor.com/ or send any e-mail to 00-BuzzFactor-subscribe@egroups.com.

Here's the blurb used by Internet marketing expert Dr. Kevin Nunley:

Kevin Nunley works with small businesses and organizations providing affordable marketing advice, copywriting, and Internet promotion. Reach him at DrNunley@aol.com or (801) 253-4536. Ask for his free report on marketing with low-cost media. See all of Kevin's articles on his Marketing Info Supersite: http://www.DrNunley.com.

Keep your author blurbs short but packed with plenty of quick details about who you are, what benefits you provide, and how readers can get more of what you have to offer. Short is essential, because otherwise many editors and Webmasters may not be willing to run them in a longer form. Present your author blurb as you would like to see it run, but don't be surprised if an editor or Webmaster proposes to shorten or edit it

Self-Syndicating Your Articles

Traditionally, when writers are syndicated, they sell their columns through a syndication company, which in turn sells the columns to newspapers, magazines, and newsletters around the world. Some popular examples of syndicated columnists include Dave Barry, Abigail Van Buren, and Ann Landers. Hungry self-promoters like you, though, don't even bother with these big-time syndication companies. In true Poor Richard's fashion, you syndicate your articles yourself.

The two best places to start promoting the availability of your free articles are through your own Web site and e-mail newsletter. The people who know you through these venues are already aware of the high-quality information you furnish. Many of these readers and visitors publish their own e-zines and oversee their own Web sites. Make it obvious to anyone who might be interested that your information is available for free.

Shelley Lowery, the self-described "Webmistress" of **Web-Source.net** (http://www.web-source.net/), shown in Figure 8.2, does an excellent job of self-syndication on her site. The page serves as a table of contents to all of Lowery's site design and Internet marketing articles. Each article can be read on its own Web page and is available by autoresponder. She even has a special e-zine set up just for people who want the latest information on her free articles. Lowery has all the bases covered. Best of all, she doesn't hide the fact that her articles are for the taking; she announces it at the top of her main free articles page.

Here is Lowery's self-syndication announcement:

Each of the articles below was written by Shelley Lowery. You have permission to publish these articles electronically, in print, in an e-book, or on your Web site free of charge, as long as the author bylines are included. If you'd like to include a photograph, you may copy the image on the right by right clicking your mouse and selecting "Save Picture As." You may request the articles via autoresponder or copy and paste them from their corresponding pages. New articles will be added on a regular basis, so check back often. If you'd like to receive new articles as soon as they're released, you may subscribe to the "Publisher Mailing List."

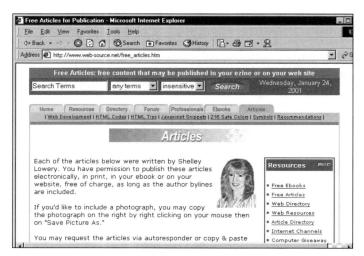

FIGURE 8.2: Shelley Lowery lets readers know right away that her Web design and marketing articles are available for use on other sites.

Damon G. Zahariades makes this similar offer to his Web site visitors:

Note to Webmasters and E-zine Publishers:

I welcome and encourage you to use any of the following articles in your e-zine or on your Web site. You can easily retrieve a properly-formatted (60 characters per line) e-mail copy of any article from an autoresponder. (You'll find the link on each article page.) I ask only that you include my full name, "Damon G. Zahariades," after the title as well as the following short signature:

Read what the experts are saying about Damon's "Web Business Today!" newsletter at http://www.WebBusinessToday.com/.

By announcing the availability of your free articles on your site, you save yourself from having to do all the work of tracking down interested Webmasters and e-zine editors and supplying them with what they need. In essence, they come to you, get permission to reprint your articles, find out what they need to do in return, and copy and paste the articles they want—all without any direct involvement from you.

You can also make a similar type of self-syndication plea in your e-zine. Every issue of Art Sobczak's *TelE-Sales Hot Tips of the Week* newsletter ends with this notice:

Reprint Permission

Copyright 2001, Art Sobczak, Business By Phone Inc. Reprint permission granted in part or whole when the following credit appears: "Reprinted with permission from Art Sobczak's "TelE-Sales Hot Tips of the Week." To subscribe free, visit http//www.businessbyphone.com, or mailto:telesales@businessbyphone.com with "join" in the subject line.

One drawback to this open-door self-syndication policy is that you don't control the quality of the vehicles that run your material. Some experts prefer to pick and choose the sites and publications that carry their articles. Others reason that any exposure is good for their brands and that lower-quality sites that carry the experts' articles probably don't get much traffic anyway. Only you can decide how much and how freely you want to give away your material.

Free Content Web Sites

Luckily, you don't have to rely only on your own site to get the word out about your collection of free articles. The following Web sites are set up to provide a comprehensive listing of free content for Webmasters and e-zine editors. Get your articles listed for greater exposure.

Article Announce
http://www.web-source.net/articles/

Ezine Articles
http://www.ezinearticles.com/

FreeSticky.com
http://www.freesticky.com/

IdeaMarketers (shown in Figure 8.3)
http://www.ideamarketers.com/

Marketing-Seek.com
http://www.marketing-seek.com/articles/

MediaPeak.com
http://mediapeak.com/

Free Article Mailing Lists

A number of e-mail newsletters are being published to announce the availability of free articles by a variety of different experts. Here are three such newsletters in which to promote your articles:

FIGURE 8.3: Sites such as IdeaMarketers list hundreds of free articles available from dozens of online experts.

Free Ezine Content
http://topica.com/lists/FreeEzineContent/

Articles Archives
http://www.egroups.com/group/articles_archives/

Free-Content
http://www.egroups.com/group/Free-Content/

Finding and Approaching Editors and Webmasters

Self-syndication is a great way to get your articles circulating via people who already know you. But your efforts to get widespread exposure through your writing shouldn't end there. You still need to seek out the following two groups of people:

- Webmasters and e-zine editors who don't yet know you
- Webmasters and e-zine editors you're currently unaware of

Of course, I'm not referring to Webmasters and e-zine editors in general. I'm talking about those who reach an audience that is likely to be interested in your identity. To get your free material published through these avenues, you'll have to hunt down the people who oversee them and make those folks aware of the valuable articles you offer. In Chapter 3, "Developing Your Branding Arsenal,"

I discussed compiling a database of the many online sources that cater to your brand's target audience. This would be a good time to open that file and start filling it with the names, URLs, and e-mail addresses of compatible Webmasters and e-zine editors.

Start by listing the sites and e-mail publications you already know about. Visit those sites and take a closer look at them to make sure you have the editor's correct name and e-mail address. Include any comments you have regarding each resource into a Notes field in your database. These comments help you personalize the e-mail messages you'll soon be sending to these site owners and editors.

Next, head to your favorite search engine and do keyword searches on terms related to your brand image. Investigate the sites that pop up and determine their potential for carrying your articles. Also, go to mailing list sites like **Yahoo! Groups** (http://www.yahoogoups.com/) and **Topica** (http://www.topica.com/) and perform similar searches to find related e-zines. Add the promising ones to your database. Here are three other ways to discover new sites and e-zines:

- Whenever you find a Web site that's worth adding to your database, look to see whether the site has a links page. Most likely, the Web sites it links to also appeal to the same audience.
- Check the signature files of people who correspond with you by e-mail. I've found many article-publishing sources by visiting the Web sites of subscribers and others who send me personal e-mail messages.
- Ask your network of online friends and business acquaintances if they can suggest a site or e-zine that might want to carry your articles.

Once you have a couple dozen or more sources in your database, it's time to start contacting them. The best way to accomplish that is with a simple introductory e-mail message. Here's a hypothetical letter from a sports trivia expert:

Dear Stan,

I just visited your TableTennis.com site. What an excellent resource you've put together. Your Ping-Pong Fun Facts page was especially entertaining!

Would you be interested in a free sports trivia column? I've been writing the Jock Talk Trivia column for two years. You can check out tons of previous columns on my Web site, JockTalkTrivia.com. I think your site visitors and e-zine subscribers would really enjoy them.

You will find complete details on how easy it is to run these columns at http://www.jocktalktrivia.com/columns.html. Remember, the columns will cost you nothing and they will give TableTennis.com fans another reason to stick around.

Cheers!
Johnny Smithton
www.JockTalkTrivia.com
Home of the "Jock Talk Trivia" column

Here are the key ingredients that make this letter effective:

- It starts with a personal salutation to the site owner that uses his first name.
- It makes a direct reference to the site. You could use a publication's title in the case of an e-zine.
- It says something favorable about the site.
- It includes a specific note about a favorite section, proving that this isn't a form letter.
- It offers the free columns and lets the site owner know where to read samples.
- It directs the site owner to a specific Web page that contains syndication details.
- It reminds the site owner of the reason to run the free columns: They will draw and keep visitors.

Now craft your own version of this introductory letter. Go through your database and personalize the message to each site or e-zine. Save this letter in a special file. Whenever you discover a new online resource that should be running your articles, add the resource to your database and send a similar version of this e-mail note.

Getting Paid for Your Articles

The more you promote the availability of your articles online, the more exposure you'll get. You'll also start getting requests from Web sites for written content above and beyond what you're offering for free. For instance, some Webmasters might ask for an article on a specific topic you haven't covered yet. Others may ask for exclusivity or the right to be the first source to run your new articles for a certain period of time. As these requests come in, weigh the pros and cons and determine whether the extra effort is worth it. If a site gets a lot of traffic and has the potential to bring you a lot of recognition, it might be smart to write a special free column for it. However, if there's no exposure benefit, you have every right to ask the site owner for compensation to write customized content.

For a couple of years, I submitted free music business columns to a site that catered to aspiring musicians. The site ran the same articles I offered to many other online sources. A larger company acquired the site. The editor wanted to beef up the editorial contributions, so he offered to pay me a modest amount to write an exclusive weekly column. On top of that, my columns still ran with the same author blurb that accompanied my free articles. That's the nice thing about giving away quality content for free. If you prove you can deliver, some sites may eventually pay you and promote you at the same time.

Several Web sites syndicate content from independent writers and publishers and sell it to online and offline publications. Profits are split with the writers. If you'd like to make a few dollars with your brand-focused writing talents, check out these sites:

iCopyright.com
http://www.icopyright.com/

iSyndicate
http://www.isyndicate.com/

ScreamingMedia
http://www.screamingmedia.com/

SubPortal.com
http://subportal.iboost.com/

Becoming a Resident Web Expert

Another way to establish yourself as an authority in your field is to get hooked up with your own section at one of the growing number of expert sites. These Internet outposts are typically set up with a broad range of categories. An expert is chosen to preside over each topic area.

Take a close look at the rules and policies on these sites. Some don't allow you to run a site that directly competes with your expert area—a restriction that would be counterproductive to branding yourself online. Some of these sites pay you; some ask you to invest your time in exchange for exposure.

For a huge list of expert sites, check out the **Ask the Experts refdesk.com** page at http://www.refdesk.com/expert.html. Here's a collection of some of the more prominent experts sites:

4advice.com
http://4advice.4anything.com/

About.com
http://www.about.com/

Abuzz
http://www.abuzz.com/

AllExperts.com
http://www.allexperts.com/

AskMe.com
http://www.askme.com/

EXP.com
http://www.exp.com/

ExpertCentral.com
http://www.expertcentral.com/

Expertcity.com
http://www.expertcity.com/

Experts.com (shown in Figure 8.4)
http://www.experts.com/

GetExpertAdvice.com
http://www.getexpertadvice.com/

iVillage.com Experts Directory
http://www.ivillage.com/experts/

Keen.com
http://www.keen.com/

Pitsco's Ask an Expert
http://www.askanexpert.com/

PointAsk!
http://www.pointask.com/

Suite101.com
http://www.suite101.com/

Yahoo! Experts
http://experts.yahoo.com/

FIGURE 8.4: A growing number of sites, such as Experts.com, feature subject-specific authorities to answer readers' questions.

Now that we've covered how to exploit the Web sites and e-zines of other content providers, it's time to turn our attention to another method of getting your personal brand message to the masses: self-publishing. That topic awaits you in Chapter 9, "Self-Publishing to Disperse Your Expertise."

CHAPTER NINE

Self-Publishing to Disperse Your Expertise

Chapter 8, "Exploiting E-zines and Web Sites of Others," discussed the advantages of writing and freely distributing how-to articles and other valuable forms of content related to your brand identity. This chapter talks about other ways to reach potential fans with useful information and samples of what you do. I use the term *self-publishing* to describe how you get your information out into the world. *Self* refers to you, since you're the one who will be creating, compiling, and packaging this information in your own inimitable way. *Publishing* relates to you finding creative ways to distribute your content to the people most likely to be interested in your area of expertise.

Here are some of the self-publishing channels I'll be addressing to various degrees in this chapter:

- E-mail courses
- Free e-books
- For-sale e-books
- Special reports
- CD-ROMs
- Affiliate programs

To get the most from your self-publishing efforts, you need to deliver information that is tightly focused on your brand. Your goal is not to take whatever information you can gather, throw it against a Web-based wall, and hope something sticks. Your expert wisdom must be crafted to provide a benefit to potential fans while showing you in the most favorable light. In addition to establishing your identity through these informational vehicles, you also want to encourage the people who read them to subscribe to your e-zine, visit your Web site, and begin a relationship with you that you hope will last a long time.

On the other hand, many people who consume your self-published materials will already be fans, subscribers, and regular visitors to your site. Therefore, another reason to distribute self-published information is to persuade fans to do some of the following things:

- Purchase your product or service
- Accept your idea or way of thinking
- Take the actions you suggest
- Share your self-published resources with others
- Recommend you, your e-zine, and Web site to friends and associates

Self-publishing won't necessarily require a big investment (in fact, many of the methods discussed in this chapter will cost you nothing at all), but it holds the potential for quickly spreading your online branding message to a slew of new and old fans alike.

Your Self-Publishing Triple Threat—*To be effective, your self-published material must hammer home the following three details: who you are, what you do, and the unique way you do it. To self-publish without trying to get these three points across would be senseless, so make sure everything you send out into the world reinforces your brand.*

Offering Free E-mail Courses

I love free e-mail courses. Once you write and set up one, an e-mail course becomes an incredibly easy and effective way to promote awareness of your brand. Like an e-zine, a course (or e-mail workshop, as I sometimes call it) makes excellent use of repetition while delivering focused information about you and what you know, but an e-mail course delivers it in more potent doses.

An e-mail course is a short series of lessons delivered, of course, by e-mail. Interested fans sign up for a course simply by sending an e-mail to an autoresponder address of your choice. To set one up, you'll need to use an autoresponder service that has follow-up message capabilities. Many autoresponders that come with basic Web-hosting packages are often of the one-shot variety. That means the autoresponder will send only one return message and that's it. You can either ask your Web host if it offers a multiple-message option, or you can use a free online autoresponder service, such as **GetResponse.com** (http://www.getresponse.com/), **SendFree,** shown in Figure 9.1, (http://www.sendfree.com/) or **FastFacts.net** (http://www.fastfacts.net/).

What type of material should you offer in an e-mail course? The best source of ideas is the list of articles you have written or are thinking about writing on

FIGURE 9.1: SendFree offers free autoresponders, which can be used to deliver e-mail courses.

your area of expertise. Let's say you're a wedding planner and you just wrote an excellent article called *Five Steps to Planning a Memorable Wedding Reception*. Each step consists of at least three or four paragraphs. Instead of offering this wonderful advice as another free article, split the steps into five lessons to be delivered via an e-mail course.

To go the e-mail course route, simply insert the wedding reception planning steps into your autoresponder files and instruct the system how to deliver them. Lesson one will always be delivered instantly whenever someone sends an e-mail to ReceptionPlans@autoresponder.com (or whatever your autoresponder e-mail address is). You determine when follow-up lessons are sent. You could send one lesson every day for five days or send them every other day to spread the course out over 10 days. If your course requires recipients to do a week of activities between lessons, you'd have the autoresponder send out messages seven days apart. The beauty of autoresponder e-mail courses is that, once they're set up, all these messages are sent to interested people without any effort on your part.

E-mail courses can reinforce your brand in all sorts of creative ways, including the following:

- A visual artist positions an e-mail course as an electronic gallery tour. Each message includes a link to an online image of a new painting with a detailed description of the medium and what inspired the artist to create the work.

- An unsigned band offers a members-only guide to unreleased tracks and studio outtakes. Fans who sign up get an e-mail every three days for two weeks. Each e-mail contains a secret URL to a hard-to-find MP3 file or new single from the band.
- An author promotes a new mystery novel by offering the first chapter in 10 daily e-mail installments.

Turn Your E-mail Course into Cash—*In addition to using free e-mail courses as promotional tools, you can sell more extensive courses. For a couple of years, I sold a self-published manual called* Creating Wealth for Creative People, *a money-making guide for artists, writers, musicians, and other people involved in the arts. Sales slowed to a trickle, so I considered ways to repackage the information. The book was arranged in 28 modules, each of which covered a specific step to success. I ended up turning the manual into a 28-day e-mail workshop called* Turn Your Creativity Into Cash. *The old version of the manual cost me about $6 per copy to print. The e-mail version costs nothing to produce, yet I still charge $19.95 for it. A for-profit e-mail course can generate income and cement your brand identity at the same time.*

Multipart e-mail courses can be more powerful than online articles and e-zines because customers give you permission to contact them repeatedly in a concentrated period of time. If you deliver high-quality content in your follow-up mailings, you have a real opportunity to embed your brand image quickly. Imagine hundreds of people anxiously awaiting your next message for several days in a row. With the welcome repetition that e-mail courses provide, you can easily turn casual observers into rabid fans. When setting up the individual messages of your course, keep these points in mind:

Use consistent subject headings—If your first lesson carries the subject line "Search Engine Ranking Tactics: Day One," don't use "More Search Engine Tactics" for the second lesson. Be consistent and use "Search Engine Ranking Tactics: Day Two." Readers will recognize your course much more easily when the lessons are consistently labeled.

Start with a short reminder notice—At the top of each e-mail message, tell recipients why they are receiving it. Especially if your segments are delivered days apart, this notice will remind people that they requested multiple mailings from you. Believe it or not, some people will forget and accuse you of sending spam. A simple notice like this should do: "This message is part of the five-step Hula dancing course you recently signed up for. Enjoy!"

Include your course's title and an author byline—Reinforce the name of the course and what the reader is about to absorb. Using the same wording that's used in the subject line would be ideal. Right below the lesson title, put an attribution like "by Fred Jones—The Geometry Geek" or "by Penny Smith, author of *50 Ways to Cheat Your Lover.*" In other words, get your name and brand identity established early in each message.

The main body of your message—Next include the meat and potatoes of your message. Here you put the useful information that will help your readers learn something new, get motivated, and get more of the juicy details your course title promises.

End with a teaser for the next lesson—Always conclude your lessons with a line such as, "Tomorrow, I'll reveal the five things the IRS doesn't want you to know about medical deductions. See you then." Create some excitement and give your readers another reason to look forward to the next segment of your course.

Include a final brand-building blurb—Use the end of your message to once again squeeze in a brand-related message. This is a good spot to use your Brand Identity Statement (BIS) and contact information. For instance, I might include a final blurb that reads, "Brought to you compliments of Bob Baker and The Buzz Factor. For more resources, tips, and tools on how to promote your band or record label, visit http://www.thebuzzfactor.com/. Have a question about today's lesson? Send Bob an e-mail: bob@bob-baker.com."

Publishing E-books

Though you're probably sick of seeing Internet-related words with an *e* conveniently slapped onto the front of them, it's time to introduce you to another *e*-word. Welcome to the wonderful world of e-books. Unlike articles posted on a Web site or helpful tips sent in the body of an e-mail, *e-books* are self-contained files formatted like the pages of a book. They can be read on screen or printed to be perused later. Some e-books are formatted for hand-held computer devices and small e-book readers. Many e-books contain only a few pages of material; others can run hundreds of pages long. E-books can be distributed by attaching them to e-mail, copying them to CD-ROMs or floppy disks and mailing them, or making them available for download from a Web site.

One of the most attractive things about e-books is the cost to reproduce them: Zilch. Nada. It could set you back thousands of dollars to print and distribute traditional paper-based books. Once an e-book is designed and formatted, though, you can reproduce and circulate an infinite number of copies for no additional expense. The ease of copying and distributing e-books has some people in the publishing industry trembling from fears of widespread copyright infringement. But for your online branding purposes, e-books are a godsend.

How to Create an E-book

While e-books have become a hot topic in recent years, the dust still hasn't settled enough to determine a clear industry standard regarding software and format. Some hand-held devices can only read e-books in text, HTML, and rich text file (RFT) formats; others can display only Palm-formatted or Windows CE e-books. Learning about e-book software and hardware can be quite confusing. To avoid a long dissertation on every available option, I'm going to give you what I consider the two best e-book creation options: PDF and HTML executable files. (If you do want to learn more about the various e-book formats, check out **Bookbooters: eBook Formats Explained** at http://www.bookbooters.com/formats.asp.)

PDF E-book Creation

PDF-formatted e-books are created using Adobe Acrobat, a program that lets you convert any document—including entire Web sites—into an Adobe Portable Document Format (PDF) file, with its original appearance preserved. In essence, Acrobat takes a snapshot of the pages in a document. That way, people who read your e-book don't have to have the fonts and images that were used to create the document. All they need to view a PDF file is the free Adobe Acrobat Reader, which comes pre-installed with most computer operating systems these days. People who don't have it can easily download the reader from Adobe's site.

The great thing about PDF is that files can be read across most operating systems. Even though you may have created an e-book on a Windows system, after it's converted to PDF, someone with a Macintosh can read it, too. Many hand-held e-book readers also support PDF files.

To find out more about Acrobat and how it works, head to **Adobe Acrobat** at http://www.adobe.com/products/acrobat/ (see Figure 9.2). The full-featured version you'll need to convert files will cost you about $250. Adobe also has an online conversion service that runs $9.95 a month. And, best of all, the site offers three free online trial conversions. Head to **Create Adobe PDF Online** at http://cpdf1.adobe.com/ to learn more about Adobe's online service options.

HTML E-book Creation

The next best option for putting your e-book together is using an HTML e-book compiler program. What you do is create a separate HTML file for each section of your e-book, which might include a title page, table of contents, introduction, individual chapters, about-the-author page, and so on. Prepare the sections as if you were creating interlinked Web pages. The table of contents page should link to all the chapters. Each chapter should include a menu of links

FIGURE 9.2: The Adobe company offers an online version of its Acrobat service, which converts common documents into PDF files.

to other chapters or simply link back to the table of contents. You can also include hyperlinks to any Web site or online resource you mention in your text. Photos and media files can also be included in the same manner they would with a Web page.

Next, place all your e-book's HTML pages and images into the same folder. By using one of the e-book creation programs listed in this section, you can convert the entire contents of the folder into a single executable (.exe) file. People interested in reading your e-book won't need any special software to view your book. They simply double-click your .exe file and it opens to whatever page you've designated as the title page. From there, readers can click through to whichever segments for which you provide links.

HTML E-book System Requirements—An .exe file can be read by almost any Windows operating system (sorry, Mac users are out of luck with .exe files). However, many of these .exe files require Windows 95 or later and Internet Explorer 4.0 or later to function properly. HTML .exe files work fine for people who have the minimum Windows system requirements, but they're not as widely user friendly as PDF files. Still, I think going the .exe route is your next best bet after PDF.

The following sites offer various e-book creation programs. Most offer free sample downloads with a fee required for a fully functioning version.

EBook Wizard
http://www.ebook-wizard.com/

EBookCompiler.com
http://www.ebookcompiler.com/

E-ditor
http://www.e-ditorial.com/software.html

eBookPro
http://www.ebookpro.com/

KeeBoo Creator
http://www.keeboo.com/

NeoBook
http://www.neosoftware.com/nbw.html

WebCompiler
http://www.webcompiler.com/

Free E-books

People are attracted to free stuff. After decades of being used plentifully by advertisers, the word *free* is still one of the most effective marketing terms in the English language. Free e-books are growing in popularity on the Internet for good reason. Here are just a few things you can do with a free e-book:

- Give it away from your site.
- Convince other Web sites and e-zines to give it away.
- Offer it as a freebie for new e-zine subscribers.
- Give it away to your current subscribers as a token of your appreciation.

Give your e-book an attention-getting title and fill it with lively information that focuses on your specialized area. E-books can even carry photos, artwork, and other graphic images, as well as audio and video files. By encouraging your fans to share your free e-book with others, your brand identity may spread faster than a chain letter.

A viruslike ping-pong effect occurred when I created a free e-book to promote my music-marketing site. I knew that many of my biggest fans and paying customers were musicians who had released their own CDs. To attract more of these types of musicians, I started giving away an e-book called *Double Your CD Sales (in 90 Days or Less)*. At the beginning and end of the book, I encouraged readers to pass along the file to anyone else who could benefit from the advice.

I also managed to generate a considerable amount of online media coverage related to the free title.

About 10,000 people downloaded the e-book from my site during the first three months I offered it. There's no telling how many others received the book as a result of file sharing, but my number of Web site visitors and new e-zine subscribers picked up considerably in the months that followed. Do you think there's a free e-book inside of you that's ready to be unleashed on the world?

Does Length Matter?—*Just because the word* book *appears as part of the term* e-book *doesn't mean you have to write something as long as* War *and* Peace *to start publishing e-books. The book you hold in your hands contains more than 100,000 words. However, you can easily produce a quality free e-book by writing only 1,500 to 2,000 words. In fact, your free e-books should be short enough for people to read in one sitting. If you make them longer, your book may get put aside until a more convenient time—a time that may never come.*

The following sites are e-book directories, e-book search engines, or sites that in some way compile lists of available free e-books. Visit them and get your title listed.

Bizinfocenter.com
http://www.bizinfocenter.com/free-ebook-directory/

eBook Directory
http://www.ebookdirectory.com/

Ebook Giveaways
http://www.ebookgiveaways.com/

EBooks Portal
http://ebooks.searchking.com/

Ebook Shop
http://ebookshop.bizland.com/

Free-eBooks.net
http://www.free-ebooks.net/

Co-Branded E-book Partnerships

Promoting an e-book and giving it away as a free download from your site can generate a lot of interest. How much more interest could you stir up if you got dozens of other people to freely distribute your e-book from their sites, too? If your book truly provides useful information, you may well find sites that are willing to promote it heavily to their audiences. However, most Webmasters are savvy enough to realize that your e-book is a promotional vehicle for you. No matter how valuable the information in your e-book is, these Webmasters will probably limit exposure to brief mentions or plugs buried on lower-level pages of their sites.

A great way to overcome this apathy is to offer co-branded e-book partnerships. Here's how they work: Make a copy of the title page file of your e-book. Open the copied file and somewhere under the title add text along the lines of "Compliments of BigCoolWebSite.com and Alex Jones." (In this scenario, you are Alex Jones.) Create a new version of the e-book with this altered title page and send it to the owner of BigCoolWebSite.com. Let her know that you'd also like to add an extra page or two to the e-book that promotes BigCoolWebSite.com in any way the owner sees fit, as long as the owner is willing to give away this customized copy to her readers.

If BigCoolWebSite.com's owner is wise, she'll see the value in having a ready-made promotional tool that not only provides valuable information, but also exposes her own brand to the masses. She would be far more inclined to actively hawk a free e-book that promotes both of you, as opposed to one that promotes only you. That's why you should repeat this co-branding offer to several more noncompeting sites. How much brand recognition could you generate if you had 10 sites actively promoting your free e-book?

You Have to Give to Receive—*Always be on the lookout for ways to help yourself by helping others, as with the co-branding partnership example described in the main text. If you're always asking people for favors without giving a lot back, your progress will be slow. The best promotions are two-way transactions. Whenever you examine a new exposure avenue, ask yourself, "What does this person need that I can supply, and what might I ask for in return?"*

For-Sale E-books

In addition to being effective promotional tools, e-books can also become a profit center for you. Many online branders, myself included, offer a combination of free and for-sale e-books. If you deliver high-impact, beneficial information to enough people through your free titles, you'll find you have a built-in audience of potential buyers. People who think enough of your brand to spend money on your products are your biggest fans, which means they are the people most likely to recommend you to others. Thank your paying customers and treat them well. They will reward you many times over.

The following sections show you where to sell e-books online, how to offer a no-risk buying plan to readers, and why giving away shorter sample e-books and cross-promoting with other experts can boost sales.

Places to Sell Your E-book

The following sites carry and sell e-books. Some of the sites are online e-book retailer shops while some, such as **ClickBank.com** and **DigiBuy**, are e-commerce sites that allow clients to sell digital content through their service:

BookLocker.com
http://www.booklocker.com/

ClickBank.com
http://www.clickbank.com/

DigiBuy
http://www.digibuy.com/

eBookMall.com (see Figure 9.3)
http://www.ebookmall.com/

Scribbler's eBookShoppe
http://www.eBookShoppe.com/

***Two E-book and Online Publishing Resources**—For more information on creating for-sale e-books, visit Angela Adair-Hoy's WritersWeekly.com site at* http://www.writersweekly.com. *Adair-Hoy also co-wrote the book* Publish and Promote Online *with M.J. Rose.*

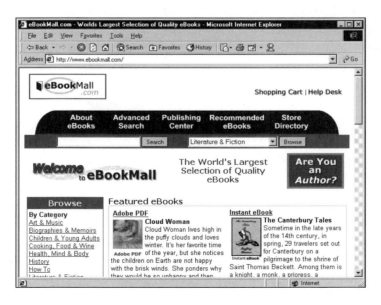

FIGURE 9.3: eBookMall.com specializes in selling e-books online. Self-published authors are welcome.

Promoting a Read-Now, Pay-Later Offer

My first for-sale e-book, *Ignite Your Creative Passion*, got off to a slow start. I put up a Web page and order form and made my e-zine subscribers aware of its existence. Beyond that, I didn't promote the book very heavily. During the first six months, I barely sold a handful of copies at $9.95 a pop. Something had to give. I knew the information was valuable. And except for the few buyers who acted, I had thousands of subscribers who were not benefiting from the contents of the book.

I took a cue from direct-mail booksellers and decided to make a free-trial offer. I invited subscribers to download the e-book risk-free, take 14 days to look it over, and decide whether it was worth $9.95. After 14 days, I asked them to either purchase the e-book or delete it from their hard drives—all on the honor system.

Instead of just supplying the download URL and hoping that subscribers would follow through, I set up a special multiple-message autoresponder. People interested in the free trial had to send an e-mail to an autoresponder address. They immediately received a message that provided the URL from which they could download the e-book. The autoresponder was set up to send a follow-up message 14 days later that served as a gentle reminder of the free-trial agreement. This follow-up message also gave recipients various options on how to purchase the e-book. I figured that one reminder message wouldn't be enough, considering how busy most people's lives are. So I also had the autoresponder send two more follow-ups, at 21 and 28 days.

The results? Sales were far from enough to retire on, but they did pick up considerably after I initiated the free-trial offer. Hundreds of people downloaded the e-book. About 25 percent of them ended up purchasing it. Another 25 percent were kind enough to send a short note explaining that they didn't have time to read it or that the book wasn't what they expected. Nearly 50 percent didn't respond at all.

By traditional standards, this venture seems like a flop. For me, it's a victory. Here are the five reasons why:

- I generated more revenue from a title that had previously showed only a minor blip on my sales radar screen.
- I now have a greater number of people who enjoy my material enough to invest in it, which gives me more potential buyers for future products.
- Even people who didn't purchase the e-book now have a greater understanding of who I am and what I offer.
- The small number of people who unscrupulously shared their copy of my e-book with others still helped me spread my brand identity further.

- The whole promotion didn't cost a dime.

Since there's so little to lose, consider promoting your own read-now, buy-later offer.

Protect Yourself from E-book Bootleggers—*There are ways to keep people from freely distributing your for-sale e-books. Adobe and other e-book creation programs allow you to use encryption and other locking features that let buyers download your e-book without being able to make multiple copies of it. However, hackers often find ways around these mechanisms, but unless you're selling millions of copies, that shouldn't affect your bottom line.*

Offer a Free Sample Version

Another creative way to generate interest in your for-sale e-books is to use a technique popularized by software marketers: offer a free demo version. Take your full-length e-book and create a sample version that includes only the table of contents, the introduction, and the first 20 percent or more of the main chapters. On the other hand, you could format the demo e-book so that it includes only short teaser sections from every chapter. Regardless of how you choose to reveal material in your sample edition, let readers know all about the useful goodies you have waiting for them in the full, paid version. And, on every page of the demo edition, provide the URL from which people can order the e-book.

Cross-Promote with Other Experts

As you network across the Internet, you'll no doubt correspond with other experts in related fields. Many of these experts are promoting their own free and for-sale e-books. This creates a perfect opportunity to cross-promote. In the marketing materials promoting your for-sale e-books, offer the other experts' free e-books as bonuses to fans who buy your book. Don't go out of your way to announce that these bonuses are usually given away. In fact, many promoters describe them in terms of being "a $15 value" or whatever dollar amount is appropriate.

Conversely, ask that these other experts offer your free e-books as bonuses to customers who buy their for-sale e-books. This creates a win-win-win situation in that paying customers receive more helpful information with their purchases, the other expert gets exposure to your audience, and you spread your brand identity to people who may not have otherwise run into you.

Getting the Most Branding Punch from E-books

E-books give you more room to educate fans and promote your brand, compared to the usual constraints of Web pages and e-mail. To help you make the best use of this space, here is a list of the primary sections of an e-book:

Title and copyright page—This is usually the first page readers see when they open your e-book. It should include the title of your book in large letters at the top, your name, and a copyright notice. Even if you're giving away an e-book, you still want to display a copyright notice to show who owns it. You don't need to register your book with the Library of Congress to copyright it. Simply placing text such as "Copyright 2001 by Chris Jones; All rights reserved," will do. Also, it's a good idea to include complete contact information. If you produce a free e-book, include a notice on this page encouraging readers to freely share the e-book. For instance, here's the notice I used in one of my free e-books:

This publication MAY be reproduced, stored in a retrieval system, AND shared with anyone and everyone without the prior written permission of Bob Baker. In fact, sharing this PDF file is enthusiastically encouraged. However, you may not alter its content or sell it for any amount of money. This publication shall remain intact and FREE of charge, so give it away.

About-the-author page—I suggest making the second page of your e-book a short biography that reinforces your brand identity. I use the following text in one of my free creativity e-books:

Bob Baker is an author, musician, workshop leader, and former magazine publisher who provides inspiration and low-cost marketing ideas to people pursuing creative fields.

On this author page you should also include a list of other e-books and resources you have available, a strong endorsement quote or two, and an enticement for readers to subscribe to your free e-zine and visit your Web site for more brand-related details.

Table of contents—If your e-book is long enough and divided into sections, a table of contents helps readers navigate your book. However, if your core information is relatively short, you can skip a table of contents and dive right into the main part of your text.

Body of your e-book—Just like the free articles discussed in Chapter 8, "Exploiting E-zines and Web Sites of Others," and the e-mail courses addressed earlier in this chapter, the body of your e-book should pack a mean punch. Don't hold back. Give your readers information, images, and inspiration that will wow them so much they'll want to rave about it to other people who share their passion for your area of expertise.

End-of-book promotional message or order form—Once you've come to the end of the hard-hitting body of your e-book, it's not time to say goodbye just yet. Use a final page or two to list some of the products, services, and resources you have to offer. Do you have print books to sell? Include the titles, descriptions, and Web pages where they can be ordered. Are you available for public speaking engagements? Promote the benefits of your live presentations and let people know how to contact you for bookings. These final pages are also a good place to encourage people to subscribe to your e-zine and visit your Web site.

Places to Promote Your E-book

Getting exposure through online reviews and e-book announcement lists is a great way to promote your e-books. Two sites that have extensive lists of e-book promotion sources are **About.com—E-Books and E-Publishing** (http://www.publishing.about.com/cs/ebooks/) and **ePublishing Connections** (http://www.epublishingconnections.com/).

The following e-zines regularly promote both free and for-sale e-books. You'd be wise to subscribe to these announcement lists and send them e-book-related press releases. (For more information on pursuing online media coverage, see Chapter 11, "Exposing Your Identity Through Online Publicity.")

eBook Directory Update Newsletter
http://www.topica.com/lists/Free_ebooks/

eBooks N' Bytes Informer
http://www.topica.com/lists/ebooksnbytes/

Ebook News
http://groups.yahoo.com/group/Ebook_News/

Deb-E-Books Ebook Newsletter
http://www.topica.com/lists/Deb-E-Books/

I Love Ebooks!
http://www.topica.com/lists/iloveebooks/

Publishing Avenue eBook News
http://www.topica.com/lists/ebooknews/

E-book Publishing Resources

The subject of e-book publishing is vast and ever changing. To get more educated on this fascinating topic and keep up with the latest e-book news, visit the following sites:

About.com—E-Books and E-Publishing
http://www.publishing.about.com/cs/ebooks/

eBook Connections
http://www.ebookconnections.com/

eBookNet.com
http://www.ebooknet.com/

eBooks N' Bytes (see Figure 9.4)
http://www.ebooksnbytes.com/

ePublishing Connections
http://www.epublishingconnections.com/

A Must-Read Book—For more in-depth information on electronic publishing, pick up a copy of Poor Richard's Creating E-Books *by Chris Van Buren and Jeff Cogswell. This book shows authors, publishers, and corporations how to make the most of e-publishing. It covers planning and creating an e-book, distribution and electronic sales, rights and legal issues, and so on. Find more details online at* http://topfloor.com/pr/ebook/.

FIGURE 9.4: eBooks N' Bytes provides resources for e-book publishers.

Publishing Profitable Special Reports

You can take the content of your e-books and offer printed hard copies for sale in the form of special reports. Even in this digital age, many people are still willing to pay a little extra to have a paper copy of a title mailed to them the old-fashioned way. In fact, when I first started offering both printed and e-book versions of my music marketing titles, I was surprised to find that more than half of my customers still opted to purchase the higher-priced hard-copy versions.

Selling special reports can be profitable because people spend money on a highly focused title, regardless of how long the printed piece is. For instance, an average small paperback book is filled with about 75,000 words and retails for around $14.95. Yet I've sold many special reports over the years for $5.00 or $6.00 each—reports that ran only 2,000 to 3,000 words. Not a bad way to profit from one's writing. Making available printed versions of your special reports gives your fans more options to devour your knowledge. For-sale reports also provide a more tangible vehicle to carry your brand name and image.

Take a look at John Kremer's **Book Publishing Reports,** http://www.bookmarket.com/reportcd.html. You'll see that Kremer has taken 27 book promotion–related special reports (worth $100) that he's written over the years and made them available on one CD-ROM for $40. He sells the titles individually as printed reports. On the CD-ROM, though, he converted them all into HTML e-books—a good way to make use of both formats. Could a self-published CD-ROM work for you?

Combining an Affiliate Program with Self-Publishing

Amazon.com was perhaps the first site to make a splash with an affiliate program on the Web. Amazon CEO Jeff Bezos figured if he offered a commission on any sales generated through referral links to his site, it might draw a lot more visitors to Amazon.com. The tactic proved to be quite successful. Now it seems every company who sets up shop on the Web offers an affiliate program on a per-sale, per-click, or per-lead basis.

The affiliate approach also works for individuals. Canadian physician Ken Evoy has transformed himself into a recognized figure on the Internet through the widespread promotion of his *Make Your Site Sell* collection of e-books and other related titles. Most of his exposure is generated by the many thousands of affiliates who each gets a cut of any sales he or she generates for Evoy's products. Similarly, Jim Daniels reports that half of the online sales of his *Insider Internet Marketing* book comes through affiliate links. Lesson: An affiliate program can be good for your brand's exposure *and* your bottom line. Consider using one to promote and sell your e-books, as well as your other products and services.

Everything You Wanted to Know about Affiliate Programs—One of the most thorough discussions of affiliate program options is written by Allan Gardyne and can be found on the AssociatePrograms.com site at http://www.associateprograms.com/search/howto.shtml. It's an exhaustive listing and explanation of dozens of ways to set up an affiliate program.

There are many ways to run an affiliate program—from online services and software that cost thousands of dollars to more modest options you can operate yourself. The most important element is having a way to track where sales come from. Each affiliate is generally assigned a unique tracking number or URL. You must have a way to ensure that every sale made through an affiliate's unique link is recorded and paid.

What follows is a brief list of affiliate service and software options:

AffiliateShop (about $300 a year)
http://www.affiliateshop.com/

Affiliate Tracking Network
http://www.affiliatetracking.com/

AffiliateZone.com
http://www.affiliatezone.com/

AutomateYourWebsite.com—Ultimate Automation ($50 a month)
http://www.automateyourwebsite.com/

Be Free, Inc. (expensive; used by the some of the bigger online retailers)
http://www.befree.com/

ClickTrade (charges 30 percent of what your affiliate gets, shown in Figure 9.5)
http://www.clicktrade.com/

Commission Junction
http://www.cj.com/

LinkShare
http://www.linkshare.com/

PlugInGo.com ($895 sign-up fee)
http://www.plugingo.com/

SimpleAffiliate.com ($29.95 software package)
http://www.simpleaffiliate.com/

Your Own Associate Program (packages starting at $199)
http://www.palis.com/new/yoap7/

FIGURE 9.5: ClickTrade allows you to set up affiliate selling relationships with thousands of other sites.

Self-publishing can be an effective and lucrative way to get the word out on your brand. In fact, if you do a good enough job of promoting your expertise through e-mail courses, e-books, special reports, CD-ROMs, and affiliate programs, you just might find yourself approached by a traditional book publisher some day. Do you think I'm kidding? That's exactly how I came to write the very book you're reading right now!

In the next chapter, "Branding Yourself Through Online Networking," we discuss even more ways to connect with people online, establish rapport with fans, and form profitable business relationships.

CHAPTER TEN

Branding Yourself Through Online Networking

Once you set up your own Web site, publish an e-mail newsletter, and distribute and self-publish articles, e-books, and other brand-building materials, you're well on your way to building a recognized identity online. However, with the exception of personal e-mail messages you get from new fans, much of your branding assault is launched from a distance. Though people may be reading your advice, hearing about you from other sources, visiting your site, and subscribing to your e-zine, they're still not communicating with you on a direct, personal level.

One way to get more involved with people online is by networking through mailing lists, discussion forums, message boards, clubs, and other avenues. Networking via these channels takes time and effort, but it can amount to time well spent. Here are three reasons to network online:

- To position yourself as a resource with people who turn to you for advice, entertainment, or guidance (in other words, potential fans and customers)
- To get to know peers and other experts with whom you share information, resources, and moneymaking opportunities
- To make yourself known to the movers and shakers in your industry

This chapter covers the best ways to network online and points out many of the pitfalls to avoid. We also talk about the differences between mailing lists, newsgroups, discussion forums, and Web communities. Along the way, we discuss how to find the best places to promote your brand and go over the rules of proper (and effective) online posting.

Networking Through Mailing Lists

The purpose of an Internet mailing list is to allow a group of people to exchange messages with each other in such a way that everyone participates. Mailing lists provide a way for people to share frustrations, achievements, advice, solutions, and more. An active group of subscribers can quickly develop a lively dialogue. But these conversations don't take place in real time as they do in Internet chat rooms. Mailing lists are more like message boards in which individual postings are delivered by e-mail. Subscribers can either sit back and lurk, observing the flow of messages, or dive in and express their views on a topic being discussed.

Every mailing list has at least one owner, usually the person who founded the list. The owner determines the topic of the list, the rules subscribers must follow, and whether individual messages need to be approved before being passed on to everyone. If messages don't need to be approved, the list is unmoderated. With an *unmoderated* list, every e-mail message a subscriber sends to the mailing list's address is disbursed to every subscriber via e-mail.

I've never run a community mailing list like this, but I admire those who do. It takes a lot of time and commitment to stay on top of this kind of wide-open interaction. Subscribers veer off topic and post inappropriate messages regularly. For instance, I once subscribed to an unmoderated list for writers that had a subscriber whose aunt was in the hospital. For days on end, subscribers sent a plethora of messages wishing her a speedy recovery. I know that lists do create a sense of community and I did genuinely feel sorry for the aunt; but I had subscribed to this list to exchange writing tips with other authors, not to wade through reams of condolences. Sending those sympathy messages privately to the person who posted the original message would have been more appropriate.

For some list owners, a *moderated* mailing list is the way to go. Subscribers can send all the messages they want, but no one receives them until the owner reviews and approves them. This option ensures that subscribers receive only messages that are relevant and focused.

E-zines Are Announcement-Only Mailing Lists—*In case you wonder why the term mailing list has popped up in different contexts, you should know that an e-zine (discussed at length in Chapter 7,* Publishing an E-mail Newsletter*) is a mailing list set up as announcement-only. With an announcement-only list, just the owner can post messages to subscribers.*

The following sites either host or catalog a wide variety of mailing lists. Most feature searchable databases that allow you to quickly find lists that may be right for your brand:

DiscussionLists.com
http://discussionlists.com/

dolist.net
http://www.dolist.net/annuaire_en.asp

List of Lists
http://catalog.com/vivian/interest-group-search.html

ListQuest.com
http://www.listquest.com/

Liszt
http://www.liszt.com/

Publicly Accessible Mailing Lists
http://paml.net/

SparkLIST.net
http://sparklist.net/

Tile.Net/Lists
http://tile.net/lists/

Topica
http://www.topica.com/

WebScout Lists
http://www.webscoutlists.com/

Yahoo! Groups (shown in Figure 10.1)
http://www.yahoogroups.com/

FIGURE 10.1: Yahoo! Groups is one of many sites with a directory of mailing lists covering a wide variety of topics.

Once you find a description of a list that seems promising, you need to subscribe to it. You can typically do this by either sending an e-mail to a specific address or by filling out a form on the hosting Web site.

Some mailing lists generate a considerable amount of activity. Luckily, most lists give you the option of receiving either individual e-mails or a daily digest. Going with the individual e-mail option can flood your inbox with messages. A digest version combines many messages in one e-mail, often with a link to an archive Web page where you can view all messages in their entirety. Some list services, such as Yahoo! Groups, also offer a *No E-mail/Web Only* option that lets you read the list's e-mail exchanges on a Web site. Think about these factors before signing up for a lot of mailing lists and being hit with an avalanche of e-mail.

Participating in Mailing Lists Effectively

When it comes to discussion mailing lists, there are certain rules to follow and specific practices that will make your networking efforts more fruitful. A lot of people with good intentions make serious mistakes when participating in mailing lists. Absorb the following steps and you won't have to worry about making online blunders.

Read the FAQ or Introductory Guidelines

Different mailing lists have varying rules for subscribers. Some owners run a tight ship while others are more lenient regarding the variety of messages that are posted. When you first subscribe to a mailing list, you'll usually receive a welcome message. Often that welcome e-mail contains guidelines that clarify the subject matter the owner wants to stay focused on. A lot of other aspects of list participation may also be covered in this message, such as rules for self-promotion. Some list owners direct subscribers to a list of frequently asked questions (called FAQs and pronounced "facts") on a Web site. Regardless of how these instructions are offered, take a few minutes to look them over. The last thing you want to do is get off to a rocky start with a mailing list because you committed a *faux pas* out of ignorance. In some cases, doing so results in getting you permanently booted off the list.

Lurk and Get a Feel for the List

Before diving in, sit back for a few days and watch the exchanges. Read and observe the way members post messages, start discussions, and respond to previous messages. Get a handle on the personality of the list in general, as well as the people who post. Is the tone lighthearted, businesslike, angry, academic, or something else altogether?

Another important thing you must do at this point is decide whether this list will help you with your branding efforts. There are only so many hours in a day, and online networking is just one of many ways you'll be branding your identity.

It's your job to figure out which lists are worth your time. To help determine the value of a mailing list, ask yourself the following questions:

- Are the topics being discussed in line with my identity?
- Do the participating members appear to be people I can help or who can help me?
- Are there other experts or authority figures among the members whom I need to know?
- Do enough people subscribe to this list to make it worth my time?
- Is this the right avenue for promoting my brand?

After dealing with a few mailing lists, you'll soon discover that many subscribers share certain traits. Personalities shine through in the way people write and post their messages. Just for fun, I'll give you a breakdown of the types of people you may observe in mailing list discussions:

The novice—This person is often new to the list and freely admits a lack of knowledge regarding the subject matter. Novices are often shy in their demeanor and impressed with the wealth of information others have to offer.

The gabber—This member posts messages that are chatty and often off-topic. Even when a gabber's comments are related to the topic at hand, they tend to ramble on far longer than is needed.

The complainer—Every active list has a few people who like to let off steam or debate others just to prove a point. Complainers are cynical and tend to look for the weaknesses in other members' suggestions. List owners usually ban members who are too rude and abusive.

The perky poster—Some mailing list members are so tickled to be alive, they find joy in the simplest things. Perky posters tell members how much their lives have been enriched from being part of the list. They are also the first ones to send other members holiday wishes or wish them good luck on new projects. With all the negativity in the world, you can't help but love a perky poster (to a point).

The seller—Every list has members who test the boundaries of good taste when working in plugs for their products and services. If these sales-hungry subscribers generally provide useful posts, members may tolerate the self-promotion. But if the advertising gets out of the hand, a member can get banned or, worse yet, be branded as a self-serving buffoon. (Near the end of this chapter, in the section titled "Posting Self-Serving Plugs without Getting Flamed," we cover the right ways and wrong ways to promote yourself in networking forums.)

The expert—Members who skillfully play the role of expert provide answers to subscribers' questions on a regular basis. Experts also freely recommend resources and offer helpful advice. The list owner is typically one of the resident experts, but a handful of other members usually rise to the top to reveal themselves as valuable contributors. From a branding standpoint, this is the role you want to shoot for.

The majority of subscribers to mailing lists play the role of lurkers. They sit back and watch the flow of comments but don't regularly participate. You may not hear a peep out of them, but it's important to know they're out there. Lurkers read your messages and come to know you every bit as well as those who post messages repeatedly. So always be on your best mailing-list behavior, because people are watching.

Introduce Yourself

Once you've spent a little time observing a list's activity and you're convinced it's a list you want to participate in, it's time for you to start interacting. The best way to make an initial splash is through an introduction, which is a common way to ease into the flow of conversation. Give your first message a simple subject line like *New Member Introduction* or, better yet, use your name in the subject line, as in *Bob Baker: Introduction*.

Use this message to let other list members know who you are, what you do, and why you joined the list. This message shouldn't be used to ramble on about your entire life's story. Respect the limited time that other subscribers have while focusing on your networking goals: to establish yourself as a brand identity online. Whether or not you're aware of it, this first message also lets members know where you fit into the mailing list personality mix; are you a novice, a seller, a perky poster, an expert, or what?

Here's an example of an introduction message someone might send to a natural herb mailing list:

Hello everyone!

I just joined the Natural Herb Discussion List a few days ago and have really enjoyed the exchanges I've read so far.

My name is Mary-Ann Turnbull. After working in the health-food industry for more than a decade, I published a book last year called 105 Home Remedies Using Natural Herbs. *I've had articles published in* Herb Quarterly *and the* Journal of Home Remedies.

I can already tell that the members of this list have a lot to offer and that many of you will become a valuable asset as I continue my research in this fascinating field. And if anyone ever has a question about herbs as they relate to home remedies, don't hesitate to ask me. I'll do my best to give the right answer.

Here's to many spicy herb discussions in the weeks and months to come!

Mary-Ann Turnbull
Author of 105 Home Remedies Using Natural Herbs
http://www.herbal-home-remedies.net/
Free herbal remedy tips by e-mail:
Subscribe@ herbal-home-remedies.net

With one message to the list, Mary-Ann has firmly established herself as a member who fits into the expert category. Make sure your introductory message accomplishes the same thing for your brand image.

Always Use a Signature File—*Chapter 4, "Maximizing E-mail for Brand Delivery," introduced the concept of e-mail sig files—those short, descriptive lines that appear after your name at the end of an e-mail message. Note Mary-Ann Turnbull's sig file at the end of her introduction message example in this chapter. Always include your sig file when posting a message to a mailing list, newsgroup, or other discussion forum. To paraphrase a traveler's check commercial, never post a message without one.*

Respond to Posts

Once you've made your presence known through an introductory message, you'll need to reinforce your identity by showing up at regular intervals in the discussions. Continue to watch the parade of messages, keeping an eye out for opportunities to subtly shine a light on your brand. In the example in the preceding section, Mary-Ann would look for posts that deal with using herbs for healing purposes, particularly within the home. When someone strikes up a conversation that's up her herbal alley, she'd be wise to jump in—as long as she has a valuable piece of information to add to the dialogue.

When you respond to someone else's post in a mailing list, you simply hit the Reply button without altering the subject line. Depending on your e-mail software, "Re:" will be added before whatever text was in the original message's subject line. That way, list members will know your message pertains to an earlier post. (Otherwise, add it yourself.) Another thing you want to do is include the text of the first message along with your reply, so readers know exactly what you're responding to. Warning: Only include parts of the original message that are necessary to put your response in context. There's no reason to make members scroll through nine paragraphs of the original message when your reply relates to only one of them.

If it's been a while since you've posted a message to a particular list, you may be tempted to fire off a quick reply post just to get your name into the mix again. Take heed. It's far better to target your comments and only respond when the message really reflects your brand. Also, only post solid information that you know is true and that you'll be willing to defend if it's criticized … or be willing to apologize for if you goof up.

Start a Discussion

In addition to being reactive and responding to the posts of others, you'll also need to be proactive and introduce new topics for discussion. As with the example in the "Introduce Yourself" section earlier in this chapter, keep your messages focused on who you are and what your brand stands for. There are many ways to start a new discussion in a mailing list, including the following:

- Ask a question with the intention of getting feedback from other subscribers.
- Express your opinion on a recent news item that relates to your area of expertise.
- Make members aware of developments in your field and explain why those developments are important to them.
- Post warnings about something that subscribers should steer clear of, as long as your comments aren't libelous.

When starting a new discussion, your priority should be providing useful information and encouragement to other members. While dishing out that information, don't ignore opportunities to support your statements and opinions with references to your brand identity. Here's an example of this concept in action, once again using the fictitious Mary-Ann Turnbull:

Since this is the beginning of cold and flu season, I wanted to pass along a suggestion for an herbal remedy that helps reduce the chances of catching the common cold. For years, I went along with the prevailing notion that vitamin C was the best thing to bulk up on to keep from getting sick. However, as I was collecting material for my book, 105 Home Remedies Using Natural Herbs, *I discovered a growing number of people raving about Echinacea, a wonderful herb that boosts the body's immune system.*

As long as it's not forced, make references to your own experiences, articles, books, and other brand-related activities. Sure, you could just provide information or express an opinion and leave it at that. But demonstrating why you're the right person to say the things you say carries more impact. Also, if you start a discussion that's likely to generate a lot of replies, be prepared to check messages often and respond to those replies.

Position Yourself as a Resource

When you effectively use mailing lists to establish your brand, you end up in a position in which many list members frequently ask themselves, "I wonder what (insert your name) thinks about this?" Subscribers look forward to hearing your take on any subject related to your identity. But the only way you earn such a respected standing is by demonstrating your expertise on a regular basis. Here are a few ways to position yourself as a valuable resource on mailing lists:

- When a subscriber posts a message looking for Web sites that deal with your specialty, do some quick research and post a reply with a list of your recommendations.
- When you run across a new Web site or news article that would be of great interest to the members of a certain mailing list, post a comment about it with a link. (Warning: Don't include an extended quote from the site or article, as this may be considered copyright infringement.)
- If someone is experiencing a problem related to your area of expertise, suggest a solution based on your knowledge of the field.
- If you've written an online article that addresses a topic currently being discussed on a list, mention the article and provide a link to it.

Sometimes, establishing yourself as an expert in a specific niche can lead people to believe you are also knowledgeable about topics related to, but outside of, your specialty. For instance, I post messages to appropriate mailing lists to reach my target audience: aspiring songwriters and bands who produce their own CDs. I provide a lot of solid advice on how these independent musicians can promote their music on a budget. Yet I frequently get e-mail from people who write something like "Bob, it's obvious you know a lot about the music business. Can you give me your opinion on a recording contract I was just offered?" I've never written about recording contracts and probably wouldn't know a good one if it walked up and bit me on the posterior.

The trick is to stay focused on your niche. Don't try to win over new fans by appearing to know something you don't. Admit your limitations. When people ask me for advice on a music industry topic that's outside my realm, I tell them that it's not my area of expertise and try to point them to a resource that can help them. I recommend you do the same.

For some additional perspectives on networking through mailing lists, read Richard Hoy's article **Why Discussion Lists Suck** at http://www.clickz.com/cgi-bin/gt/article.html?article=370 and **E-Marketing Through Mailing Lists and Newsgroups** by Shel Horowitz at http://www.frugalfun.com/m5.html.

Promoting Your Brand Through Newsgroups

Newsgroups have been around since the early days of the Internet. While they are similar to mailing lists in that there are many thousands of them that cover every conceivable topic, newsgroups are more like static online bulletin boards. Anyone can post a message and respond to messages left by others. Newsgroups don't exist on Web pages and postings aren't delivered by e-mail; instead, they reside on a special part of the Internet accessible through a newsreader interface. Don't worry, you probably already have this interface. AOL and other online services have newsreaders built into their regular features. Also, Netscape Messenger and Microsoft Outlook Express can work with newsgroup messages.

Newsgroups have strange-looking addresses, such as alt.adoption, rec.folk-dancing, and biz.entrepreneurs. These addresses usually tell you what topic the newsgroup is geared toward. For descriptions of the various types of newsgroups and a good overview of how newsgroups function, take a look at **Deja.com: Usenet Short Course** at http://www.deja.com/info/usenet_faq.shtml. For even more details on newsgroups, check out **A Usenet Primer** at http://www.mcfedries.com/Ramblings/usenet-primer.html and **How Newsgroups and Forums Work** at http://www.learnthenet.com/english/animate/forums.html.

The History of Newsgroups—Usenet (the original newsgroup and a generic term still used to mean newsgroups) was born in 1979 at Duke University when James Elliot and Tom Truscott devised a way to share research, information, and witty observations among Duke students and faculty. Other universities started using the program these two guys developed and it snowballed from there. It's estimated that more than 20 million people participate in newsgroups, posting hundreds of thousands of messages a day.

Before you can start networking through newsgroups, you'll need to track down those that best align with your brand. The following directories can help you search for appropriate newsgroups:

CyberFiber Newsgroups
http://www.cyberfiber.com/index.html

Deja.com (widely regarded as the best newsgroup directory)
http://www.deja.com/usenet/

Liszt's Usenet Newsgroups Directory (shown in Figure 10.2)
http://www.liszt.com/news/

FIGURE 10.2: Liszt's Usenet Newsgroups Directory features a searchable database of hundreds of newsgroups.

Regional Newsgroups Information Center
http://www.unicom.com/regional/

Tile.Net Newsgroup Directory
http://tile.net/news/

Usenet Info Center Launch Pad
http://www.ibiblio.org/usenet-i/

The rules for posting to newsgroups are much the same as the rules for mailing lists, covered in detail throughout previous sections of this chapter. Before posting, scan messages to get a feel for the types of people who frequent a given newsgroup. You'll probably notice that a lot of newsgroup posts are filled with self-promotional hype, depending on how well monitored the newsgroups are. If a group is littered with dozens upon dozens of blatant ads, chances are the only people seeing them are other self-serving marketers. Steer clear of these branding dead-ends. Target your efforts on the newsgroups that have some serious discussions on your area of expertise.

A couple of good articles that cover helpful tips for both newsgroups and mailing lists are **Advertising in Discussion Lists and Newsgroups** at http://www.busymarketing.com/lists.shtml and **Using Newsgroups and E-mail Lists** at http://www.tka.co.uk/search/newsgrp.htm.

Using Discussion Forums and Message Boards

When the Web exploded some years ago, a lot of smart people took the bulletin-board concept used by newsgroups and created Web-based versions. The result was online discussion forums and message boards. Like newsgroups, these online forums provide a place for people with shared interests to ask questions, express opinions, and comment on specific topics. As you may have guessed, these forums also offer another way for you to network and establish your brand identity.

General Online Forums

There are a seemingly infinite number of forums and ways to find them. The following sites host a variety of online forums covering an array of topics. Many of these sites also give you the ability to start your own forum, where you can rule the roost. Search through the various categories on each site and you'll likely find many message boards that cater to your niche:

Bianca
http://www.bianca.com/

Chat Mode Message Boards
http://boards.chatmode.com/

ChatWeb.net
http://www.chatweb.net/

CustomPost
http://www.custompost.com/

Delphi.com
http://www.delphi.com/dir-delphi/

ezboard
http://www.ezboard.com/

Fool Moon Free Family Chat
http://foolmoon.com/

Forum One's Online Community Index
http://www.forumone.com/index/index.php

HealthBoards.com (discussions of numerous health topics)
http://www.healthboards.com/

InsideTheWeb
http://www.insidetheweb.com/

NetQuantum Message Boards
http://forums.netquantum.com/

Sympatico Forums
http://www1.sympatico.ca/forums/

World Message Board (message boards for individual countries and cities)
http://netlec.com/board/

Site-Sponsored Online Forums

In addition to sites that host a wide variety of message boards, you can also find targeted forums on many highly traveled Web sites. For instance, **Music and Audio Connection** (http://www.musicandaudio.com/) is a site that caters to songwriters, musicians, and recording pros. The site also features a discussion forum. Regardless of your specialty, there are surely countless sites with forums that are right up your brand's alley. Here are more examples of site-sponsored discussion forums:

About—Talk About (more than 700 categories)
http://talk.about.com/

ClickZ Forum (discussions on e-commerce and online marketing topics)
http://clickzforum.com/

CNET Message Boards (forums on a variety of computer issues)
http://forums.cnet.com/

CNN Interactive Community Index (discussions on health, food, entertainment and the latest news)
http://community.cnn.com/

Motley Fool Discussion Boards (investing and personal finance)
http://boards.fool.com/

ParentsPlace.com Message Boards (covers child safety, pregnancy, and other parenting issues)
http://www.parentsplace.com/messageboards/

Salon.com Table Talk (discussions related to articles that appear on Salon.com)
http://tabletalk.salonmagazine.com/

That Home Site! Forums (covers a wide variety of topics)
http://www.thathomesite.com/forums/

Search Engines

Here's a nifty trick for hunting down places to post networking messages. Go to a search engine, such as **Google** at http://www.google.com/, and enter a key word or phrase associated with your brand. Add the words *forum* and *post* and string them together with plus signs. Sticking with the herbal remedies theme from earlier sections of this chapter, I entered *herbs+forum+post* and quickly came up with seven great forums. You can use this same search engine trick to uncover many forums in line with your brand identity.

Networking Through Community Sites and Clubs

Online communities are similar to discussion forums in that they provide places to post messages, but they generally provide other features, such as areas to post photos and other shared files, real-time chat capabilities, link directories, and other content related to the topic at hand. Of the sites on the following list, I have found **Yahoo! Clubs** to be particularly effective in networking my brand online. However, any one of these sites may well lead you to a community that caters perfectly to your specific niche.

eCircles
http://www.ecircles.com

Nettaxi.com
http://www.nettaxi.com/

North Sky Communities
http://communities.northsky.com/

SeriousChat.com
http://www.seriouschat.com/

TerraShare.com
http://www.terrashare.com/

Web Communities on MSN (shown in Figure 10.3)
http://communities.msn.com/

Yahoo! Clubs
http://www.clubs.yahoo.com/

Exploiting Online Networking Options

Even if you've only skimmed through this chapter, you can tell there are countless ways to network online. With choices ranging from mailing lists and newsgroups to discussion forums, message boards, and more, it's difficult to know where to

FIGURE 10.3: Web Communities on MSN hosts hundreds of categorized online communities.

start, much less how to keep up with all the messages you'll have to read and write. Use the tips in this section to help manage your networking activities.

The best approach is to settle on a handful of networking avenues that you want to dominate. After searching through the many resources listed in this chapter, you'll discover some real gems—lists and forums that are widely read and seem to be tailor-made for your brand. These posting places are heavily populated with either potential fans you need to reach or other experts and industry contacts you need to know.

Pick your top sources in this category and commit to making them your regular hangouts—your "A" list of from one to perhaps four sources. Read the messages posted to these prime lists and forums every day, if possible. Try to post a reply or a new message at least a few times a week. These are the networking avenues where you'll have a strong presence on a regular basis.

In addition to these top networking places, compile a list of sources that didn't make the "A" list but are still good places for you to make an impact. Periodically pop into these forums, message boards, newsgroups, mailing lists, and communities and see what topics are being tossed around. Of course, you'll then look for opportunities to provide helpful advice, direct people to useful resources, share your wisdom, and so on. You'll want to make time now and again to appear on these second-tier sources, just not with the frequency of your "A" list postings.

Beware of Blind Messages and Bulk Postings—In my formative years on the Internet (all of five or six years ago) I made the mistake of crafting wonderful messages and posting the exact same one to several mailing lists and dozens of newsgroups in one fell swoop. There are two problems with this approach. First, since I didn't even read the other posts, I had no idea what context my messages would be read in. For all I knew, the opinion I expressed or resource I recommended may have been soundly trounced in a recent discussion, which wouldn't make me look very alert or responsible. Second, people who visit one forum are likely to visit others that cover the same topic. If these people see your same message in multiple locations, don't be surprised if they start spreading the word that you're a spammer (someone who indiscriminately posts blatant ads in bulk). It's worth it to spend the extra time to write thoughtful, customized messages.

Posting Self-Serving Plugs Without Getting Flamed

After spending a little time on message boards and other online forums, you'll notice tricks that smart marketers use to work in self-promotional messages without stirring the wrath of spam-sensitive readers. Skillful posters slyly weave in messages that promote their brands while delivering information people want and need. Here are four ways to post such messages:

Transform ads into conversational messages—There will be times when you have something specific you want to promote. For example, let's say you want to drive traffic to your rock-climbing Web site by announcing an article you just posted. The lazy person's path to promoting through networking channels would be to write an ad regarding the article and post it to numerous forums. Here's an example of how such an ad might read:

> The 7 Habits of Highly Effective Rock Climbers
> *Learn the secrets the pros use to scale the most death-defying heights. Free article available now at:*
> *http://www.rock-climb.com/7habits.htm*

Posting a blatant ad like this one is a sure-fire way to become known as a self-serving bozo who breaks the rules of online etiquette. The wording of the message makes it clear that its only purpose is to publicize the poster's site. However, there is a way to get across the same information without making people mad. The secret: Impart the information in the form of a naturally flowing conversation. Here's an example of a more casual way to promote the article:

> *Hello everyone,*
> *There have been a lot of discussions here in recent weeks concerning the right ways and wrong ways to rock climb. I'd love to get some feedback*

from all of you regarding my take on the whole subject. I took some of the ideas I've seen posted on this forum and combined them with some of my own best practices. The result is a free article called The 7 Habits of Highly Effective Rock Climbers. *I just posted the article on my site at http://www.rock-climb.com/7habits.htm. Please check it out and click the e-mail link at the end of the article to let me know if you agree with my recommendations.*

The more conversational message still promotes the article and drives people to the rock-climbing site, but it does so in a way that includes the community of people who frequent the forum. It also goes a step further by respecting people's opinions and inviting reader feedback.

Ask for personal stories—If you're an expert in your field, you constantly gather information on your core topic. Talking to people who are pursuing the thing you specialize in should be a regular part of your research. For instance, if you coach aspiring writers on how to generate more freelance income, you should gather details on the obstacles and successes encountered by freelance writers. It would be perfectly acceptable to solicit personal stories within discussion forums. After obtaining permission, you can use these case studies in any articles, reports, or books you might write. You can also use these one-on-one interactions to establish brand-focused relationships and build a network of fans.

Offer free review copies of your work—Eager to get samples of your art, writing, music, or other skill into the hands of potential fans? Put together a free e-book, digital audio file, or graphic image and announce its availability through select mailing lists, newsgroups, and message boards. Don't write a blatant ad for your freebie. Cradle it in the same conversational tone that the rock climber did earlier in this section. Also, get people involved by requesting feedback on your free item.

Ask people to take a quiz or survey—Another way to drive people to your site is by asking readers to express themselves in a survey or test their knowledge with a quiz. As long as the topic is directly tied into the subject of the forum, and as long as you announce your quiz or survey in a friendly and helpful manner, chances are good it will be well received. If you do go the survey route, promise to post the results as soon as they're available.

Now that you know all about mailing lists, newsgroups, discussion forums, message boards, and online communities, it's time to get busy finding the best places to network and market your brand. Next up: generating publicity on the Internet—the subject we discuss in Chapter11, "Exposing Your Identity Through Online Publicity."

CHAPTER ELEVEN

Exposing Your Identity Through Online Publicity

Are you ready to transform yourself into a media darling? Would you like to get feature stories on you and reviews of your work through online magazines, industry newsletters, and news sites? Using the tips and tools in this chapter, it could happen. Even if you are already publishing your own free e-zine, distributing free articles and e-books, exchanging links with relevant sites, networking through discussion forums, and generating considerable word of mouth, you should still allow time for online publicity. Getting covered by the media stokes the fire created by your other promotional efforts and draws even more people to your brand.

You can obtain online publicity in any number of ways, including the following:

- Being interviewed in an e-zine that is directly aligned with your niche
- Having your product reviewed in a popular column on a Web site that specializes in your field
- Appearing on a Web page that highlights industry developments on a site frequented by your potential fans
- Being profiled by a columnist who writes about your area of interest for online magazines
- Getting a mention in an e-mail newsletter with a huge circulation that covers a field related to your brand

In this chapter, we look at how the media operates and why writers and editors need you as much as you want them. We talk about how to save printing and postage costs by putting your media kit on your Web site, and how to craft each element of your kit for maximum impact.

To help you hunt down appropriate members of the media, I show you some of the best free media directories available online. In addition, we look at the many options you have for delivering your news releases and personal notes to editors and writers. Finally, we discuss specific tactics for approaching the media and why taking the attention off yourself and your product or service is often the best way to get covered. We have a lot of important stuff to cover in this chapter. Let's dig in!

I Want My Radio and TV—You may alertly notice that this chapter lacks information on contacting radio and TV outlets, which are very much a part of the media at large. I discuss radio and TV separately in Chapter 13, "Exploiting Offline Branding Strategies." The chapter you're reading now focuses primarily on communicating with journalists who might give you exposure through e-mail newsletters and Web-based publications. However, you can apply most of the principles expressed in the following sections to all forms of media.

Why the Media Needs You

Many people think the media is an impenetrable fortress. Folks who feel this way have the impression that to get covered in a newspaper, magazine, or trade publication—online or off—they have to be part of a secret club or have some inside connection. Nothing could be further from the truth. Most people who have a negative attitude toward the media either have never dealt with news sources, expected too much too soon when they publicized themselves, or simply took the wrong approach when communicating with editors and writers.

Before the Internet became all the rage, we already had many thousands of print publications. The rapid expansion of cyberspace has only multiplied the number of media sources. Most established print publications now have an online presence and often feature distinct stories that appear only on the Internet. Also, the low cost of entry has allowed a multitude of would-be editors and writers to create their own online news outlets. These countless publications have audiences that are hungry for information related to the subject of the publication. Editors, writers, illustrators, photographers, and designers—many of whom are overworked and underpaid—decide what information their audiences are most interested in and do their best to deliver it.

More than 80 percent of what we read in print and online publications is reportedly "planted." No, that doesn't necessarily mean that stories are covered because of government conspiracies or because bigwigs slip money under the table. News stories are frequently planted by public relations firms, freelance publicists, and everyday people who simply contact the media with interesting article ideas.

***Be an Unselfish Media Resource**—Once you start to establish relationships with media people, occasionally offer story ideas related to your brand when you have nothing to gain. Do you know of a cool, new site or a noteworthy event? Pass the tip on to your circle of media friends, even if the story has nothing to do with you. This trait transforms you into a media resource, not just a self-promoter. When you do have something self-serving to promote, your pals in the media may be more receptive to covering you.*

For 10 years, I published and served as managing editor of my own music magazine. As much as I tried to get out and see bands perform live and stay up to date on developments in the music industry, I couldn't possibly be everywhere and know everything at all times. I often relied on the recommendations of others when making decisions on what bands and topics to cover. Sometimes one of my writers would come to me with a story concept, or a media kit from a new band would catch my eye; at other times, speaking with someone at an event or on the phone would spark an idea. I didn't manage my magazine from an enclosed fortress and neither do most of the editors, writers, columnists, and reviewers you'll contact. They need people just like you to give them ideas and information they can use to serve their audiences.

Take a look through several articles and news stories online. Rarely are these stories only about things, such as products, services, events, companies, and so on. Most good articles have a human element. In fact, journalists are taught to bring their stories to life with examples, anecdotes, case studies, and quotes from real people involved in the topic of the article. Shouldn't you be someone whom journalists turn to when they need a quote or example of someone involved in your area of expertise?

The Ugly Truth About Media Exposure

The steps I encourage you to take in this chapter are far different from the way most people pursue media coverage. Typically, someone running a business thinks, "I need to promote myself and my company. I know, I'll slap together a news release and send it to hundreds of media sources. Then I'll sit back and wait for dozens of e-mail messages and phone calls to pour in from eager editors." Guess what? When the media is approached this way, the e-mails and phone calls rarely come.

In the previous section, I mentioned that more than 80 percent of published news stories come as a result of people contacting writers and editors with press releases and story ideas. Sounds encouraging, right? Here's another statistic that provides some balance: More than 90 percent of the press releases and media kits sent to the media head directly to a slush pile or, worse, a trash can.

Although media people depend on publicists to find good news stories, a small percentage of the story ideas that are pitched ever see the light of day. Sometimes the timing is wrong or a similar story was already covered recently. Most often, though, the way the person, product, or service is presented is full of flaws. To help you avoid these shortcomings, before pursuing your publicity goals, ask yourself the following questions:

- How do I determine which media people to approach with my publicity messages?
- How should I persuade media people to cover me?

Let's examine the answers to these questions, starting with how you determine which media people to approach. Just as you have a defined image and a focused area of expertise, so do editors, writers, and reviewers. The first step to effective online publicity is to steer clear of the shotgun mentality of sending the same message to hundreds or thousands of media people. Obviously, it would do you no good to send a news release about your new Web page of auto-repair tips to food editors and restaurant reviewers. Targeting is the key. Even focusing on publications that cover your niche has many variables. Some writers cover hard technical news; some columnists prefer lighthearted, human-interest angles; some writers only review products, books, or Web sites; others specialize in interviews and people profiles. Make sure the publicity message you send is right for the person receiving it.

Next, how should you persuade media people to cover you? Before you can convince media folks that what you offer is newsworthy, it helps to know what makes them tick. In a nutshell, these four things motivate media people:

Delivering content that will best educate and entertain their audiences— The first duty for editors and writers is not to help spread the word about your brand. Their primary goal is to do their best job to retain and increase their own audiences. Try to determine what each media person needs and figure out a way to deliver it.

Being the first one in their industry to break a news story—When media people earn the reputation of being on the cutting edge, it makes them feel good. Can you position your brand as being the newest, the first, or on the verge of making a major splash? Use this angle carefully, though. Media people are always getting news releases from ego-stricken people claiming to be the biggest and the best. Be prepared to back up your claims.

Not wanting to miss the boat on something that is generating a buzz— While many editors and writers like being on the leading edge, they also like to turn their readers on to newsworthy people and things that have already proven themselves popular. Use any news coverage and accolades you've already received—as well as sales charts or popularity rankings—to demonstrate that your news story has a ground swell of support behind it.

An angle that is witty or creative enough to grab their attention—Many people have inspired the media to cover them simply because of a funny Web site name, cleverly written press release, or other promotional gimmick. The book *Web Pages That Suck* and the accompanying Web site at http://www.webpagesthatsuck.com/ garnered a lot of media coverage because of the nontraditional title. Does your brand lend itself to a publicity angle that uses wit, humor, or irreverence? Beware, though, and use cleverness only when you have substance behind the gimmick.

Compiling Your PR Database

It's time to start building a database of the editors, writers, columnists, and reviewers you will be contacting. In Chapter 3, "Developing Your Branding Arsenal," I encouraged you to compile a database of online sources related to your brand. Using contact-management software, you can easily enter and categorize many different types of people, Web sites, e-zines, and more. This database topic came up again in Chapter 8, "Exploiting E-zines and Web Sites of Others," so you may already have started a list of editors and other online media people.

If not, begin by entering Web sites and e-zines you are already familiar with, making sure to get editors' and writers' correct names and direct e-mail addresses, if available. This database-compiling process should be an ongoing activity. Whenever you encounter a Web site that seems suited to your identity, search through the site for contact information. Many online magazines feature a staff page with names, titles, and individual e-mail addresses. These details may also be found on a site's About page. Also, look through individual articles and reviews, which often carry each writer's personal e-mail address.

Three More Ways to Uncover Media Contacts—*Other methods of ferreting out useful sites include the following: First, enter keywords related to your brand at search engines and visit the sites that come up; second, look through the recommended links pages on sites that appeal to your potential fans; and finally, search through industry-specific directories to find still more sites associated with your identity.*

In the good old days, you had to drag yourself to the public library to find sources that contained lots of media listings. Either that or you had to fork over the big bucks to purchase a large media database on computer disk. Those two options are still available, but now you have the added luxury of being able to dig up lots of media contact information online. The following sites provide free information on a wide variety of media. Some just supply links to each publication's home page; some take you to each site's staff page; others provide the e-mail addresses of specific writers and columnists.

ALACARim Press Release Mega Submission
http://www.alacarim.com/getthepress/

AJR NewsLink (shown in Figure 11.1)
http://ajr.newslink.org/

E&P Media Links
http://emedia1.mediainfo.com/emedia/

Media UK
http://directory.mediauk.com/

News365
http://www.news365.com/

NewsDirectory
http://www.newsdirectory.com/

NewspaperLinks.com
http://www.newspaperlinks.com/

PubList.com (directory of print publications)
http://www.publist.com/

FIGURE 11.1: AJR NewsLink provides links to a variety of daily, business, alternative, and specialty newspapers around the world.

ThatsNewsToMe.com
http://www.thatsnewstome.com/

ZineVine (directory of online magazines that cover computers and the Internet)
http://www.zinevine.com/

For a comprehensive listing of news-link sites, check out **Google—News Directories** at http://directory.google.com/Top/News/Directories/. As you may have figured out, you could easily spend weeks compiling thousands of media names and addresses, but I caution you to focus on quality over quantity. It may seem like a good idea to enter the names of dozens of *Time, Newsweek,* and *People* magazine editors into your database, but chances are you'll be disappointed with the response. Focus on the people and online resources that are most associated with your brand identity. Start with the smaller media outlets and work your way up the food chain. Targeted publicity connections can help you reach potential fans faster, which may well pave the way for *Time, Newsweek,* and *People* magazine to contact you in the future.

If sifting through and compiling hundreds of Web sites isn't for you, there are many good media databases available for a fee. Here are four sources to consider:

Bacons.com
http://www.bacons.com/

Gebbie Press
http://www.gebbieinc.com/

mediafinder.com
http://www.mediafinder.com/

Parrot Media Network
http://www.parrotmedia.com/

Contacting Publicity Sources

After you've purchased or compiled a media database, it's time to start using it to make connections. It helps to be aware of the various options you have for communicating publicity messages. Here are the three most basic approaches to contacting the media:

One by one—You take a look at Web sites and e-zines one at a time and determine the best way to pitch your brand to each outlet. For instance, you might visit one Web site and discover it's in search of success stories related to your area of expertise. You write a short, first-person narrative based on one of your positive career experiences and submit it. While poking around another site, you find a column that regularly recommends online resources. Since the columnist's e-mail address is posted on the site, you send a friendly message suggesting that she consider your site for a future column. I advise you to spend as much time as possible using this one-outlet-at-a-time approach. It's the most personal and direct method for generating publicity online.

In bulk—You have something big to announce: a new book or music CD, the launching of a new Web site, a clever promotion that ties into a current fad, or some other major event. You need to reach a lot of media sources in a short period of time by sending the same news release to every contact in your database. This approach should be used only in cases when your news angle has the potential for mass appeal. Don't automatically fire off every PR idea you come up with to every person in your database. But when you have news that warrants it, this media blitz technique can be effective.

Through personalized mass e-mailings—You have a major PR angle you want to exploit, but you don't feel comfortable sending generic e-mail news releases to all your media contacts. Instead, you create a boilerplate letter that spells out the essence of your publicity hook. One by one, you personalize each e-mail message before sending it. You add the recipient's name and a specific note that applies to each media person. This hybrid method satisfies your need to get the same message out to many publicity sources while adding the more intimate flavor of the one-by-one approach.

If you decide to go the bulk press release distribution route, you have a few options for delivering the goods. First, you can load a long list of media e-mail addresses into the Bcc: line of your e-mail program. However, some programs won't respond well if you try to send an e-mail to hundreds of addresses at the same time. Second, you can use a bulk e-mail program such as those available from **ColoradoSoft** (http://www.coloradosoft.com/), **Email Workshop** (http://www.emailworkshop.com/), and **PostCast** (http://www.postcast.com/). Most of these bulk e-mail programs also have mail-merge capabilities that allow you to automatically customize e-mail messages with people's names and references to their Web sites. Third, you can pay to use one of the following PR distribution services, most of which will e-mail or fax your news release to select media outlets:

Direct Contact Media Services
http://www.owt.com/dircon/

eReleases ($295 to reach more than 2,500 media contacts)
http://www.ereleases.com/

Internet Media Fax (sends your release by fax for .25 per page)
http://www.imediafax.com/

Internet News Bureau (PR packages starting at $250)
http://www.newsbureau.com/

Internet Wire
http://www1.internetwire.com/

MediaMap Online
http://www.mediamaponline.com/

PR Newswire
http://www.prnewswire.com/

PressAccess.com
http://www.pressaccess.com/

Press Flash (reach Internet and high-tech media by fax)
http://www.pressflash.com/

Press Release Network
http://www.pressreleasenetwork.com/

URLwire
http://www.urlwire.com/

WebWire
http://www.webwire.com/

Xpress Press Release Distribution (shown in Figure 11.2)
http://www.xpresspress.com/

FIGURE 11.2: Xpress Press Release Distribution sends e-mail press releases to journalists who cover a variety of specialty areas.

Distribute Your Press Release for Free!—*You can find a lot of free stuff on the Internet, but publicity services are rarely among them. One excellent source for getting your news releases posted for free is PRWeb.com at* http://www.prweb.com/. *Another free press site worth looking into is Affiliated Press at* http://affiliatedpress.com/subguide.html. *For publicity related to a new or existing Web site, take a look at Click2newsites.com at* http://www.click2newsites.com/press.asp. *If you have a music business–related news story, submit it at no cost to Music Industry News Network at* http://www.mi2n.com/.

News Release Writing 101

It's time to discuss how to conceive and write news releases so that they have the best chance of breaking through the clutter and appealing to the media people who receive them. As you may know, a news release is a short announcement that spells out the essential details of a specific event, achievement, or notable topic. There are many good reasons to send a news release to the media. Unfortunately, most people who contact the media present so-called newsworthy information in an unfavorable light. As good as their intentions are, self-promoters often focus on their own needs instead of the needs of editors, writers, and reviewers. Consider the following excerpt from a hypothetical press release:

John Jones Starts Web Design Business

John Jones, a seasoned Web designer with six years of experience under his belt, is officially in business. "I can do it all," says Jones. "I can take your online content and package it in the most visually appealing and user-friendly manner allowed by law."

The approach Jones takes in this news release is typical of most marketers. The emphasis is on the promoter and how great he is. No effort is made to appeal to the writer's audience or the Web editor's visitors. Therefore, little media exposure would be gained from Jones' self-serving announcement. The questions you should always ask before crafting a news release are, "What's in it for the media person and his or her audience?" and "How can I position my story so it's most appealing to the media outlet's readers?" John Jones and his new Web-design business would benefit greatly from two things: focusing on a specific niche and offering something of value to readers, as in this example:

Expert Offers Fine Artists Free Web-Design Critique

"The caliber of an artist's Web presence can make or break a career in the fine arts," says John Jones, a seasoned Web designer. "Being an artist myself, I

know the challenges of creating a professional image online. That's why I started offering free Web-design critiques for artists."

This second treatment of Jones' news release has great potential for generating media coverage. For it to work, of course, Jones should truly be a specialist in art-related Web design and be willing to offer the critiques he promises. Beyond that, the release is effective because the focus is on providing a newsworthy benefit of interest to a specific group of media people and their readers. The second version of the press release doesn't directly pat Jones on the back as much as the first one. But since the latter will most likely lead to far more publicity, Jones' reputation is better served when he is in the background and the benefit he offers takes center stage. To get your wheels turning, here are a few angles that make for newsworthy press releases:

You're involved with something that is new or different—Are you unveiling a new section of your Web site? Have you just produced a new e-book, e-zine, or other helpful product? Have you decided how your new thing is different from competing products? If so, you may have a good opportunity to get mentioned in the media. Remember, keep the focus on reader benefits. Don't proclaim *Publisher Releases New Book on Modern Dog Breeding* when you can just as easily announce *New Book Reveals High-Tech Tips for Dog Breeders*. See the difference? Nobody really cares about the publisher or the book. What matters is what the book delivers.

You're offering something of value for free—It's the most attention-getting four-letter word in marketing: *Free*. If you can demonstrate that you have something of value that's available at no cost, media people will often share the news of your free resource with their audiences. You'll usually need to supply media people with the free item, or at least tell them how to get it if they're interested, so that they can make an evaluation. Newsworthy freebies might include an e-book with a benefit-oriented title, a new how-to section on your Web site, a useful article that's available by autoresponder, a free sample of your service, and so on.

You've just accomplished a notable achievement—Did you just get a write-up in a prominent magazine? Has your original song hit the number one spot in a music Web site's popularity poll? Did you win a prestigious award? Any of these scenarios could be ripe for media exposure. Writers and columnists like to cover the movers and shakers in their industries. If you're making waves, let the media help you tell the world about it.

Headlines and Subject Lines

The headline of a news release is like the front-window display of a department store. If people like what they see at first glance, they'll move in closer to get a better look. If nothing catches their eye, they move on to the next window display. The headlines you write for your news releases carry a heavy burden. When delivered by e-mail, the subject line serves the same function. In fact, when sending a news release via e-mail, the headline (or a shortened version of it) is the best thing to use in the subject field.

To illustrate the good, the bad, and the ugly of headlines and subject lines, we'll examine some music-related press releases I spotted online recently. Here's one that missed the boat:

Dream—Hot, Hot, Hot!

This headline was used to tout the fact that the musical act Dream had earned the Number 6 spot on Billboard magazine's Top 200 chart. The act's video was also doing well in a fan popularity poll on MTV's Web site. These accomplishments are newsworthy, but the band would have been better served with a stronger PR presentation. For starters, repeating the word *Hot* three times in the headline won't inspire most media people to read this. Headlines should get to the point quickly in as few words as possible. Consider this alternate headline:

Dream Jumps to #6 on Billboard's Top 200 and Climbs at MTV Online

Now that's a more potent message—one that's far more likely to be read. Here's another headline that swiftly gets to the heart of the matter:

Grammy-Nominated Alejandro Sanz Performed with Legendary Producer/Songwriter David Foster

This headline effectively explains what the news release is about. You know immediately that Alejandro Sanz performed with David Foster. Even if you don't know who these musicians are, the headline gives you a good idea of what the release covers. Media people shouldn't have to guess and decipher the true meaning behind a mysterious headline. Give them a clear indication right off the bat.

The person who wrote the Alejandro Sanz press releases committed one *faux pas*, though: use of the past tense *Performed*. Headlines should always be written in the present tense. *Performs* would have been far better. Otherwise, it carries the stigma of being old news. Look through any daily newspaper or magazine. Just about every news story occurred in the past. Yet, you'll read headlines such as *The Blue Jays Win 6-2* or *President Meets with Women's Rights Group*. Always use present tense!

This next headline shows that the publicist had the right idea:

Up-and-Coming Progressive Rockers Land High-Profile Gig with Star Bluesman

This release promotes the Hawaii-based band Technical Difficulties and its upcoming concert opening for blues guitarist Johnny Lang. The writer used present tense wording perfectly. But the headline is missing the meaty details. Even replacing *Star Bluesman* with *Johnny Lang* would have helped, since Lang is the bigger story that could have helped Technical Difficulties get exposure. Also, the band's name offers an opportunity to have some fun with words, such as:

Blues Guitarist Johnny Lang Encounters Technical Difficulties

Always be on the lookout for creative ways to grab attention by playing with the words available to you. Here's another headline example from a popular artist:

Cyrus Responds to "We the People" Report

An Internet site apparently reported that country singer Billy Ray Cyrus asked the Republican Party to stop using his song, "We the People," as the theme song for the George W. Bush presidential campaign. The purpose of the news release was to set the record straight and let people know that Cyrus never had a problem with the theme song and was, in fact, proud that it was used.

Lesson: When you are promoting someone who has an established name, use that name in the headline. *Cyrus* may not do it for a lot of people. The full name, *Billy Ray Cyrus*, would make this headline stronger. The same goes for "We the People Report." Not everyone may have been up to speed on what that was. This headline is stronger:

Billy Ray Cyrus Responds to George W. Bush Theme Song Controversy

Powerful headlines are short and packed with details. A good headline leaves little room for ambiguity. Here's a news release headline used to promote the Country Music Awards:

Country Music Superstar Vince Gill to Host the 35th Annual CMA Awards, Nov. 7 on CBS

This headline leaves no doubt what this release is about. Make sure your PR materials do the same.

Five Tips for Better News Releases

Here are a few more quick tips to keep in mind when writing a news release:

1. **Keep it short.** News releases should run no longer than one or two printed pages. Brevity is paramount. Lay out the important facts promptly and simply. Don't make editors wade through paragraph after paragraph of useless verbiage.

2. **Limit the scope to one angle.** A good news release doesn't tell your life story. It covers only one sliver of your activities. Don't write a release about your new Web site, your upcoming book, *and* your charity promotion. Craft a separate release for each topic.

3. **Put the meaty details up front.** The traditional advice on news releases says to include the who, what, where, when, and why in the first paragraph. If you can do that in an interesting way, go for it. I'm not such a stickler for that wisdom, but do get to the point early and make sure all basic questions about your topic are answered in the press release.

4. **Avoid jargon and buzzwords.** Journalists read news releases every day from *robust, best of breed* companies that offer *integrated solutions* and *customer-centric* technologies. These empty phrases may impress the company's CEO, but they do nothing to earn respect from editors. Write your news releases using clear, direct language.

5. **Always include contact information.** Traditionally, printed news releases have contact details listed at the top. With e-mail, you need to fit as much of the message as possible into the first screen. That's why I advocate placing contact information at the end of e-mail news releases. Include the name of the person the media should contact along with an e-mail address, Web site URL, phone number, fax number, and street address.

Are You a Buzzword Junkie?—Jargon and overused buzzwords clutter far too many news releases. The problem is so widespread, a number of Web sites have sprung up to combat the catch-phrase demons. Two of the better sites in this category are Jargon-Free Web at http://www.jargonfreeweb.com/ *(see Figure 11.3) and BuzzWhack at* http://www.buzzwhack.com/.

The following news release is one I wrote to promote my success with spoken-word online audio files. Note that the focus isn't on me and the thing I was promoting. Instead, I highlighted a larger, more newsworthy angle that spoken-word MP3 files for musicians was a new trend. Also notice that I listed a number of competing mp3.com music tips pages. Sure, it took the direct spotlight off me, but including the list helped strengthen the premise that spoken-word file sharing was a trend to reckon with.

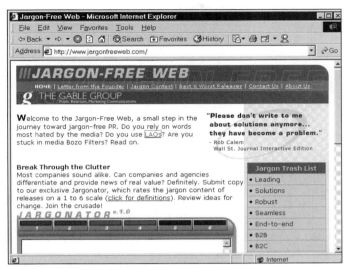

FIGURE 11.3: Jargon-Free Web slices and dices company news releases while poking fun at empty buzzwords. This site is also home to a collection of lame-ass quotes (LAQs).

Free Downloads of Spoken-Word Music Business Tips Proliferate on MP3.com

The same digital technology that drives major record companies crazy over copyright infringement is a Godsend for independent bands. Musicians without the backing of major labels have been flocking to the Internet in droves to freely distribute digital audio versions of their songs to anyone who will listen. This same technology is now being used to teach musicians how to market their music better online. A growing number of music business experts are sprouting up in the Books & Spoken Word section of mp3.com, one of the most heavily traveled music Web sites.

"Musicians are accustomed to using their ears to hear and play music. It only makes sense that they'd also use their ears to soak up motivational messages and valuable information," says Bob Baker, whose inspirational track "Become Successful This Minute" claimed the #3 spot on the Self-Help charts of mp3.com for four straight days. The file is one of five spoken-word tracks available on Baker's page at http://www.mp3.com/Bob-Baker/.

"'Become Successful This Minute' has really struck a positive chord," says Baker, who is Webmaster of The Buzz Factor at http://www.thebuzzfactor.com/ and author of The Guerrilla Music

Marketing Handbook *and* Poor Richard's Branding Yourself Online, *among other titles. "The track reminds you that you don't have to wait and get anyone's permission before pursuing a career in music. You're worthy of recognition and success simply because you believe it is so."*

The Books & Spoken Word section of mp3.com doesn't get as much attention as the music sections. But there's been a developing interest in the many new self-help pages popping up on the site to help music people, including http://www.mp3.com/bardscrier/, http://www.mp3.com/audioguide/, http://www.mp3.com/MBI/, and http://www.mp3.com/NMABasicTrainingEC/.

"This spoken-word popularity trend is bound to continue," Baker adds. "As more musicians take to the Internet to promote their music, the need for solid advice in a digital format will continue to grow."

What Happens Next?

What happens after a media person receives your initial news release or personal PR message? Will you follow up with an e-mail message at a later date or send a review copy of your product? Would you like the media person to call you, send an e-mail, come to your public appearance, take a look at your Web site, or wait for your follow-up call? Whatever it is, let the media person know what should happen next. That doesn't mean media people will automatically do what you want; more often than not, they won't. But at least you've provided some expectations that interested journalists can work with.

I regularly receive e-mail messages that proclaim the existence of a new product or Web site. These e-mails often go into great detail about how great the product or site is without any indication of what the sender wants or what comes next. You don't want to tell media people what to write about or how to do their jobs. On the other hand, some of my most effective PR campaigns occurred when my e-mail notes spelled out specific follow-up details. For instance, when trying to generate more media reviews of my e-books, I send an introductory e-mail to targeted reviewers that explains who I am and what my book is about. But I don't stop there. I also include a line that states the following:

If you'd like a free review copy, let me know right away and I'll send one to you.

For high-profile media contacts, I may send a note that includes this statement:

I'm putting a printed copy of the book in the mail today. It should arrive by Friday. Please let me know if you have any questions or comments by replying to this e-mail.

The key is to be respectful to media people while trying to gently steer the publicity transaction in your direction. Don't leave media people guessing whether they'll hear from you today, next month, next year, or not at all. Spell out the things you have to offer media contacts and then kindly nudge them to do something or let them know what they can expect from you next.

Your Online Media Kit

At the risk of sounding like an old-timer, I must tell you that back in the early years of running my music newspaper there were only a couple of ways for publicists to deliver full media kits to me. They packaged their PR materials in a nice folder and either shipped it by mail, sent it by courier, or delivered it in person. The Internet has given PR people a new option that eliminates printing, postage, and paper cuts: an online media kit.

You should still produce those hard-copy kits for select media outlets and others who request them, but you'll do yourself and your media contacts a favor by also placing your publicity materials on your Web site. That way, in your PR e-mail messages you can mention, "For more information, visit my online media kit at ..." On your site's home page, you can also direct interested visitors to your media kit pages. What follows are the three essential elements of an online media kit and how to present them.

Bio

As you may know, *bio* is short for biography. An effective bio gives detailed background information on you and spells out the current state of your career. Keep the following key points in mind when writing your bio:

Limit the length to one or two pages—An informative bio should use enough space to tell your story, but don't think of it as an encyclopedia. I've seen many bios that run a few pages long; however, they usually contain more facts than a media person needs to know. One or two pages at the most is plenty to recount your history and philosophy.

Stay focused on your brand—Bios are no place to boast about everything you've ever accomplished. Save the little league home-run stories for family reunions (unless you're a little league home-run expert). Only details that reinforce your brand identity should be included in your bio.

Write your bio like a well-crafted article—I've always enjoyed reading (and writing) bios that have the feel of a feature story in a newspaper or magazine. Media people don't want a list of dry facts and accomplishments, but they do like to discover those things as they read an interesting tale about your career. If you're not a good writer yourself, find or hire one.

Use quotes from key people—Intersperse exposition with quotes from the main players in your story. Quotes add life to any bio. Even if you write your bio yourself, be sure to quote yourself, as I did in the sample news release in the previous section. Weaving in positive quotes from published reviews is also acceptable in a bio.

Be positive, but don't overhype yourself—Your bio should put an optimistic spin on your brand-related activities. Crossing the line and being too boastful, though, can work against you. For example, writing that your band *has been causing a stir in Chicago with energetic live shows* is cool. Saying you're *the hottest thing since the Beatles and Elvis* is downright silly.

Write your bio as if a publication might run it—Another reason to go easy on the hype is because many small Web sites and e-zines may run some or all of your bio as an article. Many people who produce publications are stressed out and short on time. There is always a shortage of well-written material to publish. Give editors a bio that's objective, cleanly worded, and interesting—and they just might run it as is!

Photos or Graphic Images

If a Web site does a feature story on you, the editor will likely want to run an image of you along with it. Few sites send a photographer to take your picture. You'd be smart to have photos ready for any publication that requests them. Print media typically asks you to mail photos or e-mail high-resolution digital files, most likely in a TIF format at 300 dots per inch (dpi). Web sites, on the other hand, require low-resolution image files, usually in JPG or GIF format at 72 dpi.

Media Webmasters will love you if you already have your photo images posted on your site. Doing so allows them to download the pictures from your site and have them available immediately to use on your article's Web page. Whether you use a digital or film camera, keep the following photo tips in mind when planning your online images:

Zoom in for better pictures—Generally speaking, the best photos are up close and personal. A tight shot on someone's head and shoulders is far more appealing than a wide-angle view of a person running through a field. Keep the shapes and images in your photos simple and large, and let them fill up the frame.

Keep backgrounds simple—The emphasis in any promotional photo should be on you and the attitude that radiates from you. Unfortunately, most pictures show people posed in front of busy, mind-numbing background scenes. Picking a location that has atmosphere and texture is great, as long as you stand out against it.

Avoid predictable poses and straightforward angles—If your photographer asks you to stand with your hands folded in front of you while he or she shoots at eye level, run the other way. Don't use a predictable, bland picture unless you plan to give out smelling salts with all your photos. Getting a good shot takes time. You may have to take 50 photos to find one that works well. Try a variety of things during a photo session. Try sitting, lying down, or climbing on top of something. Have the photographer shoot from a high angle for some shots and a low angle for others. Have some fun, take some chances, and work to find an eye-catching image.

Make sure the image reinforces your brand—Long before you arrive for a photo shoot, get a handle on the type of visual image that best demonstrates your identity. Dress accordingly. Also, your facial expression needs to gel with your brand. Every photo you make available to the media should complement the image you want to portray. The bottom line is, have a consistent look and attitude.

Positive Quotes Page

Once you start getting news coverage online, you're going to want to tell media people about it. By demonstrating that other Web sites and e-zines have covered you—especially if they've showered you with praise—you give credence to the idea that you're worthy of further coverage. Whenever you land a feature story or review on the Web, it's a good idea to describe the coverage and provide a link to it. Don't run an entire story or review on your site without first getting permission from the site that originally ran it. What you can do, though, is post a collection of glittering excerpts from articles that have been written about you.

To put together a positive quotes page, go through the stories that have been written about you online and in print. Take a cue from major motion-picture marketers and pull out the best one- or two-sentence quotes from a variety of media sources. Here are two examples of such quotes that I found on the **Christine Columbus** site (at http://www.christinecolumbus.com/), an online catalog for women travelers:

"The one and only catalog for women travelers."—Cooking Light
"A traveling woman's dream."—Complete Women

Take these quotes and place them in large letters on a single Web page. You might put a headline at the top that reads, "Here's what the media is saying about (insert your name here)." Having all these quotes on one page is more effective than asking people to surf to individual articles at different sites. By providing a dozen or more glowing excerpts on one page, you allow media folks to get a quick overview of what other news sources have been saying about you.

Creative Quote Generation—*How do you create a positive quotes page if you haven't generated any publicity yet? Approach people you know in the industry— such as other experts, authors, people who head organizations, even satisfied customers—and ask them for a comment that you can include in your online kit. Directly soliciting quotes is the best way to start when you're short on traditional media quotes.*

Online Publicity: Additional Tips

You now have plenty of tools to help you garner media attention on the Internet. Before we leave this subject, I'd like to give you a few more quick tips and ideas. For instance, you can often get a write-up in smaller e-zines or Web sites by first giving them a plug. I stumbled on this concept by accident. Over the years, I've reviewed and recommended a lot of Web sites and e-zines through my writings, often without the site or e-zine owners being aware of the coverage. I noticed that when I did send an e-mail to the owner of a source I recommended, I frequently got a return plug, even if it was just a quick blurb mentioning that the source had been reviewed in my e-zine. Now I make it a habit to send a low-key note to anyone I mention in my e-zine, on my Web site, or in any articles I write. I don't demand a reciprocal mention. I don't have to, because many people automatically return the favor.

Let's cover a couple of no-nos. While you're compiling your database of online media contacts, keep an eye out for notices that request you send hard-copy news releases by regular mail. Some journalists prefer not to receive news inquiries by e-mail. Respect those wishes and contact media people in the manner that they prefer. Also, always include your news release or personal note in the body of an e-mail rather than as an attached file, unless a media person has specifically requested it. Every week I get cryptic e-mail messages with a news-related note in the subject line, no information in the body, and an attached file I never asked for. Can you guess what happens to these e-mails?

Whenever you visit an online magazine, check to see whether the site lists an editorial calendar. Many publications plan the themes of their issues a year ahead of time. If your brand identity fits an upcoming theme, start thinking about an angle you can pitch to an editor.

Finally, what if you go all out to generate publicity and nothing happens? What if nobody responds to your e-mails or appears interested in your story? It happens to the best of us, so be prepared. The media will never be as interested in you as you are. It's a fact of life that gaining publicity is often a slow process, especially in the beginning.

One thing to keep in mind when you're faced with media exposure silence is that your name and identity are still making the rounds. Editors, writers, columnists, and reviewers may not be biting just yet, but they are reading your personal notes and news releases. Your name will slowly start to sink in. By contacting the media on a regular basis, you pave the way for future recognition and opportunities for exposure.

Need more information on getting media exposure? Take a look at the following online resources:

About.com Public Relations
http://publicrelations.about.com/

Gebbie Press—How to Write a Press Release
http://www.gebbieinc.com/wwwww.htm

Workinpr—The Premier Jobsite for PR Professionals (shown in Figure 11.4)
http://www.workinpr.com/industry/career/car_prtools.asp

FIGURE 11.4: The Workinpr site provides several helpful articles on how to create a media kit and manage a PR campaign.

If you use all the tips in this chapter, before you know it you'll be a media darling. When combined with your other online activities, publicity will help carry your brand identity message even further. In the next chapter, "Other Online Branding Tools and Techniques," we'll discuss a final array of creative tricks you can use to establish your name in cyberspace.

CHAPTER TWELVE

Other Online Branding Tools and Techniques

If you've read this book from the beginning and now are thinking that we've surely covered every aspect of branding yourself online, think again. We still have several important elements left to discuss regarding how to use the Internet to become recognized in your chosen field. In this chapter, we cover the following topics:

- Five strategies you can use to inspire other Web sites to link to yours
- The pros and cons of online advertising and the various ways to utilize banner ads and e-zine sponsorships
- The art of receiving and presenting Web-based awards
- Exposure opportunities with freelance talent Web sites
- The power of a brand-focused visual appeal
- The importance of networking with your industry's movers and shakers
- Why you need to unleash an Ongoing Branding Assault

If you're serious about carving a unique identity online, you'll need to employ a variety of tactics to get your message across. As important as a great Web site and a free e-zine are, you'll need to reinforce your distinct image through multiple channels before your brand makes a significant impact. The tools in this chapter arm you with the extra ammunition you'll need to succeed.

Linking Strategies

Let's talk about links and why you need to pursue them. Because of the almighty hyperlink, the Internet has become a vast network of interconnectivity. From your Web site, with one click you can send visitors to any number of other sites that you recommend or mention. Likewise, each of hundreds of other Web sites can supply a link to your site. The Web is like a giant cross-referencing party with everyone giving and receiving links. The thing is, some sites receive a lot more links than others do. Generally, the more popular or useful a Web site, the more likely it is that many sites will link to it. Perks that come with getting numerous links include the following:

- A lot of incoming links often means a lot of new visitors, which is good for your brand's exposure.
- Many search engines give higher rankings to sites that have many other sites linking to them, which can also increase the number of visitors to your site.

In Chapter 6, "Designing Your Web Site for Brand Impact," we talked about the importance of offering a list of recommended sites and how sending people to sites closely related to your identity positions you as a resource. In this section, we focus on incoming links and how to motivate hundreds of targeted Webmasters to provide links to your site.

How Well Linked Are You?—*Want a quick way to find out how many sites are linking to yours? Go to LinkPopularity.com at* http://www.linkpopularity.com/. *Enter your URL and the site will show you results from three search engines: Infoseek, AltaVista, and Hotbot. You can also go to the AltaVista* (http://www.altavista.com/) *or Google* (http://www.google.com/) *search engine and enter link:www.yourdomain.com. You'll get a list of Web pages that contain links to your site. The results won't be all-inclusive, since search engines won't catch every page linking to you, but it will give you a good idea.*

There are many ways to receive incoming links from other Web sites, including the following:

- Getting mentioned in online articles about your area of expertise
- Having your self-promotional author blurbs appear with articles written by you
- Being included in directories of recommended links
- Getting listed on free link directory sites
- Appearing in archived issues of your e-zine if you use one of the online mailing list services
- Appearing in archived issues of other people's e-zines
- Being mentioned in online reviews of your Web site, product, or service
- Having your site appear in news releases posted on news sites
- Appearing in the sig file that accompanies your message board posts
- Running banner and text ads

When many people think of generating lots of incoming links, they think about link swaps. This common approach involves Webmasters making an "I'll link to yours if you link to mine" offer to countless site owners. Link swaps can lead to your site being listed on a lot of other sites, but there are problems associated with this tactic.

People who employ the swap technique usually set up a special page to list all the outgoing reciprocal links. This page gets increasingly chaotic as the number of site owners wanting to exchange links swells. If you follow this course, the sheer quantity of outgoing links begins to degrade the quality of them and you end up with many links that are loosely related or completely unrelated to your brand identity. Supplying a jumbled, unfocused links page will turn off your visitors and cause them to question the value of the information you offer. That's a road you don't want to travel. Here are the five linking strategies that I recommend:

Provide outgoing links only to sites you strongly endorse—The sites you recommend say a lot about who you are. Like all of the other elements on your site, your outgoing links should be focused and directly related to your identity. If you're a tax specialist, don't offer a link to a clip art site just because the owner claimed he or she could send lots of traffic your way. If a site isn't precisely intertwined with your brand, or if a site is of questionable quality, don't link to it. Only provide useful links that will help your visitors and strengthen your online image.

Communicate with sites that you recommend—When you think enough of a site to include it on a recommended links page, you should do so without requiring a reciprocal link. Don't reduce yourself to sending messages that state, "Hey, I'd like to add your site to my links page. All I need in return is a link to my site. Let me know when you have mine set up." If you discover a site that will be valuable to your fans, list it. However, after you add sites to your links page, contact the site owners and make them aware of the plug. Provide the URL where the site is listed and tell the owner a bit about what you do. You might even include a note that says, "If you feel my site would be of value to your visitors, feel free to mention it or include it on your links page." This approach is far different from the tactic of demanding a ransom for freeing a link. You're likely to get quality incoming links when you plug great sites related to your brand with no strings attached.

Find alternative ways to plug other sites—In the course of your online travels, you'll come across many good sites that are related in some way to your identity. However, only a small percentage of them will be of a high enough caliber to warrant including on your recommended links page.

Instead of writing off the rest of these sites, think outside the box. How else can you plug them without listing them on your page of top-notch links? You might post a short Web site profile of the week or write an article called "12 (insert your area of expertise) Web Sites You Need to Know About." Using this method, you'll plug additional worthwhile sites without cluttering your recommended links page. Of course, you should contact the owners of these secondary sites in the same manner outlined in the previous strategy.

Simply ask for a link or editorial mention—If you discover interesting sites that don't qualify for your recommended links page or an alternate plug, it doesn't hurt to contact the site owners and simply make them aware of your site and what it offers. Kindly ask to be included on the sites' link pages or to be kept in mind for a future editorial mention. You won't accomplish much in life if you don't politely ask for things, so get in the habit. If the owner of one of these low-priority sites responds with a request to receive a reciprocal link, graciously explain that you won't be able to do so at this time but that you'd still appreciate a mention if the owner sees fit.

Promote links to individual pages and articles—If you're like most people, you probably think of generating incoming links as a way to drive visitors to your home page. That's a worthy goal, but don't overlook linking opportunities for specific pages. For example, among the free articles available at author Marcia Yudkin's Web site is a Publicity FAQ. The article answers common questions asked by people who are new to the public relations field. Yudkin has had a lot of success getting PR sites to link directly to this FAQ page. The bottom line is that sometimes you may have better luck suggesting a link to a specific page on your site as opposed to pitching the site in general. If your cooking site has a great recipe for low-carb beef stroganoff, contact the many low-carb sites on the Internet and make them aware of the page that contains the recipe. These sites probably aren't interested in plugging generic cooking sites. But if you have a specific page that's right up their alley, tell them about it and ask for a link.

Giving and Getting Online Awards

One often-overlooked avenue for getting exposure online is the Web site award. In case you didn't know, thousands of awards are handed out every day—from major awards such as CD Now's Cool Cosmic Site of the Week and USA Today's Hot Site to much lesser-know awards dished out by a wide variety of Webmasters. Winning one or more of these awards allows you to exploit the recognition in many ways, including the following:

Announcing the win on your Web site—When an objective, third party deems you to be *cool*, it adds credibility.

Spreading the news through your e-mail newsletter—Your fans should already know how cool you are, but it doesn't hurt to remind them.

Driving new traffic to your Web site—The bigger the source of the award, the more traffic you'll get.

Alerting the media through a news release—Winning an award provides an excellent reason to connect with the media.

To win an award, you must submit your site to one or preferably many of the award sites. Chances are good you'll win some, too. Award sites need to recommend and award new sites every day, week, or month. They're often hungry for new suggestions.

What follows is a sampling of Web sites that give awards based on everything from fun and crazy themes to top-notch design and other criteria. Don't automatically submit to every one. Look through these and other award sites and pick the ones for which your brand is best suited.

AdZe's Cosmic Sites (awarded to sites that are uncommon, thought-provoking, or entertaining; submit by e-mail to suggest@www.adze.com)
http://www.adze.com/site-of-the-night.html

Best of WWWomen Sites
http://www.wwwomen.com/feature/bestwww.shtml

Cool Site of the Day
http://coolsiteoftheday.com/

Cruel Site of the Day (daily link to the world of the perturbed, peeved, pensive, and postal)
http://www.cruel.com/

Dr. Webster's Cool Web Site of the Day (innovative, useful, or just plain cool sites; submit by e-mail to: mmcdonald@123go.com)
http://www.drwebster.com/

Ellen's Place—Potpourri of Links
http://www.ellensplace.net/potpourr.html

Fun Site of the Day (silly, weird, humorous, amusing, and absurd sites; submit by e-mail to: submit@fungame.com)
http://www.fungame.com/fsod/

The Lycos Top 50 (submit by e-mail to: fholznagel@lycos.com)
http://50.lycos.com/

NetGuide (submit by e-mail to: fun@netguide.com)
http://www.netguide.com/

Project Cool Sightings (recognition for sites with great design)
http://www.projectcool.com/sightings/

Selectsurf
http://www.selectsurf.com/

Too Cool Awards
http://toocool.com/

USA Today (submit by e-mail to cyber@usatoday.com; shown in Figure 12.1)
http://www.usatoday.com/life/cyber/ch.htm

Web 100 (reviews of sites and ratings by users)
http://www.web100.com/

Webby Awards
http://www.webbyawards.com/

Yahoo! Pick of the Week (submit by e-mail to: suggest-picks@yahoo-inc.com)
http://www.yahoo.com/picks/

FIGURE 12.1: Every weekday, *USA Today's* Web site selects a Hot Site, as well as recognizes fun and useful sites. Getting such awards can drive a lot of traffic to winning sites.

For a more in-depth list of award sites, consult the following directories. Some of these resources simply catalog award sites; others allow you to submit to multiple sites using a single form:

Award-It!
http://www.award-it.com/

Award Sites
http://www.awardsites.com/

Google—Web Site Awards
http://directory.google.com/Top/Computers/Internet/WWW/Best_of_the_Web/Site_Awards/

RefDesk Cool Site Awards
http://www.refdesk.com/textcool.html

Website Awards
http://websiteawards.xe.net/

Why be content with just receiving an online award? A creative thinker (you are one, aren't you?) always looks at opportunities from different angles—even upside down and backward. Therefore, if receiving awards is so great, why not present one of your own?

Here's how it works: Let's say you're a rock-and-roll memorabilia expert who specializes in Elvis collectibles. Instead of hoarding all the recognition yourself, start giving some away to other Elvis-themed Web sites. Offer an Elvis site award. Give it a clever name that ties into your brand name, such as Pete Rogers' Hip-Swiveling Site of the Week Award. Send news releases about your new award and promote it on your Web site and in your e-zine. Next, review a lot of Elvis-related sites and start naming weekly winners. Send a message to winning sites letting them know about the honor that has been bestowed upon them. Create a catchy looking award logo that winners can display on their sites along with a link to your site.

When Web sites win awards, their owners will take many of the steps I suggested earlier in this section. The owners of the sites will brag about the award in their newsletters, send news releases to the media, and announce it on their sites. In other words, they'll give you free exposure simply because you recognized them as having a cool site. Yes, online awards can lead to as much recognition and traffic for the site presenting the award as for the one receiving it.

Online Advertising

You may have noticed that most of the Internet branding techniques covered in this book require an investment of time and energy, not cash. There's a good reason for that. For one thing, keeping spending to a minimum gels with the Poor Richard's philosophy of simplicity and frugality. In addition, you'd be wise to steer clear of the media saturation mentality that in recent years led to countless Web sites overspending, losing their shirts, and summarily closing up shop. There are many ways to progressively build your online reputation without spending a fortune on advertising.

However, advertising can enhance your online efforts. In this section, we'll examine the pros and cons of Web site banner ads, e-zine sponsorships, and search engine keyword advertising. When used in the right places and at the right times, each of these advertising forms can help promote your brand.

Unfortunately, many Web-based entrepreneurs think that spending a ton on paid ads will provide a shortcut to brand recognition. That might be true if people didn't routinely tune out anything that resembles advertising on the Internet. And the fact that consumers are often skeptical of claims made in advertisements doesn't help. Your best bet is to advertise sparingly. And when you do run online ads, make sure the ads appear in places frequented by your ideal fans—and preferably in places where people have likely already heard of you through other means.

Banner Ads

Banner ads are one of the first things that come to mind when people think of advertising online. It's tempting to think about having your name and URL proudly displayed in a banner ad across the top of your favorite Web site. The only thing is, banner ad effectiveness is in a sorry state. In the early days of the Web, as many as 1 visitor in 10 would click a banner ad to find out where it led. Today, some advertisers are lucky if 1 out 500 visitors clicks their banner. Considering that most Web sites charge per impression (each time the banner is displayed), banner ads aren't your best ad investment.

Luckily, there is a way to display your banner ad on other sites free. Just hook up with a banner exchange program. These programs act as an advertising barter arrangement whereby you run banner ads on your site in exchange for having your ads run on other sites. If you're interested in this no-cost ad option, take a look at the following banner exchange sites:

123Buttons
http://www.123buttons.com/

1for1 Banner Exchange
http://www.1for1.com/

BannerMall
http://www.bannermall.com/

BannerExchange Network
http://bannerexchange.mycomputer.com/

LinkBuddies
http://site.linkbuddies.com/

The drawback of banner exchange programs is that you usually have little control over which sites your ads run on and what ads run on your site. If you'd like more control and your budget allows for it, you might consider running paid banner ads on sites that cater to your audience. You probably already have sites in mind where you feel your ads would be most effective. Contact the Webmasters of those sites and ask for rates. You might also offer your own one-to-one banner exchange directly with the site to keep costs down.

If you don't want to go it alone and need guidance, the following sites can help you set up a more extensive banner ad campaign:

Adbility
http://www.adbility.com/

BURST! Media
http://www.burstmedia.com

Fastclick
http://www.fastclick.com/

Pennyweb
http://home.pennyweb.com/

ValueClick
http://www.valueclick.com/

E-zine Ads

E-zine ads have grown in popularity in recent years because they have generally proven to generate higher response rates compared to banner ads. The more prominent e-zines are well read. E-zine text ads—sometimes called sponsorship ads, classified ads, or line ads—visually carry the same weight as editorial content. Since subscribers must scroll through an e-zine issue to read it, the ads are more likely to be noticed, as opposed to Web page banner ads that are mixed in with lots of competing content.

As with banner ads, you may already be aware of e-zines that reach your audience. Contact the publishers for rates. Otherwise, the following sites provide e-zine advertising advice and lists of e-zines that offer ads:

Eyesmail
http://www.eyesmail.com/

E-zine Ad Auction
http://www.ezineadauction.com/

E-Zine AdSource Directory
http://www.ezineadsource.com/

EzineAdvertising.com
http://ezineadvertising.com/

Free Directory of E-zines
http://www.freezineweb.com/

Free E-zine Advertising Directory
http://www.free-ezine-advertising.com/

Lifestyles Publishing Directory of E-zines
http://www.lifestylespub.com/

Zineconnection.com
http://www.zineconnection.com/

Search Engine Advertising

In an earlier era—back when *Yahoo!* was a term you only heard shouted at rodeos—an Internet search engine was a free service that objectively displayed a list of Web pages based on the keywords that a person entered. Thankfully, search engines are still free, but a growing number of them are not so objective when it comes to displaying search results. Some search engines now run paid text ads alongside their regular results; others show search results based on who has bid the highest for the selected keywords. Some charge advertisers per impression; others charge only when a surfer clicks an advertiser's link.

Search engine advertising is a relatively new but growing online marketing method. With its relative low cost, paying for search engine placement is worth looking into, especially if you only pay for keywords that relate directly to your brand image. Check out the following list of search engines that feature text ad placement:

Ask Jeeves
http://www.ask.com/

FindWhat.com
http://www.findwhat.com/

Google (shown in Figure 12.2)
http://www.google.com/

GoTo
http://www.goto.com/

HootingOwl
http://www.hootingowl.com/

Kanoodle.com
http://www.kanoodle.com/

Sprinks
http://www.sprinks.com/

FIGURE 12.2: Google allows advertisers to buy boxed text ads that appear to the right of search results when select keywords are used.

Regardless of what advertising method you choose to pursue, it's important to craft your ads so that they get the best response. One of the biggest mistakes is to simply list your site's URL along with a bland description. Sorry, but *www.GreenThumb.com for all your gardening needs* won't cut it. Put a little pizzazz in your ads and dangle a benefit or two in front of readers. For instance, *Backyard Gardening Secrets Revealed* or *10 Free Resources for Backyard Gardeners* might attract a bit more attention.

Use Ads to Inspire Action—*Don't run ads just to get your name out there. Nike might be able to afford to run image ads, but you can't. Your ads need to inspire action and get people to visit your Web site, download your free e-book, subscribe to your free e-zine, or connect with you in some other meaningful way. Also, don't try to sell a product or service directly from an ad. Use your ads to lure people closer to you. After you've won them over by displaying your skill and expertise, you can try to sell something.*

Respect Privacy and Earn Trust

Many folks are leery about venturing onto the Web. People are fearful of hackers and frauds and dealing with sites that may go out of business tomorrow. That's why it's important for you to conduct business ethically online and go out of your way to calm people's fears. A growing number of sites are including a link in their navigation bars labeled Privacy Policy. This page lets visitors know how the site captures personal information and how that information will be used. The privacy policy page used by the **Bakersfield Californian** newspaper at http://www.bakersfield.com/privacy/ provides a good example of the type of details that should be included. For more information on healthy online business practices and consumer rights, check out the following sites:

Direct Marketing Association
http://www.the-dma.org/

Online Privacy Alliance
http://www.privacyalliance.org/

Privacy Rights Clearinghouse
http://www.privacyrights.org/

Another way to instill trust is to earn and display a seal of approval from a recognized online source. The following sites dispense such seals based on a variety of criteria:

Academy Internet Seal of Approval
http://www.academyinternet.com/seal/seal.cfm

Better Business Bureau Online
http://www.bbbonline.org/

ePublicEye.com
http://www.thepubliceye.com/

Internet Seal of Approval
http://www.isamember.com/

TRUSTe
http://www.truste.org/

VeriSign Inc.
http://www.verisign.com/

WebTrust
http://www.cpawebtrust.org/

Keep in mind that many industry-specific associations award their own seals. One may be suited to your site and brand identity.

Your Online Visual Image

Admittedly, I place a lot of importance on establishing a brand identity by providing expert information and allowing your personality to shine through your written words. After all, I am a writer, so I may be biased. However, you should know that your online identity can be greatly enhanced by your brand's visual image, as well. The visual aspect of your brand can take many forms, including the following:

Your logo—Having a recognizable logo works for McDonald's, Coke, Yahoo!, and many other companies. If your name and image lend themselves to using a logo, consider having one professionally designed. Then display it wherever your brand message appears.

Your Web site design—A cooking site targeted to mothers should have a look and feel that's different from a site dedicated to pro wrestling. Make sure the colors and design elements you use on your Web pages are consistent with the quality and tone you want to project.

Your photo—Consumers are capable of making a connection between a person's name and what they stand for without a visual reference. For instance, most people who read best-selling novels have no idea what the authors look like. But if you provide your fans with a face to go with your name, you add another layer of recognizability to your brand. Especially if you're pursuing an identity as a model or actor, a visual component is crucial.

A Picture Is Worth a Thousand Gigabytes—*Some enterprising people make excellent use of a visual image to embed a brand identity into the public consciousness. Take a look at Matthew Lesko and Information USA at* http://www.lesko.com/, *which is illustrated in Figure 12.3. There you'll find Lesko sporting a bow tie and dressed in a colorful, one-of-a-kind suit covered with question marks. It's a zany approach, but it's one that matches his personality. He's consistently used the outfit for years. Whether you see Lesko on a television program, at a book signing, or on his Web site, there he is wearing the bow tie and multicolored question marks.*

FIGURE 12.3: Matthew Lesko uses a bow tie and a colorful suit covered with question marks as part of his visual brand image.

Would your brand benefit from a visual counterpart? If you're a food expert, consider wearing an attention-getting apron. If your nickname is the Comedy Commando, dress in camouflage. If you're a swimsuit model, pose in a swimsuit. Get the picture? Even if you only want to use a straightforward headshot, pick out the most flattering photo and use it often. Make your visual identity as clear and consistent as every other aspect of your brand.

Exploiting Talent Sites

Another way to promote your brand image is through one of the many freelance talent sites on the Web. Most of these online resources allow you to post a resume and portfolio of your work, along with additional information that can help you establish an identity as a pro in your chosen field. While these sites vary somewhat in the type of talent they allow, please note that most of them are geared to freelance writers, advertising copywriters, editors, graphic designers, marketing consultants, and so on. Here's a list of some of the more prominent talent sites:

Aquent
http://www.aquent.com/

Creative Freelancers
http://www.freelancers.com/

eWork
http://www.ework.com/

FreeAgent.com
http://www.freeagent.com/

Fast Company's Go Free Agent
http://www.fastcompany.com/career/free.html

Guru.com
http://www.guru.com/

Mediabistro
http://www.mediabistro.com/

SkillsVillage
http://www.skillsvillage.com/

Smarterwork
http://www.smarterwork.com/

The Write Jobs
http://www.writerswrite.com/jobs/

Writer's Resource
http://www.writersresource.net/

Another type of online freelance service is the talent auction site. Generally, this type of site allows people needing the services of a specialist to post information about their projects. Freelancers can respond to these posts by stating their credentials and bidding on the jobs. Usually, the information supplied by bidders is available for everyone to see, which makes it a great place to hammer home your brand. Some sites, such as Monster Talent Market, offer a reverse auction, where talent buyers bid on the freelancers they want to hire. Here are some talent auction sites to consider, most of which cater to the same writing, designing, and consulting talents as the previous list:

GovCon's BidRadar
http://www.bidradar.com/

BrainBid.com
http://www.brainbid.com/

Bullhorn.com
http://www.bullhorn.com/

eLance (see Figure 12.4)
http://www.elance.com/

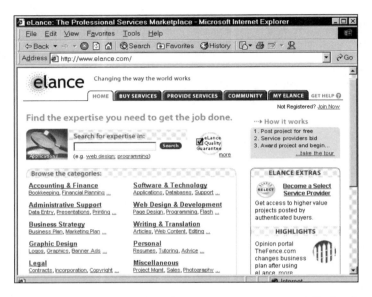

FIGURE 12.4: On the eLance site, talent buyers post projects while freelancers promote their expertise and place bids.

Farm
http://farm.ants.com/ants/

Monster Talent Market
http://talentmarket.monster.com/

TalentBanks.com
http://www.talentbanks.com/

TheCentralMall.com
http://www.thecentralmall.com/

UBidContract.com
http://www.ubidcontract.com/

WorkExchange Technologies
http://www.workexchange.com/

Interacting with Peers and Other Experts

We've talked a lot about communicating with potential fans, current customers, members of the media, and so on. Now let's discuss another form of online communication that can work wonders for your brand: interacting with movers and shakers in your field. In the offline world, people frequently attend trade shows and conferences to meet other people who are active in their line of business. These connections often lead to wider exposure and more paid work. While it's still a good idea to attend industry events, the Internet allows you to instantly gain access to just about any human being in the civilized world by using only e-mail—no airfare and hotel expenses and no jet lag to contend with.

Even with the convenience of e-mail, many folks are too shy to contact influential people in their field. With no one to pave the way with an introduction, even the most enthusiastic Internet entrepreneurs feel they lack the clout to make themselves known to people they admire. My advice: Get over it! Start making connections with other experts and people experiencing success in related fields. Sure, some won't respond. Some may only e-mail back a quick, cold reply. Others, however, will turn out to be warm and friendly people who enjoy getting to know others with similar aspirations.

Some of the authors who supplied testimonials for this book, as well as many of the experts who contributed to Appendix A, "Online Success Stories," came to know me because of introductory e-mails I've sent over the years. They initially didn't know me from the proverbial Adam, but that didn't stop me from sending a cordial message letting them know who I was and how much I admired their work. You should do the same.

As you communicate with other experts, authors, the heads of industry organizations, and people who run prominent companies in your field, your circle of influence will grow. These movers and shakers will eventually talk about you and recommend you to others. Having a network of friends in your industry will expand your brand's reach a hundred fold.

Your Ongoing Branding Assault

When you pursue only a handful of the online promotional options available to you, you cheat yourself out of the magic created by an Ongoing Branding Assault. To succeed in branding yourself online, you must regularly hit potential fans with your targeted message from as many different angles as possible.

Keep in mind that the people you're trying to attract are slapped with thousands of messages every day. From television, magazines, and junk mail to radio, billboards, and ads on city buses, they are literally bombarded with marketing intrusions. To cut through that clutter, you have to reach them not just once or twice, but several times with your well-defined brand message.

That's why it does you no good to be timid about your approach, and why it's futile to expect that a few attempts to reach your audience will have much of an impact. According to a study by Bell Labs, a single issue of *The New York Times* contains more information than an adult in the 16th century had to contend with over an entire lifetime. It takes a lot to get people to pay attention—even to things they're excited about. To keep from getting lost in the shuffle, you have to reach potential fans with your message on a regular basis.

The best way to make an impression is to connect with people repeatedly through a variety of online channels. Only then will many of these people recognize that what you have to offer is beneficial to them. As you may know by now, your Online Branding Assault can be accomplished using a variety of online tools and techniques, including the following:

- Your free e-zine
- Your brand-focused Web site
- Your free e-book
- Articles written by you on other Web sites
- Your postings in high-traffic discussion forums
- Coverage you procure in the media

Your mission, then, is to come up with an ongoing plan that covers your target audience with a series of marketing coats. Each one builds upon previous coats by making still more people aware of what you do, and by making more of an impression with those people you've already reached.

Consider a songwriter who sets up a Web site and then lands favorable reviews in two music e-zines. Would those accomplishments be enough to catapult her to stardom? Not likely. But they would be a good start if she can follow them up with publishing her own e-zine, giving away free music downloads of her songs, writing a regular music column for a popular music site, and winning an online songwriting contest.

Find a way to get members of your target audience to see your name (and your well-defined brand image) at least several times within the course of a year. And make sure they hear about you from a variety of different sources. That's what an effective Ongoing Branding Assault is all about.

Now that we've covered a full range of online branding activities, let's turn our attention to the many ways you can use offline promotional tactics to enhance your online accomplishments. These topics are covered in Chapter 13, "Exploiting Offline Branding Strategies."

CHAPTER THIRTEEN

Exploiting Offline Branding Strategies

Thus far in this book, we've covered a full spectrum of ways to use the Internet to turn your name into a brand name with a tightly focused image. But even in a book that concentrates on personal branding from a cyberspace point of view, we can't ignore the importance of promoting yourself in the real world. So let's now turn our attention to the realm we live in, the world of flesh and blood and three dimensions. In this chapter, we'll take a look at the following important offline branding tactics:

- Using free and paid seminars and workshops to share your expertise
- Attending trade shows, fairs, and conferences to network and make lasting personal connections
- Presenting events that you organize and sponsor
- Designing and printing promotional materials, including business cards, envelopes, brochures, tips sheets, and more
- Using direct mail in a sensible and cost-effective manner
- Getting widespread exposure through radio and TV interviews
- Putting telephone branding techniques to good use
- Getting the most from face-to-face communication

Entire volumes have been written about non-Internet marketing tactics. This chapter doesn't pretend to cover every aspect of offline promotion, but it does give you some of the best ways to strengthen and reinforce your online branding efforts.

Branding Yourself Through Events

There's no denying the impact of face-to-face communication. Even if you provide compelling words and appealing graphics on your Web site, and even if you excel at creating a warm and personal online style, people still miss the human factor. Meeting people at events is a superior way to add an extra dimension to your brand's impact. At events, you'll meet people who soon become a part of your online fan base. Another rewarding aspect of events is that they often allow you to meet people who previously knew you only through your e-zine or Web site. Making face-to-face connection with fans leads to stronger bonds and a stronger brand image.

In the following sections, we cover a variety of ways to use live events to promote yourself. We talk about how to use public speaking to educate people and establish your identity. We also cover why you should attend trade shows, fairs, and conferences related to your industry. In addition, we discuss the advantages of organizing your own event, fundraiser, or celebration.

Public Speaking

One of the most powerful ways to project your identity in the offline world is to take on the role of teacher and give live seminars and workshops. High-profile speakers can command thousands of dollars in speaking fees. If you're just starting out, though, you'd be wise to get in front of groups for little or no money. For one thing, you need a lot of practice to hone your public speaking skills. Take advantage of every opportunity to get in front of an audience that may be interested in your brand identity.

Another reason you want to get a lot of speaking experience is to overcome any fear you may have. Anxiety over public speaking is regularly cited in surveys as people's number one fear—greater than the fear of heights, snakes, or even death. If apprehension is keeping you from pursuing this excellent promotional avenue, just realize that most professional speakers initially had similar fears and that regular practice, taken in small steps, will melt those fears away.

Your presentations will be stronger if you limit the scope of your talks to one or two themes. Mix in personal anecdotes with examples and quotes that illustrate the points you want to make. Allow for audience interaction by asking questions throughout your talk and having a question and answer segment at the end. Have an outline and use notes, but avoid reading from a script. I've only scratched the surface of public speaking tips here. The following sites offer articles and advice for delivering better seminars and workshops:

Advanced Public Speaking Institute
http://www.public-speaking.org/

How to Write and Deliver a Speech
http://www.selfgrowth.com/articles/Rando13.html

Toastmasters—10 Tips for Successful Public Speaking (shown in Figure 13.1)
http://www.toastmasters.org/tips.htm

FIGURE 13.1: Toastmasters International is an established organization with chapters around the world that help people with public speaking and presentation skills.

From a branding standpoint, make sure the title of your presentation offers a benefit and clearly reflects your identity. Offer handouts that attendees can take with them. Of course, these handouts should contain your name, Web site address, e-mail, phone number, and other contact information. Find creative ways to capture attendees' names and addresses. Ask everyone to throw their business cards into a fish bowl or have them fill out short forms at the beginning of your talk. When your presentation is over, pick a card or form out of the bowl and award a prize (your book, special report, sample of your craft). Follow up with everyone by e-mail or postal mail and ask all attendees to subscribe to your e-zine or visit your Web site.

Getting Paid for Your In-Person Advice—Once you gain a reputation as an effective speaker, you may be able to start charging for your presentation skills. Companies and trade-show organizers may contact you to speak. Many experts hold their own workshops and charge fans to attend. Some well-known authorities go a step further and offer weekend retreats for people who want to completely immerse themselves in a topic. For instance, photographer Philip Douglis hosts retreats on journalistic and business photography in Arizona. Every quarter Dan Poynter holds a two-day, 20-hour workshop for up to 18 authors and small publishers who pay $695 each to attend. Once you've established yourself as an expert, people will pay to get up close and personal with you.

Trade Shows, Fairs, and Conferences

Meeting people who are involved with your area of expertise offers an ideal way to introduce yourself and make a good brand-related impression. Presenting your own workshops, as discussed in the previous section, can inspire people interested in your specialty to come to you. On the other hand, trade shows, fairs, and conferences allow you to go where your targeted audience gathers. Make it a point to attend as many events related to your industry as possible. The connections you make can pay off immensely.

Just about every industry has at least one annual event. An author I know is organizing a national gel candle conference. I'm not talking about a general craft-related event that includes candle makers. The entire conference is just for people who make and sell a particular type of candle made of gel. Certainly, there's an event geared to your talent that draws a lot of people. Most likely, some of the more prominent Web sites related to your industry compile lists of annual trade shows. The following online directories list shows, fairs, and conferences in a variety of categories:

CultureFinder
http://www.culturefinder.com/

Festivals.com
http://www.festivals.com/

TSCentral
http://ww0.tscentral.com/

WhatsGoingOn.com (shown in Figure 13.2)
http://www.whatsgoingon.com/

Worldwide Holiday and Festival Site
http://www.holidayfestival.com/

If you sell art, crafts, photography, or other visual treats, you'd benefit from displaying your wares at fairs and other exhibition opportunities. At these events, you can connect with potential fans as well as network with other artists. Some industry events won't put you in touch with fans at all. Trade shows, for instance, are typically made up of business buyers and sellers. For example, Book Expo America is a big annual event in the publishing industry. I attend this trade show not to mingle with consumers who will eventually purchase my book, but to rub elbows with bookstore people, book reviewers, and other authors— people who need to know about me and what I do.

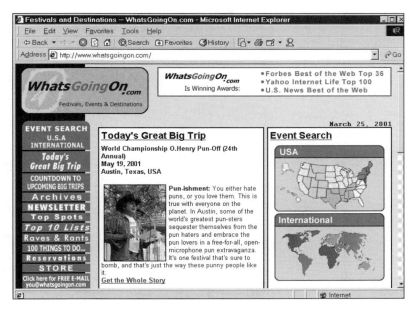

FIGURE 13.2: The WhatsGoingOn.com site provides a comprehensive database of festivals and events around the world.

Conferences are usually designed for educational purposes. People interested in a particular subject gather to attend panels and workshops presented by experts and industry power brokers. Ideally, you should be attending a conference as one of those expert panelists. But if you haven't reached that level yet, you should still attend to mix and mingle with like-minded people and to meet some of the panelists and power brokers.

I've attended many music industry conferences over the years. Rarely do I come away from such an event without meeting someone who ends up playing a role in a future stage of my development. You just can't beat meeting people involved in your industry face to face.

To make the most of attending events, come prepared to shake lots of hands and hand out tons of business cards; or, better yet, have a bright post card or useful handout to give to people you meet. At most conferences, attendees are encouraged to wear nametags or laminates that display their names and affiliations. Many enterprising marketers concoct their own unique version of a nametag. Authors have been known to hang large color copies of their book covers around their necks. Consider using a special pin-on button or sticker that asks a provocative question—anything that might help strike up a conversation about who you are and what you do.

Presenting Your Own Event

For five years, I organized an annual music conference in St. Louis that featured a combination of live music showcases at night and music industry panels during the day. It was a massive undertaking, but it certainly helped solidify my standing as a music business mini-mogul in my hometown. Every year, in the weeks leading up to the conference, I could count on using the event to work my way into several radio interviews and newspaper articles. (For details on media exposure, turn to Chapter 11, "Exposing Your Identity Through Online Publicity.") Since the musical acts that performed at the event came from Missouri and about 10 surrounding states, the conference also helped establish my name and identity outside of my immediate region.

You may not be willing to take on the challenge of organizing an entire conference, but you can present a smaller event that may bring you and your brand some attention. In fact, I did this in the years prior to starting my conference. Every so often, I put together a local concert featuring several bands at one nightclub in one night. I also organized a music business seminar once or twice a year that covered a single topic in one evening. These lesser events didn't have the media drawing power of the larger conference, but they still helped me establish myself as a St. Louis music proponent with a targeted audience.

What sort of event could you stage to promote your brand? Are you a fitness instructor? Hold an amateur body-builder contest. Do you produce your own barbecue sauce? Organize your city's largest outdoor barbecue event. Every brand identity can benefit from some type of public celebration. Here are a few more ideas for attaching your name to an event:

Present an award—Let's say you're an aspiring fashion designer. Like Mr. Blackwell, you could present an annual best- and worst-dressed people list for your city or state. Invite the media to a press conference at which you announce the winners, followed by a fashion show featuring top models from your area.

Bring in an established celebrity—If you're an expert on 1970s American pop culture, hold a small exhibit of 1970s collectibles and hire Barry Williams, the actor who portrayed Greg Brady, or another notable character from the era to make an appearance and sign autographs. Be sure to accompany the celebrity on any media interviews.

Organize a fundraiser for a local charity or cause—Doing good deeds not only makes you feel good, it can also bring you recognition. Every month or so, I hear of a radio station in my town that has teamed up with a music venue and several area bands to raise money for a worthy cause. The bands' names are mentioned regularly in promotional spots. Especially in the months leading up to the holidays, these types of events run rampant. Is there a worthy cause you'd like to support? If so, how can you associate your identity with the fundraiser?

Donate prizes to charity auctions—Another way to approach the fundraiser angle is to contribute one of your products or services to be auctioned off to the highest bidder.

Volunteer to help with a small part of a big event—Let's say a corporation is sponsoring a dog show in your area. You are a child-safety expert who raised two kids in a house with three dogs. Contact the dog show's organizers and offer to present a free workshop as part of the event on how to arrange a safe home environment for kids and dogs. Ask that the workshop and your name be included in the event program.

Another creative way to present an event is to tie your brand into an anniversary, a well-known person's birthday, or a recognized day, week, or month of celebration. For instance, April 12 is Stupid Pet Tricks Day. If you operate a pet store or dog grooming shop, you'd be smart to create a contest that coincides with the date. April 8 is Buddha's birthday. If your expertise is Zen philosophy or ancient Eastern culture, how could you take advantage of the birthday? Other event-worthy dates include April 7 (No Housework Day), April 4 (Ballroom Dancing Day), March 22 (International Goof-Off Day), and February 28 (Clark Kent's birthday). Can you see the possibilities?

***Turn a Date into a Special Occasion**—Two excellent online directories of birthdays, celebrations, and special holidays are Celebrate Today at* http://www.celebratetoday.com/ *and Chase's Calendar of Events at* http://www.chases.com/ *(shown in Figure 13.3).*

Promotional Materials

Printed promotional materials are some of your top offline branding tools—whether you hand them to people, make them available to be picked up in high-traffic areas, or mail them. They serve as physical reminders of who you are, what you do, and the unique way you approach your identity. The good news is that you don't have to reinvent the wheel when creating promotional materials. If you follow the advice in Chapter 6, "Designing Your Web Site for Brand Impact," your site should have a look and feel that suits your identity well. Your site should also contain words that describe what you do as well as helpful tips for potential fans. When creating offline promotional materials, you can recycle much of that same information and create an identical look and feel on paper.

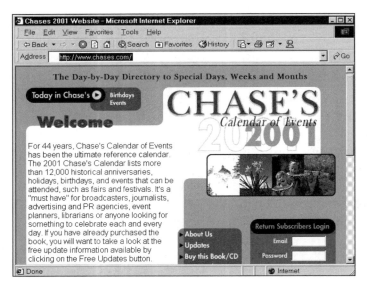

FIGURE 13.3: Chase's Calendar of Events, a print version of which is available at many public libraries, is a comprehensive directory of birthdays, anniversaries, celebrations, and special observations.

The key to branding yourself online and off is consistency. Once you have a persona, color scheme, and group of descriptive words that work, use them again and again. Your offline promotional efforts should mimic and reinforce everything you do online. Here are just some of the printed materials you might use:

Business cards—The workhorse of self-promotion is the business card. Have some printed and never leave home without them. Be sure to give one away to anyone you speak to about your brand. Of course, you want the text on your card to include your name and complete contact information, especially your Web site and e-mail addresses. In addition, be sure to add your Brand Identity Statement (first discussed in Chapter 2, "Crafting Your Best Brand Identity"), a short slogan that describes exactly what you do with a corresponding benefit. For instance, on my music marketing business cards, I might include, "Free marketing ideas for songwriters, musicians, and bands on a budget." A good business card should instantly tell people what you do and why they should care. The following three sites allow you to design and purchase business cards online:

Business Cards Express
http://www.businesscards-express.com/

Design Your Own Card
http://www.designyourowncard.com/

FullColorBusinessCards.com
http://www.fullcolorbusinesscards.com/

Letterhead—Whenever you send a letter, print it on paper that complements not only your image, but also your business card and the envelope the letter goes in. It's a good idea to coordinate and purchase your cards, letterhead, and envelopes at the same time. You may be amazed at the variety of paper choices you have, from neon yellows to muted earth tones. As long as these printed items match each other and support your identity, have some fun selecting them.

Envelopes—Many people simply print a name and return address in the top left corner of their envelopes. To better promote your brand, take an extra step and add some envelope teaser text or a sticker. Consider putting your Brand Identity Statement or similar enticing wording on the outside of the envelope to encourage recipients to get excited about what's inside.

Brochures—Brochures come in all shapes and sizes, though a common version is a letter-size sheet of paper folded in thirds. Again, the paper you use should complement your other promotion materials. Take a look at the words you use to promote and sell your identity on your Web site, then see how you can rearrange those words into a multipaneled brochure. Avoid using distant references such as *Customers will enjoy greater comfort when using this mattress.* Instead, use a more friendly, one-on-one approach, as in *You'll be a lot more comfortable sleeping on one of our mattresses.*

Fliers—You can pin fliers on bulletin boards, staple them to telephone poles, tape them to storefront windows, and hand them out at events. Use them to promote seminars, announce a new product or service, or simply let people know about you, your Web site, and free e-zine. Use a large headline and striking graphic element to grab attention. In addition to different types of papers, try experimenting with various shapes. Design and print your fliers on 11" x 17" sheets of paper and cut them in half lengthwise (to create tall, thin fliers) or cattycorner (for triangular shapes).

Tip sheets—An effective promotional item to hand out, particularly after you give a seminar, is a tip sheet. Take one of the articles you've written and print it on one side of a sheet of paper. Numbered how-to titles like "12 Ways to Lower Your Taxes" or "10 Things Every Parent Needs to Know about Child Safety" are especially potent.

Newsletters—Go through recent issues of your e-zine and select several short excerpts that you can compile into a printed newsletter. Even if you don't regularly publish a paper newsletter, presenting your information in a newsletter format gives you and your brand a professional look. If you offer useful or entertaining details in your newsletters and tip sheets, people will hang onto them—serving as an ongoing reminder of who you are and what you offer. Make sure your Web address, e-mail address, and other contact information is included on every promotional item you distribute.

All the promotional materials in the previous list can be printed on any number of specially designed papers. Think long and hard before settling on the paper choices that will represent you. The following sites offer a wide array of papers that can be used for letterheads, newsletters, brochures, fliers, and more:

Artpaper.com
http://www.artpaper.com/

Crane
http://www.crane.com/

Paper Direct
http://www.paperdirect.com/

Paper Showcase
http://www.papershowcase.com/

Paper Zone
http://www.paperzone.com/

PaperAccess.com (shown in Figure 13.4)
http://www.paperaccess.com/

SelectPaper.com
http://www.selectpaper.com/

***Sticky Promotional Items**—In addition to printed marketing tools on paper, you might consider using a novelty promotional item. Some possibilities include bumper stickers, calendars, bookmarks, pens, and so on—with your name, description, and contact information printed on them. One effective item that can get lots of exposure in people's homes is a refrigerator magnet. If a fan slaps one on the side of a kitchen appliance, it could result in ongoing exposure for months or years to come. Three Web sites that specialize in promotional magnet items are Custom Magnets at* http://www.custom-magnets.com/, *Magnetic Imprinted Products at* http://www.magnets-imprint.com/, *and MisterMagnets.com at* http://www.mistermagnets.com/.

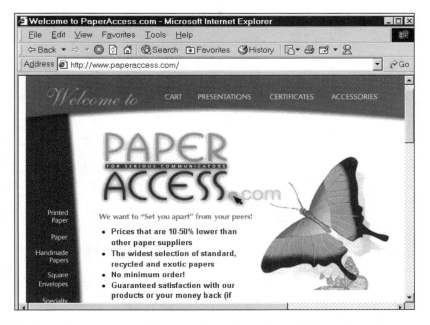

FIGURE 13.4: PaperAccess.com offers a wide variety of specially designed papers that can be used to project an offline brand identity.

Direct Mail

Just as you regularly solicit and compile names and e-mail addresses for your online promotional efforts, you should also compile names and postal addresses for offline marketing activities. Direct mail can be expensive, so I don't advocate that you invest heavily in a mailing campaign. But there are some creative and sensible ways you can use direct mail to help spread your brand recognition. Here are two of those ways:

Personal letters—Typically, big companies send form letters to hundreds of thousands of people at a time. Mail merge functions allow marketers to customize their mailings so that each recipient's name appears in the letter. That's great, but you're not a big, mass-mailing entity. Instead, you're a person who is trying to connect with other people who share an interest in your area of expertise. You'd be better off sending personal letters to individual people. For instance, if you hit it off with someone you meet at a conference, send a letter with a personal note instead of a quick e-mail. If one of your e-zine subscribers sends you a message raving about the quality of your information, respond with a personal letter along with some printed tips sheets. The idea is to build stronger, more meaningful business relationships by treating individuals as the special people they are.

How to Get Names and Addresses—*To use direct mail on a significant scale, you need a list of names and postal addresses. Most of the people you communicate with online only supply you with an e-mail address. So how do you compile offline addresses? First, if you sell a product or service, you most likely get your paid customers' contact information. Add those details to your database. Second, people who e-mail you will sometimes include their physical addresses, especially if they run a business. Compile them. Also, you can offer a printed version of a tip sheet to your subscribers for free or a small fee. Add the names and addresses of those who respond. Finally, you can rent a mailing list from magazines or organizations that cater to your target audience.*

Post cards—Post cards seem so simple, yet they pack a mean punch. Because of their low cost, post cards are the most affordable type of direct mail. The greatest thing about post cards is that your information gets across immediately. There's no envelope to open and no chance your message will get buried. The post card *is* the message. If you see the post card, you have been exposed to the words and images on it. If you are interested in doing mass mailings, I suggest using post cards instead of form letters, brochures, or catalogs. As with all forms of promotion that you pursue, make sure the message on your post card is sharply focused on your identity and the benefits you offer fans. Two good post card printing sources are **Modern Postcard** at http://www.modernpostcard.com/ and **Postcard Press** at http://www.postcardpress.com/ (shown in Figure 13.5).

Radio and TV Interviews

Thousands of radio, television, and cable TV talk shows across the country and around the world regularly feature guests. Hundreds of authors and experts of all kinds have used broadcast media interviews to boost their careers. During the 10 years that I published a music magazine, I was frequently invited to appear on local shows to talk about the state of the music scene in my town. I established a relationship with media people who came to view me as a resource on local music issues.

Several years ago, a city official created an uproar when he suggested that his department would start cracking down on musicians who performed without a business license. The media jumped on the story and I suddenly found myself being asked to comment on the controversy on the air. Lots of people heard those interviews, which served to further develop my standing as a local music aficionado.

FIGURE 13.5: Postcard Press prints four-color post cards from digital files.

Greg Godek, author of *1001 Ways to Be Romantic*, uses talk show appearances to sell thousands of books. "My job is not simply to write books," he says. "My job is to communicate my message to as many people as possible. This means conducting as many media interviews as humanly possible. I do whatever I can to bring my message to the media. Radio interviews via phone are a great way to get the public to recognize your name and to build relationships with the media." Godek is right. Television interviews require a lot more travel and preparation in dressing right and looking confident on camera. Radio interviews, on the other hand, require only your voice and a phone. You can do a dozen interviews in four time zones in one morning without leaving your bedroom.

To make the most of interviews, Godek transforms the material in his romance books into entertaining tips, lists, and quizzes. His goal is to make the radio station phone lines light up so that he's invited back as a regular guest. He also tries to tie his media appearances into a current event or holiday, plus he's always creating new material so he has a fresh angle every time he makes a return on-air visit. Could Godek's approach work for you?

To help you search for radio and TV talk shows, consult the following online directories. Some of these sites provide only radio station listings; some focus only on television stations; some cover both. Most of these directories will link you to the Web sites of individual stations, where you can investigate specific shows and get contact information.

100,000 Watts
http://www.100000watts.com/

123World Radio Stations
http://www.123world.com/radiostations/

NetBroadcastCenter.com
http://www.netbroadcastcenter.com/

Radio-Locator
http://www.radio-locator.com/

Sol Musical
http://www.solmusical.com/

WebcastPilot
http://www.webcastpilot.com/

In addition to hunting down talk-show information and approaching stations yourself, you may also want to take advantage of the following sites, most of which provide talk-show producers with a handy list of potential guests and experts.

Business Wire—ExpertSource
http://www.businesswire.com/expertsource/

CheapPublicity.com (shown in Figure 13.6)
http://www.cheappublicity.com/

ExpertPages.com
http://www.expertpages.com/

GuestFinder
http://www.guestfinder.com/

InterviewTour.com
http://www.interviewtour.com/

National Press Club—Directory of News Sources
http://npc.press.org/who/sources.htm

National Talk Show Guest Registry
http://members.aol.com/ntsgr/homepage.html

Profnet
http://www.profnet.com/

Radio Guests
http://www.radioguests.com/

Radio-TV Interview Report
http://www.rtir.com/

Yearbook.com
http://www.yearbook.com/

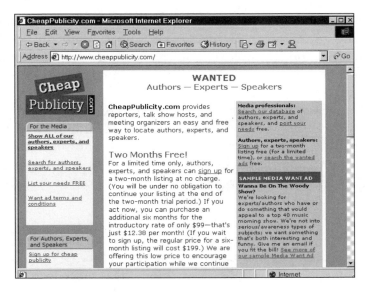

FIGURE 13.6: CheapPublicity.com offers free and fee-based exposure opportunities for authors, experts, and public speakers.

Host Your Own Show

Another way to get on the air is to become a media person yourself. Hosting your own major network TV show may be unrealistic if you have little media experience, but there are many opportunities with not-for-profit, community radio stations and local access cable channels. Community radio stations typically use volunteer talent. Because of the elevated status given to people who host their own radio shows, there may be a lot of competition for open slots. Still, if you serve a unique niche and can speak eloquently on your area of expertise, you may find yourself with your own weekly radio show.

Commercial radio stations used to be legally required to commit a small amount of their programming to community issues. Even though that requirement no longer exists, many stations strive to generate goodwill by providing programs that cover diverse issues. These community-themed shows are often aired at off-peak times, such as early Sunday mornings. However, since these segments are low on the station's priority list, you may be able to pitch an idea for a show that will work in one of those time slots.

Hosting your own TV show can be a bit trickier, but through the wonder of local access cable stations, it is possible. For four years, I hosted my own cable music video program. The music magazine I published at the time was called *Spotlight*. The cable TV show I hosted was called *The Spotlight Video Show*. It wasn't the most creative show name, but it did tie directly into the product I most wanted to promote at the time. The show reached a couple hundred thousand homes every time it aired. There were many dedicated viewers, although I'm sure most people stumbled upon it while flipping channels between *Seinfeld* and *M*A*S*H* reruns. Still, the program provided some great exposure for my music magazine and me.

Most local-access cable channels have limited resources to help you produce your own show. Your best bet is to find a young videographer who has access to cameras and editing equipment and is willing to work for little or no money to gain experience and notoriety. Then contact the cable companies in your area and find out the proper procedure for submitting programs for potential airplay.

Branding by Phone

In the offline world, the telephone remains as one of the more powerful communication tools. Even though a growing number of people are using e-mail instead of making phone calls, don't think you can get away from using the telephone altogether. After face-to-face meetings, phone calls are the best way to establish rapport with people and communicate your brand-related message.

Telephone Tips—Art Sobczak has dispensed useful advice for telephone sales reps for years through his BusinessByPhone.com (http://www.businessbyphone.com/) Web site, newsletters, seminars, books, and other products. Sobczak offers suggestions that could help you with your offline branding efforts: "The secret to telephone sales success is determining and understanding what someone wants and then showing how to get it. That means gathering information before and during the call. Then, when it's time to make your recommendation, you know it's on target." This advice works whether you're talking with a fan, an editor, or another expert. Keep the other person's interests in mind and try to deliver value. Doing so will put you in the best position to get what you want from the transaction.

There are right ways and wrong ways to use the phone. One of the biggest mistakes people make is not having a specific, predefined purpose for making a call. Calling just to touch base is fine when you call to chat with a buddy, but when you get a media person or someone prominent in your industry on the phone, make sure you have an action plan. "Hi, it's Norman Jones here just calling to check in" won't cut it. This statement, on the other hand, would be more powerful: "Hello, Mr. Smith. I'm Norman Jones. I just published a book on how to run better business meetings, and I'd like to give free copies to 20 of your employees." Have an objective that reinforces your brand identity before you pick up the phone.

In addition to being concerned about the calls you make, think about the calls you take. How do you answer incoming phone calls? If you promote a business phone number that is answered by a human being, make sure whoever answers the phone does so with enthusiasm and a smile. If you answer your own business line, do you simply say "Hello" or do you confidently state your name? Using your name and being upbeat makes a far better first impression than answering the phone using whatever mood strikes you at the time.

What happens when you're not available to answer the phone? Hopefully, you use voice mail. If so, does your outgoing voice mail message reinforce your identity? "Sorry I'm not here—leave a message" isn't good enough. Write and record a brand-focused message, such as "Hello. You've reached the office of downhill ski instructor Sarah Kelly. Sorry I'm not here to take your call. I am very interested in hearing your skiing questions and comments, so please leave a message and I'll get back to you as soon as I can." Use every opportunity to reinforce your name and the benefit you offer. The following two Web sites offer free voice mail and other services: **Onebox.com** at http://www.onebox.com/ and **Hotvoice.com** at http://www.hotvoice.com/.

Offering a toll-free telephone number not only provides a convenience for your fans and business partners, it can also be used for branding purposes. Business phone numbers of all types are often transformed into words using the letters on a phone keypad. For example, Enterprise Rent-A-Car uses 1-800-RENT-A-CAR as its branded phone number. The ideal branding situation would be having your name, Web site URL, and toll-free number the same. To contact Cars USA, for instance, you can use 1-800 CARS-USA or http://www.carsusa.com/. Branding efforts work better when everything is in sync.

For many years, 800 was the standard area code for toll-free numbers. In more recent years, the phone companies have been offering other toll-free numbers, too, and more will follow. The wider availability of numbers increases your chances of finding a toll-free number that corresponds to a word or phrase related to your brand. (Keep in mind, though, that you can also apply this numbered phrase technique to regular local phone numbers as well.) Two sites that allow you to search for available toll-free numbers are **AnyWho—Reverse Lookup—Telephone** at http://www.anywho.com/telq.html and **Toll Free Phone Search** at http://www.tollfreephone.com/. Setting up a toll-free number isn't as expensive as you might think, with average rates starting at just several dollars a month. When you're ready to take the toll-free number plunge, look over the following sites to set one up:

1-800 Discount Phone Service
http://www.usapunet.com/one800.htm

4800use.com—800 Numbers
http://4800use.com/800numbers.html

AT&T Small Business
http://www.att.com/smallbusiness/

GreatPhoneRate.com
http://www.greatphonerate.com/1800index.html

***Toll-Free Alternatives**—Here are a couple of interesting 1-800 options. For $15 a month, 1800.com (http://www.1800.com/, shown in Figure 13.7) can give you a URL that matches your toll-free phone number. For instance, if your number is 1-800-555-6789, you could set up the Web address www.1800.com/5556789/. In addition, by using Yahoo! by Phone (http://phone.yahoo.com/) you can offer a free 800 number and get a free voice mail box. The drawback is that the 800 number is the same one used by all Yahoo! by Phone users; callers have to enter a seven-digit ID number in addition to the seven-digit 800 number.*

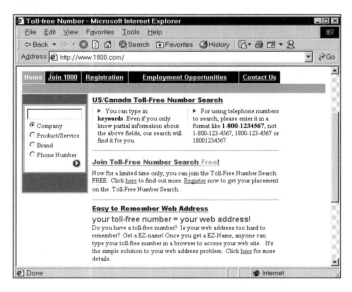

FIGURE 13.7: 1800.com can help you brand your toll-free phone number and turn it into a Web address.

Personal Interaction

The biggest difference between online and in-person communication is the extra dimension of the real world. In the offline world, people aren't limited to your words and a two-dimensional photo. They have you, in the flesh, standing right in front of them. Whether people meet you at a seminar, before or after some other public performance, at a high school reunion, or during a chance meeting at a grocery store, think about the impression you make on people and how it affects your brand.

In addition to your ideas about yourself and your identity, you must also consider the way you look, your posture and body language, the way you speak, and so on. I'm not suggesting you become overly self-conscious, but you should at least consider the many ways your in-person communication style influences your identity. The following list contains four key areas of personal interaction:

Your introduction—When you meet someone who asks you what you do, how do you respond? Do you hem and haw and mutter something like "Well, I do a variety of things that are hard to categorize"? Or do you try to impress people with empty, nonsensical buzzwords, as in "I provide integrated solutions for best-of-breed companies"? Hopefully, you don't do either of these things. I suggest you create what's called an elevator speech. Doing so allows you to succinctly explain who you are, what you do, and how you do it in the time it takes for an average elevator ride (about 20 to 30 seconds). If you can't quickly and effectively explain your identity in that short timeframe, you need to rework your explanation or rethink your brand image.

The way you dress—Looks are important. Whether it's right or wrong, the way you look and the manner in which you dress influence the impressions that people have of you. Throughout the 10 years I published my music publication, I wore jeans and a t-shirt to the office. So did my small staff. The people working for the music stores and recording studios that were my biggest advertisers also dressed casually. Therefore, when I went on sales calls, I usually dressed to complement their styles and my comfort. However, in later years, I dressed more formally when going on sales calls. Lo and behold, when I spiffed up my look, my sales numbers increased and I seemed to be taken more seriously. I've also heard of authors who reported selling more books when they wore a suit during a talk compared to appearances at which they wore jeans and a sports jacket. Consider upgrading your look to match the level of respect you feel you deserve.

Your social skills—I've always admired people who have magnetic, life-of-the-party personalities. Meeting new people and instantly connecting with them seem to come naturally to these social creatures. If you possess such people skills, consider yourself lucky. Most of us, though, have to work at our social abilities. Since I've played in rock bands, hosted my own video show, and achieved a modest level of success, many people assume I have a driven, type-A personality. Not so. I'm not a wallflower at networking events, but it sometimes takes effort to muster the courage to mix and mingle. However, I like meeting new people, and I've learned to interact effectively with others by staying positive, smiling a lot, and asking a lot of questions. Don't think you have to talk a mile a minute to be liked. The best conversationalists are usually the best listeners. The next time you're at a networking function, get busy introducing yourself, smiling, asking questions, and listening. And when the conversation turns to you, be ready with the quick elevator speech I mentioned earlier in this section.

Your enthusiasm—Above all, your positive attitude about life and your sincere interest in your brand identity should shine through everything you do. Whether you are running into a business acquaintance at a conference, doing a live radio interview, or giving a speech, let your enthusiasm show. A person's excitement level can be contagious. Mary Kay Ash, the founder of Mary Kay Cosmetics, once said, "A mediocre idea that generates enthusiasm will go further than a great idea that inspires no one." Put your enthusiasm to work in pumping up your fans about your area of expertise.

Now that we've talked about using the offline world to help establish and reinforce your online identity, it's time to turn our attention to setting online goals and reaching them. Once you have your branding activities firing on all cylinders, you'll need the advice in this next chapter to remain focused and stay on track.

CHAPTER FOURTEEN

Setting Online Goals and Reaching Them

We all know people who are gifted at a particular skill, whether it's making music, writing novels, dispensing advice about dating, or some other ability. However, it seems that only a small percentage of these talented folks ever rise above the fray and experience substantial success. Even people who are smart, personable, and driven often run out of gas and settle for working on their craft in obscurity. This dilemma of lost dreams is especially true on the Internet, where talented people wear out their fingertips on keyboards and strain their eyeballs on computer screens, only to give up in desperation. Why is that?

After meeting and observing many successful people, I've come to the conclusion that individuals who move above and beyond ordinary levels of achievement do a few simple things differently. The actions they take and the attitudes they possess may be simplistic, but these basic success traits make all the difference in the world.

In this chapter, we examine some of these traits as they relate to goal setting, including the following topics:

- Why having a burning desire is crucial to online branding achievement
- How setting realistic goals that challenge you will inspire action
- Why having an online game plan is important
- Why your Master Planner and Daily To-Do List may be your most potent weapons
- How persistence can make or break an online brand identity
- How failure plays a positive role in all success
- Why taking a long-term view is essential in accomplishing short-term activities

Develop a Burning Desire

Have you ever excitedly put a new business plan together, started a writing project, or launched a new service, only to find some weeks or months later that your passion and motivation to continue had sadly melted away? If so, what happened? Most likely, you lost one of the most powerful tools in your success arsenal: burning desire. You may claim to still desire doing the thing you started, but you obviously let go of the reasons why you started it in the first place. Or, quite possibly, your original reason for pursuing a line of work wasn't that strong to begin with.

Desire is the rocket fuel of your online success. It's the magnet that pulls you toward what you truly want out of life. It's burning desire that gets you up early and keeps you up late working on your chosen brand identity. Without it, your inspiration sputters and your progress slows, leading to heaps of frustration and self-doubt. Therefore, before you jump headlong into a new online branding endeavor, make sure you have good answers to the following questions:

- Why do you want to pursue this particular brand image online?
- Whom are you going to serve and whom will you have to become to serve them well?
- How will you grow into the part and enjoy the process?
- How will your brand identity gel with your personal beliefs about people, family, travel, and life in general?
- How will you react if you get negative criticism or rude comments about your line of work?

Fully answering these questions arms you with powerful reasons for pursuing a particular niche on the Internet. The answers also give you the energy you need to market aggressively and proudly display your chosen identity. If you're timid and unsure of yourself, it will reflect in your online presence. You must believe to the core that your image is the right one and best one for you.

To help keep your desire burning, immerse yourself in your field. If you're an aspiring children's book writer, for instance, subscribe to children's book–related e-zines, spend time on book-related discussion forums, introduce yourself to appropriate publishing industry people via e-mail, attend book-related conferences, and more. Every time you make some small progress, your desire builds.

Regardless of your chosen field, surround yourself with upbeat, ambitious people. Your attitude and upbringing may influence your state of mind, but to a great extent, you also become like the people with whom you spend the most time. Negative, directionless people have a way of draining you of your ambition. (No offense to your uncle; you know the one I'm talking about.)

The best way to develop desire is to fully examine the reasons why you want to pursue your brand image. Make sure the identity you plan to promote is in line with your personal beliefs, passions, and lifestyle. Have a plan for interacting with people involved in your area of expertise, expanding your knowledge, and fueling your enthusiasm. Cultivating a burning desire will propel you toward your goals and help you survive the challenges you will surely face.

Set Realistic Goals

Once your mind and attitude are focused and determined to achieve success, and once you've chosen the online identity that's best for you, it's time to get busy pursuing your fair share of fame and fortune. Great, but how much fame and fortune amounts to your fair share? If your only answer is "As much as I can handle" or "Whatever I can get," you may be in trouble.

If you want to avoid becoming an online wannabe who only talks about staking a claim on the Web, you must have a specific destination in mind. In other words, you must set branding goals. You must determine what you need to accomplish in advance so that you know if your progress is on track. There are different types of goals you can set and different criteria for measuring them. The following list offers several tangible categories in which you might set online goals:

- Number of e-zine subscribers
- Number of Web site visitors or page views
- Number of sites and e-zines running your free articles
- Number of incoming links
- Number or dollar amount of sales
- Number of media mentions or reviews you generate
- Number of people who download your free e-book, image, or sound file

You may also consider other important but less tangible goals. For example, you might set goals to learn various aspects of HTML, read a certain number of books on marketing, or to take a Web design class. Along the way, you may also gauge your progress by the reputation you feel you are building among your core audience or by the frequency of positive fan e-mail you receive. Only you can determine what criteria will best indicate how well you are doing at branding yourself online.

Regardless of the measurement standards you choose, setting branding objectives is important for the following three reasons:

They keep you focused on your branding efforts—Setting goals gives you a sense of direction. Without them, you'll aimlessly plod through promoting your online identity without knowing which tasks deserve the most attention.

They give you a gauge by which to measure your progress—After you've engaged in branding activities for a month or two, you need to know whether you should celebrate or go back to the drawing board. If you're attracting more attention than you expected for a few weeks in a row, it's probably time to increase your exposure objectives. If you're falling short of the goals you've set, that's a sign that you need to rethink your approach.

They make sure you don't slip into poor work habits—You've probably heard the cliché about working smarter, not harder. One of the worst things you can do is continue to engage in online tactics that aren't working. Branding goals help you monitor your progress so that you can avoid wasting your time on less-fruitful activities.

You should also write your goals in yearly, monthly, weekly, and daily amounts. For instance, if you want to add 10,000 new e-zine subscribers in the coming year, you'd have to attract 833 subscribers per month, 192 per week, and about 27 per day. Doing the math ahead of time lets you know what you need to accomplish and breaks the amounts into bite-size chunks. Mentally, it's a lot easier to focus on generating 27 new subscribers a day than to worry about the entire 10,000 for the year.

Goals Should Be Specific—When making plans for your online success, the more specific you are the better. Don't write down fuzzy goals such as "Be more active in online discussion forums" or "Get media exposure." Those aspirations are too vague. Instead, write plans more along the lines of "Visit Bill Smith's oil painting discussion forum three times a week" or "Contact two editors or reviewers every day for the next three weeks." Details give your goals clarity.

Different people have different definitions of success. Some would be happy with 2,000 Web site visitors a month, while others would need that many visitors *per day* to be happy. You should set realistic branding objectives based on your situation. You shouldn't set the bar too high and then be disappointed when you can't reach it. On the other hand, setting goals that are too easy to achieve will leave you feeling unchallenged. Set your online goals so that you have to stretch a bit to reach them; the payoff will be that much sweeter.

If you're interested in some free advice on setting goals, check out the following three online articles:

Mind Tools—Setting Goals Effectively
http://www.mindtools.com/pggoalef.html

SmartBiz.com—Success Through Goal Setting
http://www.smartbiz.com/sbs/arts/exe92.htm

Top Achievement—10 Best Ideas for Setting Goals (shown in Figure 14.1)
http://www.topachievement.com/hiltonjohnson.html

FIGURE 14.1: The Top Achievement site offers articles on goal setting and other online success traits.

Have a Game Plan

The best way to explain the importance of having a game plan is to talk about taking a vacation. Let's say that you and your family have set aside one week to go on a vacation together. The designated week is five months away and between now and then you all manage to save $6,000 to spend on the trip. Finally, the first day of your vacation arrives and you all gather at your house.

What happens next? Do you look at your family members and say, "So, does anybody have a good idea on where we should go?" Do you all stand around debating whether you should rent a van or book a flight to your destination? Does your sister suddenly blurt out, "Oh man, I forgot to pack a suitcase!"

Some adventurous folks may enjoy hitting the road without a game plan, but if you're like most people, you go to great lengths to prepare for a vacation. By the time the chosen week rolls around, you have airline tickets reserved, hotel rooms booked, and complete itineraries planned. You probably know how far the hotel is from the airport, what types of attractions are in the area, what the weather is like, and how much it costs to dine out. Why all this planning and fuss? There's a lot riding on a vacation, including the amount of money that's been invested in it, the expectations of family members, and the desire to make it a pleasurable experience for everyone.

Vacations prove that most people have at least some goal setting and planning abilities. Why, then, do the majority of smart people never use these skills to further their personal passions and careers? When it comes to plotting out the course of their lives, they just let things happen randomly, hoping for a decent outcome. Then, 10 years down the road, these people wonder why they're not much better off than they were a decade earlier.

If you suffer any discontent regarding your lack of recognition or respect, chances are you don't have a grip on the big picture that represents your major objectives. If you don't have a series of specific steps you work on every day to move yourself closer to your online goals, how do you expect to get there? Right now I want you to make a commitment that, starting today, you begin treating your life's work with the same precise goal setting that you employ when you plan a vacation—only with a commitment to the long haul.

"To succeed in any area, you've got to have a plan," writes Tod Barnhart in *The Five Rituals of Wealth.* "Just as you can't exercise once and expect to be fit for life, in your financial life you must constantly know where you are, where you're going, and how you're going to get there." The same principle applies to the life of your Internet brand.

Create Your Master Planner and To-Do List

Two simple but essential tools are your Master Planner and Daily To-Do List. The form these tools take is unimportant. You can use a computer program, a Web-based service, a basic paper notebook, or a three-ring binder.

Your Master Planner is where you store all your online branding plans, ideas, goals, brainstorms, and lists of tasks. You may also use this planner to jot down new names, e-mail addresses, Web sites, books, and other resources you hear about. If you're like me, you're guilty of writing notes to yourself on separate scraps of paper that have more of a chance of getting lost than getting things done. Through proper use of your Master Planner, though, every idea, task, and notion you record is available in one convenient source.

While you may use some of your Master Planner to collect random information, you should separate sections in the planner dedicated to the various branding activities you engage in on a regular basis. Some of the possible categories might include Web page design, e-zine content, article ideas, publicity angles, discussion forum themes, linking strategies, and so on. Anytime you think of an idea or task regarding your branding endeavors, write it in the appropriate section. Before long, you'll have a comprehensive record of everything related to your online identity.

But the goal-setting journey doesn't end here. All you've done so far is organize and focus your thoughts and planned activities. Now comes the time to put them into action. If your mind works like mine, you probably didn't have any trouble filling up the pages in your Master Planner. That's a good sign; it shows you're immersed in what it really takes to succeed. However, you may be intimidated by the size of the list you've compiled. Flipping through page after page of numerous notes, you might find yourself overwhelmed by the mountain of actions that you need to take. You may not know where to begin. To overcome this paralysis, you must apply the same tactic a mouse uses to eat a brick of cheese: consume it one nibble at a time.

Your Brand Organization—*To get the most out of planning and goal setting, you must be organized. You should not only have your major goals and ideas recorded, but you should also have your computer and paper files in order, as well as your workspace. Three sites that dish out lots of organizing tips are GetOrganizedNow at* http://www.getorganizednow.com/ *(shown in Figure 14.2), OrganizedHome.com,* http://www.organizedhome.com/, *and OrganizeTips.com,* http://www.organizetips.com/.

FIGURE 14.2: Goal setting is easier when you clear away the clutter. The GetOrganizedNow site provides free articles, tips, and discussion forums related to organizing your home, office, and life.

Your Daily To-Do List helps you weed out the high-priority tasks and gives you a road map to follow. Even if your online branding efforts are part-time, you should strive to do something every day to work toward your goals. Here's the best way to make a Daily To-Do List work: At the end of each day's branding work period, look ahead to the following day. Look through your Master Planner and decide on the most important tasks that need to be accomplished. List only 5 to 10 activities; no more. Then number them in order of importance.

When it's time to start working on your branding goals the next day, you'll already have your plan of action. You won't waste time trying to remember what you need to do or squander away the hours on low-priority tasks. Your job is to get working on the activity you've marked as your number one priority. Stay at it until it's done. Then move on to number two and so on, until as many of the day's priorities as possible are completed.

Before you stop working for the day, take a few minutes to look again at your Master Planner and plot out the next day's activities. Move any of the current day's uncompleted tasks to the new day's list, as long as they're still a priority. Make sure to note any scheduled appointments, then work your priorities around them. Once again, when it's time to start working the following day, get busy on your list. I guarantee you'll feel good as you triumphantly cross off each activity after completing it. Using this plan consistently every day will allow you to nibble away at your online brand-building goals. While each day may seem like a small step toward meeting those goals, after six months to a year, you'll be able to look back and see how incredibly far you've come in a relatively short time.

Are you interested in storing your Master Planner or Daily To-Do List online? The following Web sites provide free online planning and organizing capabilities:

eOrganizer
http://www.eorganizer.com/

JointPlanning (depicted in Figure 14.3)
http://www.jointplanning.com/

Palm.net
http://www.palm.net/

ScheduleOnline
http://www.scheduleonline.com/

Yahoo! Calendar
http://calendar.yahoo.com/

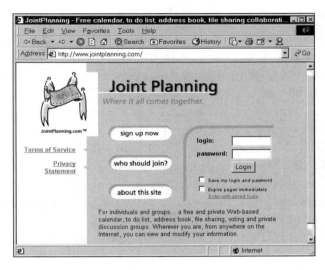

FIGURE 14.3: JointPlanning offers free Web-based calendar, to-do list, address book, and file-sharing features.

If you're willing to buck up for a professional organizing system, check out these sites:

Day-Timer
http://www.daytimer.com/

FranklinCovey
http://www.franklincovey.com/

OrganizeYourWorld.com
http://www.organizeyourworld.com/

Be Persistent

If you're in the early stages of developing an online brand identity, you probably have a head full of ideas, a to-do list filled with success-inducing activities, and more enthusiasm than should be allowed by law. Before long, you'll be fully immersed in the thrill of pursuing your Internet goals. Enjoy this exciting stage of your new vocation.

However, what happens when certain aspects of your online campaign turn sour? How will you react when people you thought you could trust let you down? How will you feel if things progress at a slower rate than you expected? If you're like most people, you'll be tempted to feel like a failure—like your well-intentioned efforts have been wasted. If you face enough challenges, you may even think of giving up your online branding dreams altogether.

As hard as it is to believe, these times of despair often bring us the most strength. For me, low points were usually followed by explosive bursts of achievement. It's not that I love being under pressure or that I ignore the bad stuff that happens. On the contrary, I examine it in detail—which, frankly, can lead to frustration and even mild depression. The key is to strengthen your resolve after you allow yourself to feel some pain—and then use that pain to motivate yourself to do things better in the future.

For five years, I organized an annual music business conference in the Midwest called the St. Louis Regional Music Showcase. It was an enormous undertaking. Every year, I gathered a team of volunteer organizers who helped me manage the event. Just about every year, I assigned organizers who bailed out late in the planning stages, leaving their aspects of the conference in disarray. It was quite frustrating. But instead of getting too worked up, I either found a replacement or ended up doing the job myself. Since I mentally prepared myself for this inevitability, I was able to find a way to work through it.

Inevitably, we all encounter potholes along the path to pursuing worthy goals. Successful people, though, have certain traits that allow them to get over slumps. Most importantly, most successful people have a personal drive and a positive mental attitude that make the ride a lot less bumpy. Marsha Sinetar wrote a book called *Do What You Love, the Money Will Follow*. That wonderful title can be reworked to read "Create the identity you love, the recognition will follow." The philosophy behind those words has been adopted by many prosperous people— from fashion designers and filmmakers to songwriters and performance artists. The longer you persist, the greater the likelihood you'll experience widespread notoriety.

To have faith that the recognition will follow, you must also accept the premise that you may be branding yourself online for a while before the recognition factor catches up. While I've given you hordes of ideas and proven strategies for speeding up the process, chances are you'll still have to deal with the lull between engaging in branding activities and receiving a substantial payoff. During this lull persistence will help you immensely.

When tough times are upon you, give yourself a break. Feel free to take a few hours or a day off to regain your center. At the very least, take a few minutes to clear your mind. After this cooling-off time, think about the questions I posed in the "Develop a Burning Desire" section earlier in this chapter. Examine the reasons why you chose your online identity. Focus on the original vision you had for serving others and enjoying the process. Then get busy making a list of ways you can make things better. That's what persistence is all about: feeling the bumps and then going to work to make your success vehicle sturdier and ready to take the next bump in the road.

When the Going Gets Tough—*The best way to endure obstacles is to prepare a slump-busting game plan. You might make a list of things you'll do to give yourself a break when times get tough. Remember, you're not running from or avoiding your problems—you're just giving yourself a chance to regain a clear head. Here are some possible ways to refresh your soul: pay a visit to a favorite book store, museum, or art exhibit; call or visit a friend or relative you haven't talked to in a long time; take a long walk through a nearby park; or exercise. One effective thing I do to reenergize is look through a file of raving fan compliments. These activities may not be high-tech, but they do serve to cleanse the mental palate.*

View Failure in a Positive Light

No one likes to fail. We avoid it at all costs and feel like rejects when we become its victim. I believe it's the fear of failure that keeps at least half the population from going after truly worthy goals. Why should human beings take the risk of failing, when they can just play it safe and keep doing the routine, comfortable tasks that have been earning them a living all these years?

The point that all these fearful people keep missing is that failure has as much to do with achievement as success does. People who succeed have tried more things and have put themselves on the line more times than the average Joe or Jane. By doing so, they open themselves up to the possibility of stumbling and not getting everything right—in essence, they almost assure themselves of failure.

Author Chad McGrew collected more than 300 rejection letters from agents and editors over the course of eight years. That would be enough failure to convince most people to choose another vocation. Undaunted, McGrew self-published small quantities of two of his novels and landed a few positive reviews in the media. Using those reviews, he eventually attracted the attention of a literary agent. Five days after taking McGrew on as a client, the agent secured a six-figure, two-book deal with a major publisher. Now there is major interest from a Hollywood producer to turn one of his novels into a movie.

In the sports world, consider the case of the most successful baseball players. If players maintain a consistent .300 batting average, they are usually some of the better hitters in the league. That means, on average, they don't get a hit 70 percent of the time they go to the plate. Seven out of 10 times they pick up the bat, they fail. They have to put themselves on the line and fall short that often just to get enough successful at-bats to become the best among their peers.

The same goes for any career that's worth pursuing. How many sour notes did it take B.B. King to get good enough to impress others and make money doing what he loves? How many lousy scenes or questionable movies did Tom Hanks have to go through before reaching the point where he was respected within the movie industry? Behind every success story, you can bet a thousand failures lie. Take chances, learn from your mistakes, and watch your progress unfold.

Do This Failure Exercise—Get out your Master Planner. Start listing some of the failures in your life and work. Especially list the failures associated with your online branding pursuits. Begin with the most recent and work your way back. Don't feel bad if you come up with a lot of them; that just means you're ambitious. Can't think of any failures? Dig a little deeper. Think about times that you took risks or occasions when you embarrassed yourself. Once you have a good list, go through each failure and ask yourself what you learned from the experience. Write down your thoughts and answer these questions:

- *How did going through the negative experience help you along the path to where you are now?*
- *What positive things can you say about the negative situation?*
- *How many of your perceived failures turned out to be blessings in disguise?*
- *How different would your outlook be if you used the words "blessing," "project," or "challenge" instead of "failure" or "problem"?*

Examining your attitude toward failure can be therapeutic. Some healthy introspection may help you overcome the stigma of feeling defeated and enable you to view your failures as the productive lessons that they are.

Pursue Long-Term Planning

In the "Create Your Master Planner and To-Do List" section earlier in this chapter, we discussed using a Daily To-Do List—a tool that allows you to take the many entries in your Master Planner and weed out the most important tasks for each day. As important as short-term action is, your efforts are strengthened when your immediate goals are directly tied to a long-term plan. Think of your long-term plan as an entire highway that stretches for miles and disappears into the horizon. Your Daily To-Do List is generally concerned with the road along the next mile, while your long-term plan takes into account the whole journey.

Plans are meant to evolve. The action steps you come up with when goal setting may change as you work toward them. Years ago when I set a goal to publish my own local music publication, I had no idea that it would lead to becoming a published author and, eventually, the owner of a highly traveled music-related Web Site (in fact, in those days, Web sites didn't even exist). Had I not set out on my initial publishing goal, I may never have ended up where I am today.

Coming up with an idea, visualizing it in your mind, and acting on it drives you to accomplish something. While the final destination isn't always the one you expected, it's usually the outcome for which you're the most thankful. By motivating yourself to head in a specific direction—whatever direction that is—

you create the opportunities from which real success can be realized. By waiting for things to happen, though, you set the stage for stagnation. That's why long-term planning is so important.

What follows are 10 tips for getting the most out of your long-term plans:

1. **Decide specifically what you want.** Before you set out to conquer your branding goals, you have to know what it is you really want. Do you have a clear idea of what you're going after? Vague concepts about some day being an online celebrity lead to vague, weak actions in attaining them. However, detailed target goals—such as selling 500 copies of your e-book, doing 10 radio interviews a month, generating 2,000 downloads of your free PDF file—keep you focused and on track.

2. **Visualize what you want as if you already have it.** To be truly successful with goal setting, you must have a clear picture of the eventual outcome in your mind. Close your eyes and imagine what being an online success would be like. Immerse yourself in that picture and feel the sensations. What would your typical day be like? What would it look, sound, feel, taste, and smell like if you were already in that enviable position? Locking in on these mental images sets you on an unstoppable course.

3. **Write down your plans.** Don't only keep goals in your head. Put ink to paper or fingers to a keyboard and commit your aspirations to a tangible form. Writing down your goals adds another element of conviction to your intent to reach them. All of my accomplishments—publishing my music magazine, writing this book, producing a widely read e-zine—started as notes to myself jotted down in a notebook. Don't overlook the power of the pen.

The Daily Brainstorm—*Your mind is like a well-toned muscle. To keep it fit and flexible, you need to give your brain regular workouts. Set aside 20 minutes or so at a specific time each day to write random ideas in a notebook. Use the time for brainstorming new ways to promote your Web site, creative marketing ideas, or concepts for your next site redesign. However you approach it, spend time generating fresh concepts every day. Then incorporate the best ideas from these sessions into your long-term action plans. For more information on brainstorming, check out Creative Think at* http://www.creativethink.com/ *(shown in Figure 14.4), a site presented by Roger von Oech, author of the creative-thinking book* A Whack on the Side of the Head.

---

4. **Make a list of what's in it for you.** This is a fun exercise. Compile a list of ways you will benefit from achieving your branding goals. Will you be rewarded with recognition, self-fulfillment, money, fame, or creative expression? By listing the benefits, you examine your true motivation for wanting the goals in the first place. Sometimes you'll discover the reasons

FIGURE 14.4: Roger von Oech's Creative Think site inspires visitors to examine challenges and opportunities in a fresh light.

that drive you aren't the most productive (such as being lured by the prospect of making gobs of money, even though your heart isn't really into it). However, when you have a goal that's fueled by a genuine desire and true belief in your ability to attain it, you'll be energized and ready to take on the challenges.

5. **Identify the information and resources you need to achieve your goals.** You may already know that it's a good idea to have a database that includes Web sites, e-zines, experts, organizations, and so on. In addition, you should make a list of the things you need to learn to reach your goals. For instance, if you want to add a subscription form to your home page, do you know the proper way to use CGI scripts to create one? If you want to produce a free e-book, do you know how to convert a Word file to a PDF format? Look through your list of goals and figure out whether a lack of knowledge is keeping you from making progress. Then get busy acquiring the information you lack.

6. **Set deadlines.** Remember how you always got off your butt and went to work the night before a term paper was due? Deadlines have a way of motivating us to act. So do commitments we make to others and ourselves. Set a time limit for achieving each stage of your goal-setting action plan. Then do whatever it takes to meet those deadlines. Make sure your

deadlines are realistic. They should strike a balance by being far enough away to allow you time to reach them, but soon enough to motivate you to meet them.

7. **Create your plan.** To write the first draft of an action plan, start with the goal itself and work backward through the process. Keep breaking down every stage of the plan into its most basic tasks, such as gathering rate information, sending e-mails, registering domain names, and writing articles. Next, make a short list of the primary things that need to be done first, making sure they're attainable steps. For instance, if your goal is to get major media exposure, you wouldn't make calling *Time* magazine your first task. You'll take a whole series of preliminary steps long before you get near a major media outlet. (Media coverage is discussed in detail in Chapter 11, "Exposing Your Identity Through Online Publicity.")

8. **Re-examine and refine your plan.** Long-term plans are not set in stone the moment they are written. They should be revised and improved. The first step to refining your plan is to get away from it for a while and let the details float around in your subconscious mind while you work on other things. Then come back to the plan with a fresh eye and start evaluating the logic in your sequence of events. For instance, have you really allowed enough time for designing your Web site? Does your plan have you juggling too many or too few projects at the same time? Also ask yourself what additional help you might need with technical support, software purchases, artwork, writing media releases, and other tasks. Then plot out your second-draft plan as best you can. It doesn't have to be perfect. Don't fool yourself into thinking you can't get started just because you don't yet know a few things. Trust your abilities and know you can handle challenges when they come up.

9. **Take action.** Before long, you have to get busy working on the plan you've just created. It's tragic, but a lot of great ideas wither away because the person who came up with them never takes action. Don't let this be your fate. Don't wait for nature to takes its mystical course. Vow to yourself that every day you will take some action based on your branding plan. Even if you think you don't have time or you aren't feeling motivated, do at least some small deed every day. Even if it's only tweaking one of your Web pages or sending one e-mail message to a fan, do something every day.

10. **Measure your progress.** Once you come up with your Internet branding plan and start working on it every day, you have to know whether your actions are leading you in the right direction. Are you moving closer to your goal or further away? Is the pace slower or faster than you anticipated? The

only way to answer those questions is to evaluate your plan and measure your progress regularly. If you find that you're way behind schedule on getting things done, ask yourself what you can do to get the result you really want. Making adjustments to your plan is an essential part of the goal-setting process. Be prepared to measure often and come up with solutions. When something is working, fit more of it into the plan. When other aspects prove to be duds, cut back or drop them completely. Fine-tuning is what goal setting is all about.

You Don't Have to Start Your Plan from Scratch—*Creating a branding action plan takes a lot of work. The good news is that I've provided you with a sample road map in Appendix B, A 12-Month Action Plan. Use this one-year plan as a starting point. Alter it to suit your own experience level and long-term goals.*

Final Thoughts

If you've read most or all of this book, it's safe to say you have a serious interest in creating an online identity based on who you are and what you do. Congratulations! By investing some of your time in this book, you've separated yourself from the majority of people who never move beyond fleeting daydreams of making a name for themselves. You are taking action on your desires, and for that you should be proud.

Most people live their lives without a sense of purpose. Multitudes long to do something that gives them a feeling of contribution—to engage in an activity that improves the lives of others while enriching their own lives. That longing is an admirable aspiration and one that you have every right to want to pursue.

This book gives you the tools you need to achieve your online branding goals. You now have the basic technical knowledge to gain access to the Internet, set up a Web site, publish an e-mail newsletter, network through online forums, communicate with the media, and more. You also have suggestions on how to determine and direct your personal passions, craft the best online identity for you, set realistic goals, and so on.

What now? Will you tuck this book away in a drawer and go back to dreaming about making an impact on the world? If you've already been online for a while, will you continue to operate in a way that confuses readers and visitors and slows your progress? Or will you take the tools and ideas in these pages and act on them to focus your efforts and improve your lot in life? The decision is yours.

The online world will continue to evolve and grow in the years to come. What changes lie ahead may be unclear, but one thing is certain: The Internet is here to stay. I encourage you to jump in, stake a claim, and make yourself known to the many thousands of people who are ideally suited to become your new fans.

I'd also like to hear about the successes you achieve and the challenges you face as you brand yourself online. I'll post some of your best stories at a special Web site set up for this book at **Branding Yourself Online** at http://BrandingYourselfOnline.com/. Please visit the site. You may also write or e-mail using the following addresses:

Branding Yourself Online
c/o Bob Baker
P.O. Box 43058
St. Louis, MO 63143
E-mail: bob@bob-baker.com

I wish you the best in creating a focused identity for yourself and hope you get what you really want from your online branding efforts—and from your life!

Online Success Stories

Sometimes, the best way to pursue a goal is to learn from others who have ventured down similar paths. This appendix features questions and answers from 13 people who know a thing or two about crafting an online identity, including the following:

Larry Chase—He started the first online ad agency, is the co-author of *Essential Business Tactics for the Net, 2nd Edition,* and publisher of the widely read e-mail newsletter *Larry Chase's Web Digest for Marketers.*

Ilise Benun—She is perhaps best known as the editor and publisher of the print newsletter *The Art of Self Promotion.* Ilise is also author of the book *Self Promotion Online.*

Rob Frankel—He is a branding consultant, speaker, and author of *The Revenge of Brand X.* Rob also moderates **Adventive.com**'s I-Branding discussion list.

Angela Adair-Hoy—She is the co-owner of **WritersWeekly.com** and **Booklocker.com**, as well as the co-author (with M.J. Rose) of *How to Publish and Promote Online.* Angela has been covered in such high-profile media outlets as *Time* and *Wired* magazines, and she generates more than $5,000 a month in e-book sales.

M.J. Rose—In 1998, she self-published her erotic thriller, *Lip Service,* and promoted it almost exclusively on the Internet. The book created such an online buzz, it ended up being a featured selection of the Doubleday Book Club and was later published by Pocket Books.

Nick Usborne—He is an e-commerce consultant and speaker. Nick also writes regular columns for ClickZ and other Web-based and print publications.

Brian Alt—He publishes and moderates the E-mail Publishing Digest and is the former managing editor for **Ezine-Tips.com.** Brian is also author of *The Insider Guide to Power Ezine Promotion.*

Laura Ries—Along with her father, Al Ries, she is a partner in the brand strategies consulting firm Ries & Ries. The father–daughter team has written two books, *The 11 Immutable Laws of Internet Branding* and *The 22 Immutable Laws of Branding*.

Damon G. Zahariades—He is the author of *The Special Report Bible*, a manual on how to write, package, and sell specialized reports. Damon also publishes a popular e-mail newsletter called *Web Business Today!*.

Raleigh Pinskey—A veteran speaker and marketing consultant, she is the author of many books, including *101 Ways to Promote Yourself*, *The Zen of Hype*, and *101 Ways to Get On Talk Shows*.

Jim Daniels—He is the author of *Insider Internet Marketing* and *Make a Living Online*. As the Webmaster of **BizWeb2000.com**, he's been featured in *Entrepreneur* and *Smart Computing* magazines. Jim also publishes an e-zine called the *BizWeb e-Gazette*, which generates about 1,000 new subscribers a week.

Geoffrey Kleinman—He operates two successful Web sites: **The Kleinman Report**, a resource for new Internet users, and **DVD Talk**, an online source for DVD movie news. Geoffrey's wife, Heather, runs two sites: **Heather Kleinman's Cosmetic Connection** and **The Makeup Diva**, both of which feature cosmetic product reviews and beauty tips.

Carla Hall—She is a singer-songwriter who has used the Internet extensively to promote her career. She is the author of *The DIY (Do-It-Yourself) Guide to the Music Biz* and frequently presents music business seminars in New York City.

As the previous list demonstrates, some of the people featured in this appendix are celebrities in their own right; some are authors or marketing experts; others are up-and-coming online personalities—but all of them offer a perspective that should help you with your Internet branding efforts.

Larry Chase

After 16 years of working for New York advertising agencies, Larry Chase started the first online ad agency in 1993. Since then, he's been frequently quoted regarding Internet marketing issues in major media outlets such as CBS, CNN, the *New York Times*, *Business Week*, and *Inc.* magazine. Larry is the co-author of *Essential Business Tactics for the Net, 2nd Edition*, and publisher of *Larry Chase's Web Digest for Marketers*, a widely read e-mail newsletter. Visit his Web site, **LarryChase.com**, at http://www.larrychase.com/ or e-mail him at me@larrychase.com.

What's the first thing people should know about online branding?
The Internet is a huge environment—too large for any one person to fully comprehend. Therefore, you shouldn't be concerned with branding yourself to

every being on the Net; that's too unfocused. Your mission is to laser-target one, two, or three niches within that huge biosphere and concentrate your power, your expertise, and your brand within those spaces.

In this way, the Net is like a small village. UNIX wizard Chris Graham calls this "tribal marketing." In this tribe or village, reputation is everything. You don't want to risk your reputation for short-term gains at the expense of losing your long-term face. Contribute to your tribe. Figure out what your target tribe needs, and then fill it with a Web site, an e-mail newsletter, or a moderated discussion list. For example, John Audette moderates the I-Sales discussion list and has garnered a reputation that goes far beyond his 8,000 participants.

Should marketers expect immediate results on the Internet?
No. Often, people visit a book site or movie site and not buy the book or go to the flick. Nevertheless, they are left with an impression of the brand. Even though they didn't buy the product that time, a visit to a site for information on, let's say, the *Batman* movie, may well pave the way for the next sequel. In other words, the visit today may help next year's sale. Think of it as a placeholder in a future customer's mind.

Can you explain the importance of giving potential customers what they want?
One of the most critical keys to branding to your constituency is to respect people's time. Since many of us don't have the reputation of Procter & Gamble or IBM, we're obliged to tell a Web site visitor what we do, why we do it, and how we do it. While it's not intentional, I've noticed that many personal and small-company Web sites come across as oblique when telling visitors exactly what they do. I often run into flowery mission statements that sound too self-absorbed: "This company was founded on a deep-seeded philosophy that everything is everything...." Readers may just get bored and end up going elsewhere. It's imperative to predict what visitors to your Web site want and when they want it. In short, be your customer or potential customer; then create a Web site that you would want to visit.

If I visit your site, I'd ask myself, "Is my time on your Web site well spent?" If I have to grope around to find your point, the time isn't well spent. If I have to wait for your graphics to load on my slow or average modem connection, the time isn't well spent. But if you give me a speedy experience that pays off in adding value to me, it is. Figure out what visitors want and serve it up sooner than later.

What are some online branding pitfalls to avoid?
Whether in a discussion list of your peers, in a one-to-one e-mail, or on your Web site, people in this medium respect you for doing your homework. If you

ask questions of a discussion list that could've been found elsewhere with ease, you're either a newbie or lazy. If you're a newbie, the people on that list will hopefully treat you with respect and point you to the information you requested. If you're lazy and repeatedly take without giving, you start to tarnish your personal brand in that community, which consists of people you wish to influence.

What's your best advice on marketing a personal brand name online?
When naming your firm or Web site, give it an obvious name from a branding perspective. Larry Chase's *Web Digest for Marketers* tells you exactly what you get. It's also helpful for the search engines. Clever names are too cryptic. People like names that spell out exactly what a company does, such as Danny Sullivan's Search Engine Report or John Kremer's Book Marketing Tip of the Week.

Ilise Benun

Ilise Benun is a self-promotion specialist and publisher of a quarterly print newsletter called *The Art of Self Promotion*. She is the author of *Self Promotion Online* (North Light Books), as well as two handbooks: *133 Tips to Promote Yourself and Your Business* and *Making Marketing Manageable*. Her articles have been featured in magazines such as *Working Woman*, *HOW* magazine, and *Nation's Business*. Ilise has two Web sites: **Art of Self Promotion** at http://www.artofselfpromotion.com/ (shown in Figure A.1) and **Self-Promotion Online** at http://www.selfpromotiononline.com/. She can be reached by e-mail at ilise@artofselfpromotion.com.

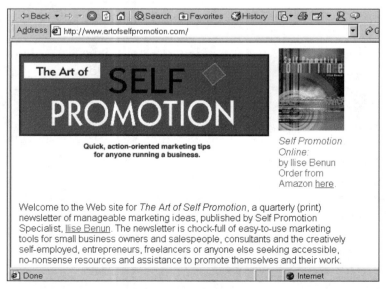

FIGURE A.1: The Art of Self Promotion announces the availability of Ilise Benun's newsletter and book about online promotion.

You made the transition from publishing a print newsletter to both a print and an online presence. What challenges do individuals face when promoting themselves online after years of offline marketing?
The biggest challenge was taking the offline identity I'd created and transferring it to the Web. Many people get bored with their identity and want to give it some spice. But if you change it too much, it won't be recognized as the same brand and you'll lose the equity you've invested over the years. There must be a connection between what people see online and offline.

What's the best way to describe your own brand identity and how did you determine that identity?
I help creative people get the word out about their work. I determined that by integrating what I was doing with the response I was getting to my self-promotion. I started putting the word out in as many places as I could and the most enthusiastic response I got was from the creative community, in particular graphic designers, illustrators, and other commercial artists. I responded by targeting them more actively and directly, and it snowballed from there.

Should people find specific segments within their market to make a splash in?
It is essential to choose a niche and promote yourself as an expert in that niche. That makes it easier for people to understand what you do. Yes, they pigeonhole you and may not be able to see you as anything else, but that option is better than the fuzzy feeling someone may have about you if you don't choose a niche. If all people can say about you is, "He does some kind of computer thing," there's no way they'll be able to spread word of mouth about you.

How important is using basic e-mail to one's online success?
An e-mail address is the most important marketing tool—one that can work for you or against you. Sometimes, your e-mail address is the only thing people see. They may see it on a list, in a directory, or in their e-mail inbox. If it doesn't say clearly who you are and what you do, they may not inquire further. Also, people I've interviewed say they determine whether to open an e-mail message by the return e-mail address. If they recognize it, they open it; if they don't recognize it, they delete it.

My e-mail address, ilise@artofselfpromotion.com, says a lot about me. *Ilise* tells recipients my name, not just my initials or some cryptic form of my name. *Artofselfpromotion.com* tells them the name of my business as well as what my business is about. The fact that it's a domain name also indicates that a Web site may be available and they just may take a moment to visit.

However, if your e-mail address is the pet name your husband calls you, your Buddhist name, or a fancy wordplay on something you do, like *songfull@* or *singfeld@*, you may miss the opportunity to interest someone who may look at that and be confused. Also, sharing an e-mail address with someone so that the address is a combination of your names is fine for personal use. But for business use, it comes through as unprofessional and, worse, doesn't provide useful information.

You've addressed storytelling in your writings. What is that and how can storytelling be applied to online branding?
I recommend that people use stories to describe their services and products instead of spouting a list of features and benefits. There is a time and place for both, but stories are much more engaging and, therefore, more likely to be read and understood. Stories about how you helped a client or how you turned a project around quickly could be posted on a Web site page called Success Stories or included in an e-mail message. Stories can also be used effectively to respond to the simple introductory question: What do you do?

Why are tip sheets such strong, identity-building tools?
Tip sheets—and their online sibling, tip-filled e-mail newsletters—are strong marketing tools because they tie useful information to a person's identity. Instead of a brochure that says, "I know about this and that, blah, blah, blah," which anyone can say, tip sheets prove that point and therefore imply expertise.

Why should freelancers pursue speaking opportunities?
Public speaking extends the power of tip sheets by proving your expertise even further. The best and clearest impression you can make on someone is in person. That's why face-to-face meetings are so effective. That's why salespeople just want 10 minutes of your time. Imagine, then, the effect of making an impression on a group of people. Your chances of finding customers multiply. Also, because so many people are afraid of public speaking, people are impressed by anyone who has the guts to get up in front of a group and give a presentation.

What do you consider the most important things a person can do to create a brand identity online?
Four things come to mind as being the most crucial:

- Include a signature file in all outgoing e-mail messages that includes a seven-word blurb that succinctly describes what you do and who you do it for. For example, "I help creative people promote their services." Seven is an arbitrary number, but you get the point. This reinforces your identity every time someone gets an e-mail message from you.

- Make examples of your work available online, either on your Web site or someone else's.
- Post testimonials from customers and clients.
- Participate in discussion forums and mailing lists in a way that demonstrates your expertise. Contribute on a regular basis, answer questions, offer resources, and be generous with your information.

Rob Frankel

Rob Frankel is a branding consultant, speaker, and author of *The Revenge of Brand X*. He is the self-described "moderating dictator" of two discussion lists: **FrankelBiz** at http://www.frankelbiz.com/ and the I-Branding list hosted by **Adventive** at http://www.adventive.com/. Rob also publishes a weekly e-zine called *FrankelTips*. His personal Web site is **RobFrankel.com** at http://www.robfrankel.com/. Reach him by e-mail at Rob@robfrankel.com.

Is establishing an identity as a person similar to establishing an identity as a company?
It's not just similar; it's identical. The problem is that few people really know what branding is. A brand for a business is more than a name and a logo. Likewise, you as a person are more than your name and your face. People forget that branding is 100 percent nonrational. The quirks, personality, habits, and mannerisms that brand a business are the same as those that people use to determine if they love you, hate you—or worse—don't care. Remember, advertising grabs minds. Branding grabs hearts. Branding is what cultivates devotion and loyalty, and turns users into evangelists.

What are the biggest mistakes people make when branding themselves?
First, people confuse *branding* with *awareness*. You have to create your brand first. Then, once it's created, you can start publicizing it. That's the only time you should advertise. Awareness is only part of the equation. Cancer has high awareness, but that doesn't mean everyone wants it.

The second biggest mistake is that people try to create their own brands. In my book, I list Frankel's Laws of Big Time Branding. The first law is that "Brands are not about you; brands are about them." That means brands are for the people who don't know you. You already know how great you are, so why waste time stroking yourself? Brands have to be done from the outside in, by a disinterested third party.

What are the top things a person should do to establish a focused identity online?

- Create a brand.
- Deploy the brand consistently throughout your enterprise. Ask yourself, are we doing it the (insert your name) way? You'll find the brand lives in the tiniest details.
- Establish yourself as a leader in your field and back it up with hard evidence. For example, I have a book, tapes, a client list, articles, and more packed into my site.
- Give. I make sure nobody leaves my site empty-handed. I offer free access to my article archive, free participation in my branded community, **FrankelBiz.com**. I also present a one-hour, real-time chat every Monday morning called Frankel's Free Clinic.

How important is writing style when conveying one's personality online?
The best advice I can give is write the way you talk. If you try to impress people, most of them get turned off. Eventually, they're going to meet you anyway. You might as well let them see the real you through your writing. That way, the people who would never hire you go away faster; the people who dig your style sign up that much faster.

What are your thoughts on the importance of focus and specialization—not trying to be all things to all people?
Everyone freaks out about losing business because every customer calls for something different. In my tapes, I talk about the Bridge to Leadership, which basically says you have to prioritize one thing so that people will know why they should call. It doesn't mean you have to stop doing everything else, but you should lead with one thing so that customers can follow. Otherwise, nobody knows why they should call.

Don't forget that search engines work on a keyword basis. People type in exactly what they're looking for. If you're all over the map, you rank lower. Last week, Google ranked me number one for "branding" because that's what I stress. (See Chapter 5, "Creating Your Personal Brand Web Site," for a discussion of search engines and keywords.)

Can you explain the difference between customers and evangelists?
Customers buy because they have to. Evangelists not only buy from you, they gladly pay a premium for the same product and encourage their friends and associates to do the same. A prime example is Apple Macintosh. For years, everyone predicted Apple's demise. But Mac users insisted on buying them and

wouldn't consider going to PCs. It's the brand that will not die, despite the claims that "they don't make enough software" or "they're more expensive than PCs."

Angela Adair-Hoy

Angela Adair-Hoy is the owner of **WritersWeekly.com,** http://www.writersweekly.com/, an e-zine and Web site that provide writers with freelance job listings and offer dozens of books for writers, many of which are written by Angela. She also owns **Booklocker.com** at http://www.booklocker.com/, a site that primarily sells e-books written by independent authors and publishers. Angela has been covered in *Time* magazine, *Wired, Publisher's Weekly*, and hundreds of other media outlets. She generates more than $5,000 a month in e-book sales alone. Angela also co-authored an e-book with M.J. Rose (featured in the next section of this appendix) called *Secrets of Our Success*. The e-book garnered so much attention that several traditional publishers bid to win the rights to publish it in paperback. It has since been published by Griffin as *How to Publish and Promote Online*. Reach Angela by e-mail at angela@writersweekly.com.

How did you make the switch from publishing a monthly print newsletter, ***The Write Markets Report,*** **to existing primarily online?**
I simultaneously published in print and online in the beginning. I made the jump to electronic distribution only after I determined that I could drop the price of *The Write Markets Report* and increase the profit margin at the same time.

Can you explain the role that publishing e-books had in your growth?
In 1997, when I self-published one of the first e-books ever, *How to Be a Syndicated Newspaper Columnist,* my sales increased dramatically. With the second e-book, sales doubled; with the third, they tripled, and so on. I realized that the same readers would buy every book I wrote.

How important is your free e-zine to your online success?
WritersWeekly.com, the e-zine, is the means of my financial survival. If I didn't have a way to remind customers every Wednesday that I'm here for them, I'd be out of business.

What's the best way to sum up your brand identity and how did you determine that identity?
WritersWeekly.com is known as me, Angela Adair-Hoy. I portray a personal image and my readers feel like they know me; like they're in my home office visiting me each Wednesday. I am genuinely friendly and kind to strangers and

this has helped to build the brand and make my e-zine and site a personal place to obtain writing assignments and help.

The WritersWeekly brand was determined by accident. I had no idea that my personal touches would build the site into such a huge empire. I now have 800 authors on **Booklocker.com** and 46,000 subscribers to *WritersWeekly.com*.

What are some of the most effective ways you attract attention online?
I provide what nobody else wants to spend time providing. I interview magazine editors to obtain market listings for writers and uncover each editor's current needs. Nobody else does this online to the extent I do. Most of my competitors simply reprint writer's guidelines. Writers know that to get a writing assignment this week, their best bet is to check out the current issue of *WritersWeekly.com*.

Any thoughts on the importance of remaining focused and consistent with a brand image?
It's tempting for creative people to branch out and try new things. Unfortunately, often these new things are out of focus with the company's line of business. If the new product or service you're considering doesn't complement the rest of your company, find something that does.

What do you do offline to market your activities?
Everything I do is online.

What are the most important things an individual can do to create a brand identity online?
Be yourself; don't treat customers like numbers, answer every single e-mail, and find something different—your own niche that will make people take notice.

M.J. Rose

M.J. Rose is widely recognized as one of the first authors to get a major book publishing deal after self-publishing exclusively on the Internet. When traditional publishers shied away from her erotic thriller, *Lip Service*, she decided to promote it herself.

In the summer of 1998, she set up shop on the Internet and began targeting female-friendly Web sites with an interest in books and erotica. At first, she sold *Lip Service* as an e-book and later self-published a printed version that became a best-seller on Amazon.com's small-press list. The book became a featured selection of the Doubleday Book Club and the Literary Guild. Soon after, Pocket Books offered the author a substantial advance to publish her book in hardcover and paperback.

Her e-publishing exploits have been covered extensively in the media, from *Forbes* and *Time* magazines to *USA Today* and the *Wall Street Journal*. M.J. Rose has since written two more novels, *Private Places* and *In Fidelity*, and co-authored *How to Publish and Promote Online* with Angela Adair-Hoy (see the preceding section of this appendix). Her Web sites include **MJRose.com** at http://www.mjrose.com/ and **The-Intercom.net** at http://www.the-intercom.net/. Reach her by e-mail at MJRoseauthor@aol.com.

What steps did you take to reach readers when you started self-publishing online?

For more than six months, I spent about six hours a day, six days a week, targeting reviewers and Web sites that reached the type of people who I felt would be most interested in my book.

What are some of the top things a person can do to establish a focused identity online?

Use your URL everywhere. Make your identity as unique as possible and tie it into your major area of expertise or service. Also, join and maintain a relationship with as many mailing lists and newsgroups as you have time for—and be generous with your information. Give a lot away for free when you start out. Never be rude or flame anyone online. It lives forever in some database. Also, make sure your identity is easy to understand. Don't try to be many different things—be an author *or* a lawyer *or* a harmonica expert, but not all three. (See Figure A.2 to see how M.J. distinguishes herself online.)

FIGURE A.2: M.J. Rose displays her name prominently on her Web site and uses a striking photo to connect her image with her name.

If someone is not a writer per se, what's the importance of writing style in conveying one's personality online?
Online, there is nothing but words. Your words can be simple; in fact, they should be simple. Nothing needs to be exotic or fancy. If you can't write to save your life, hire someone who can.

What advice do you have for people who are in the early stages of promoting an identity online and may be frustrated by slow progress?
It is a slow build, but Internet marketing is also a free ride. Very little costs money online, so it's not as if you're spending $20,000 and getting nothing back for it. It took me about five months—once I figured out the right way to do it—to go from having no Web presence to having a very respectable one. If you are not patient, the Internet isn't the marketing opportunity for you.

Nick Usborne

Nick Usborne is an author, speaker, and consultant in the area of e-commerce. He helps marketers see the customer's point of view and writes extensively on the power of words to communicate online and off. He writes a weekly column for **ClickZ** at http://www.clickz.com/. Visit Nick's Web site, **NickUsborne.com**, at http://www. nickusborne.com/. Reach him by e-mail at nick@nickusborne.com.

How important is writing style in conveying one's personality online?
It's everything. Well, not quite everything. Design also has a lot to do with crafting a personality online. But in terms of ongoing communication of your personality through your site and your e-mails, writing is the simplest and most flexible way to express who you are. Words are your voice. They are the expression of your character.

Why is dry, lackluster prose so commonplace?
Because nobody is paying attention. The early, crazy years of doing business online were dominated by the investment of billions of dollars into software *solutions*. For a while, everyone figured that he who invested the most in the best software would win. That turned out not to be the case. Who, in that climate, would invest in words? Words are commonplace; they are open source. With words, there's nothing to patent and no great upswing for your investors.

Lackluster prose is ineffective on the Internet, because dry prose is invisible. Nobody bothers to read it. So many sites compete for our attention. Writing styles online have been crafted through the process of keyboard rap—millions of users sending billions of e-mails and instant messages. The language of the Net has been determined not by the advertisers or big companies, but by hundreds of millions of regular people. Their writing has spontaneity and energy and they expect no less when they go to Web sites or receive e-mails and newsletters. Yes, they want content and clarity, but they also crave character.

Is a conversational writing style good—and if so, why?
A more informal approach to writing helps when you're online because the online environment is close to you. If you write a brochure for someone to read thousands of miles away and months after you wrote it, there is no proximity. In that scenario, you write formally. The Web and e-mail give you far greater proximity. When we're close to the person or people to whom we're communicating, we tend to become more conversational—we communicate in a way that is closer to how we talk. Look at instant messaging. It's informal and close to speech.

From a branding standpoint, what should someone do before sitting down to craft the words that appear in an e-zine or on a Web site?
First, be honest and sincere about who you are. People sniff out a fraud quickly. But within that honesty, have a little fun. Build yourself as a cartoonist draws a caricature. It's you, but more so. Make the most of those things that make you a *character*. If you want to be noticed, you need to stand out from the crowd.

What are some of the biggest misconceptions or mistakes that people make when creating a brand identity online?
They believe that their character or personal brand can be static. It can't. You can't put a photo and some text on your home page and think the job is done. The Web is not a brochure. You have to *be* your character and your brand. As they say, "Don't tell me you're funny, tell me a joke." Don't try to *build* a personal brand—be it, relentlessly, daily.

What are the top things a person should do to establish a focused identity online?
Have something worthwhile to say. Find an audience that gives a damn. Love your audience.

Brian Alt

Brian Alt is the founder and CEO of **Email Possibilities**, http://emailpossibilities.com/, a provider of e-mail publishing solutions. He also publishes and moderates the **E-mail Publishing Digest** at http://epdigest.com/, which features a daily article and a discussion community for e-mail publishing professionals. Brian is author of *The Insider Guide to Power Ezine Promotion* and a former managing editor for **Ezine-Tips.com**, http://www.ezine-tips.com/. Reach him at brian@emailpossibilities.com.

What role does an e-zine owner's personality play in branding an online identity?
It's vitally important. It's not personality in the traditional sense of the word, but rather the e-zine publisher's voice that shows through his or her writing. There are literally thousands of e-mail publications. One good way to make yours stand out is to bring something unique to it. This, of course, assumes that you are already publishing the best content possible. Readers become accustomed to a certain style of writing, and consistency in this area encourages subscribers to become loyal readers. For most people doing business online, personality is expressed in their written words. So it's important for online business owners to express themselves well in writing.

Is branding far more challenging if the e-zine owner is a lackluster writer or uses mostly freelance writers for content?
Absolutely. I recommend to all of my readers and clients that the owners have some personality stake in their e-zine. Meaning, even if they use content from freelancers or staff writers, they should also contribute themselves, even if it's simply in the form of an "Intro from the Publisher." If freelance or staff writers produce most of your e-zine content, make sure to create incentives for them to stick around. Once other writers establish the personality of your e-zine, it's not in your best interest for them to leave.

What are some of the most important things a person can do with an e-zine to carve a focused identity?
For starters, provide unique, top-notch content to your readers. Give them something they can't get elsewhere. Publish on a consistent schedule and make sure that the issues are frequent enough to engage the audience. Monthly e-zines, for example, are published so infrequently that they really need to be something special to cultivate a loyal following. Weekly e-zines stand a much greater chance of keeping an audience enthusiastic about each issue. Subscribers won't forget about the existence of the e-zine between issues.

E-zines are also great for generating feedback from readers. By asking for feedback and responding to it, e-zine publishers develop super fans that not only stay loyal, but create other loyal readers through recommendations.

What are your thoughts about the importance of focus and specialization as it applies to e-zines?
Too many e-zines aren't focused enough. I usually recommend that if an e-zine can't be the first or best in a given category, try to narrow or modify the topic and create a new category. Here are some examples of e-zines with a highly specialized focus that have done well:

MarketingExperiments.com (http://www.MarketingExperiments.com/) is a new but super high-quality marketing e-zine. It's a perfect example of taking a common topic—marketing—and giving it a fresh spin. Marketing Experiments is better than most of the marketing e-zines out there, and it's the only one I know that tests specific marketing programs. The uniqueness of its content gives it its value.

Boogie Jack's Almost a Newsletter (http://www.boogiejack.com/) is another one of my favorites. Dennis Gaskill, the publisher, mainly covers Web design topics, but with his unique spin on the subject. If you want an example of personality done well in an e-zine, check out this one for the perfect case study. The publisher keeps you laughing the whole time you're learning about Web site design, which isn't easy to pull off.

DiscoverBellyDance.com (http://www.DiscoverBellyDance.com/), a weekly e-zine for belly dance enthusiasts, is very specialized. In addition to the quality weekly content, there's an incredibly successful online community built around the e-zine. The quick growth of this e-zine and site is due to the publisher finding a unique niche and serving it well.

What are the biggest reasons readers unsubscribe from e-zines?
The most common reason I hear is, "I get too much email." E-zine publishers need to be perceived as vital or their subscribers may not have time for them. There's an absolute glut of e-mail publications, and there will be twice as many in the future. Only the best, most consistent publications will retain a loyal, engaged audience.

What are some creative things people can do to keep readers interested?
Build a community around the e-zine. Give readers a chance to contribute and help build the success of the publication. If they have a stake in it, they're far less likely to go elsewhere.

How can a good e-zine and a Web site work together to create a brand image?
A Web site and an e-mail publication support each other. A Web site is usually the primary source of new subscriptions for an e-zine. An e-zine is the best method for driving repeat traffic back to the Web site. Assuming your Web site and e-zine have similar names (reflected in the site's domain name as well), they reinforce each other to create a unified online image.

What do you consider the most important things an individual can do to create a brand identity online?
Register a domain name. If you're trying to brand yourself, get YourName.com if possible. Otherwise, get YourBusinessName.com and use it everywhere. (See

Chapter 5, "Creating Your Personal Brand Web Site," for details on how to register a domain name.) Stay in constant contact with your audience. Listen to their feedback and respond personally to as much of it as possible. The service you provide your customers or e-zine readers won't stop there. Impress them and they'll tell everyone about you.

Laura Ries

Laura Ries and her father, Al Ries, are partners in the brand strategies consulting firm Ries & Ries. They have written two books, *The 11 Immutable Laws of Internet Branding* and *The 22 Immutable Laws of Branding*. You can find the **Ries & Ries** Web site at http://www.ries.com/. (See Figure A.3.)

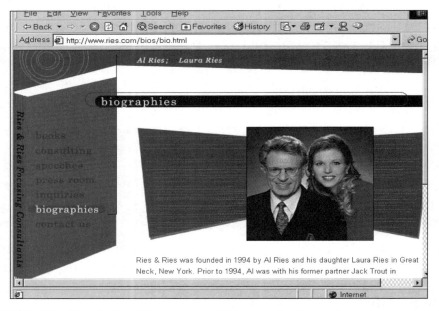

FIGURE A.3: The Ries & Ries Web site establishes author/consultant Laura Ries and her father, Al Ries, as "focusing consultants."

What are the top three things people can do to brand themselves online? The first thing to do is ask yourself "What do I stand for?" You want to express that idea in a single word or concept. The second thing is to ask yourself, "What are my credentials?" In other words, where is the proof that you own the concept you want to stake out in the first place? The third thing to do is ask yourself, "Does my name help express the single concept I want to communicate?" Ralph Lifshitz could have never become the world's leading designer. So he changed his name to Ralph Lauren.

A solo entrepreneur should follow the same principles as a large corporation. Michael Dell started in his college dorm room as a solo entrepreneur selling personal computers. By focusing on a single distribution channel—direct marketing—Dell Computer became the largest personal computer manufacturer in the United States.

What advice do you have for people who worry that having too narrow a brand focus will limit the amount of attention and business they can generate?
In theory, that might be true, but in practice it is almost never true. By limiting itself to mobile phones, Nokia has 34 percent of the world's mobile phone business. Motorola, on the other hand, makes semiconductors and many other products besides mobile phones. Motorola's share of the mobile phone business is just 13 percent. Nokia is worth much more than Motorola on the stock market.

Why did so many Web ventures, which spent huge ad budgets and received lots of media coverage, not make it?
Big ad budgets and media coverage are means to an end. The end is establishing the brand and what it stands for in the mind of the prospect. Unless you can do that, all your efforts are wasted.

What's the difference between finding a niche and finding a focus?
Finding a niche and finding a focus are the same. However, when you call the segment of the market a *niche*, you are telling yourself that it's always going to be a small segment. Why would you want to do this? Think big. Think focus. Call your strategy a focus.

How important is conveying one's personality online?
A site should reflect the strategy of the brand. If you are an artist, for example, the site should be primarily visual. If you are a writer, on the other hand, it should be primarily verbal.

Damon G. Zahariades

Damon G. Zahariades is the author of *The Special Report Bible*, a manual on how to write, package, and sell reports on specialized topics. He also publishes an e-mail newsletter and Web site called **Web Business Today!** at http://www.WebBusinessToday.com/. Reach Damon at Damon@webbusinesstoday.com.

What's the best way to sum up your brand identity?
Business insight with an extra scoop of wit; hold the hype. Seriously, that's what I concentrate on. For example, when I write articles, I have two purposes. I want

either to educate or entertain my reader base. Hype can kill credibility, and without credibility, I'm sunk. When folks read my stuff, they know they're getting something they can use or chuckle at.

Determining my identity happened without my thinking about it. First, let's address the "business insight with wit" aspect. A lot of folks publish articles these days. Some writers are so good they make your toes curl when you read their articles. But most stink. No personality. No chutzpah. Just blah. I hate boring writing. So when I write I try to add value in some memorable way.

Now, let's talk about the "no hype" angle. People use hype to pimp products. I don't pimp products and I don't like it when others do. Encouraging a personal identity of being anti-hype is really just a natural extension of my own personality. Therefore, you won't find it in my newsletter.

How did you get involved with doing business online?
Several years ago, I read an issue of *PC Novice*. Keep in mind, this was back when the Web was a mystery to most folks. There was a section in this particular issue about entrepreneurs who were building businesses online. One of the people featured in the magazine was Jim Daniels (featured later in this appendix). He was mentioned as a self-publisher. That grabbed my attention because that's what I wanted to do.

You display a distinct writing style. How important is that when establishing an online identity?
Writing style is critical. It's all you have. When you meet someone for coffee or dinner, your personality is made up of all your facial expressions, body movements, smile, and so on. Online, it ain't that easy. All you have are your words and the way you express them. If you're being yourself, that's a good thing. People like you or hate you based on your personality. It doesn't matter whether you're having coffee with them or talking by e-mail, you have to be yourself.

For example, take Paul Myers of **TalkBiz** at http://www.talkbiz.com/. This guy's writing cuts straight to the heart. No beating around the bush. He knows his stuff and writes about it with credibility and conviction. When you read his material, you get the feeling he's talking to you—and only you. That's his personality.

Next, consider Dr. Ralph Wilson and his **E-Commerce and Web Marketing** site at http://www.wilsonweb.com/. Like Paul, Ralph knows his stuff in spades. In his writing, he carries the image of a friendly professor. He's not necessarily the kind of guy you want to hang out with at the local pool hall, but Ralph has such a treasure trove of knowledge between his ears, you can't help but take what he says as gospel. That's his personality.

How do you generate newsletter subscribers?

I use two methods. First, I rely on good ole word-of-mouth. If you like my newsletter, I want you to tell the folks who are in your circle of influence. Second, I let other e-publishers use my articles in their newsletters. They get content; I get exposure—a good deal for everybody involved.

I have a different philosophy than most e-publishers. Everyone is trying to get subscribers. They dream of having a list of 100,000 subscribers they can hawk their products to. In my dream, I have a group of *responsive* subscribers. That's why I rely on word of mouth and the use of my articles. Subscribers who find out about me via these strategies tend to be more loyal. After all, they know what to expect.

Subscriber retention is just as important as subscriber attraction. I could use classified ads, ad swaps, joint thank-you pages, and so on to attract subscribers, but those strategies don't promote as much retention value as word-of-mouth and free articles.

What is the importance of delivering great content through an e-zine or Web site?

Don't underestimate your audience's intelligence. People online are savvy and they lack patience. The shenanigans that they might tolerate offline have no place online. Also, write with your own personality. You don't have to be witty. You don't have to be funny. You don't even have to be smart. Just write as if you were talking to one of your friends.

You wouldn't know it from my writing, but I sincerely believe the "less-is-more" mantra. I've read 800-word articles that have bored me to tears and I've read 150-word tips that have hit me like a brick.

Here's another tip: Know your audience. What turns them on? What turns them off? Do they want long, dry articles filled with resources or do they want quick, punchy articles filled with your personality? Know what they want and give it to them. Or know what you want to give and find the right folks who want it.

On your Web site you announce that your articles are available free for reprint. How effective has that strategy been for you?

It's been one of my smartest moves. Lots of e-publishers and site developers won't use your articles if they're not absolutely sure that they have your permission. I know some writers who don't want their material used all over the Net. If someone wants to use my articles, be my guest. They're more than welcome as long as they include my full name at the top of the article and the short blurb at the bottom.

Is it okay for self-promoters to alienate some segments of the population?
Absolutely. For instance, the folks who enjoy reading my stuff *really* enjoy reading my stuff. And those who think my stuff stinks will unsubscribe from my newsletter, which is fine. I'd rather have 5,000 loyal readers than a list of 100,000 folks who couldn't give a rat's behind about my material.

What do you consider the most important things an individual can do to create a brand identity online?
The following four are the top things I feel people should focus on:

- Be careful with your words. Once you say something online, you can't take it back. It's often archived. And chances are, people will read your words 20 years from now.

- Consider how you want to be perceived. Do you want to be thought of as smart? Funny? Helpful? Resourceful? For example, if you want to be known as helpful, you need to cruise the high-traffic discussion forums on a regular basis. You have to get your name out there with valuable content. How? By answering questions, posting survey results, and more. Be consistent. Know the difference between being helpful and being a pest.

- Provide value. Educate or entertain. If you're not adding value to people's lives in some way, they'll send you to the street.

- Be consistent. A brand identity is an image. It's a picture that people have in their heads when they think of you, and you promote that picture by being consistent. If you do something off-the-wall or completely at odds with your brand identity, you're sunk.

Raleigh Pinskey

A self-described "Viz-Ability marketing specialist," Raleigh Pinskey is a speaker, consultant, and author of many books, including *101 Ways to Promote Yourself*, *The Zen of Hype*, and *101 Ways to Get On Talk Shows*. Her Web sites include **RaleighPinskey.com** (http://www.raleighpinskey.com/) and **PromoteYourself.com**, http://www.promoteyourself.com/. Reach her at Raleigh@promoteyourself.com.

What's the biggest misconception about branding?
People don't understand that they can promote themselves in the same way that big companies do. The number of employees and the bank account may be different, but the marketing aspects are the same. Regardless of your size, consumers and the media will always ask, "Well, what makes you different?" That's a branding question. And the way you answer that question influences your brand image.

Individuals have every right to brand themselves, just like big companies. In fact, successful solo business people have been doing that all along; we just haven't been using the word *branding* to describe it. Some people call it *name recognition*, a *unique selling proposition*, or a *hook*. The buzzword nowadays is *branding*. However, many people still don't understand what branding is. I encourage any self-promoter to read all the wonderful books on branding and marketing so that they understand the concept. Rob Frankel's *The Revenge of Brand X* and *Dan Janal's Guide to Marketing on the Internet* are two good ones.

There are different definitions of branding. The original marketing term—brand—referred to a product. You as a person are a product too—a product defined by what you do, how you think, and what you are. How you dress can be a brand. How you talk can be a brand. You can brand by your name or by your attitude. It applies to everything that you do, including the way you describe yourself, as I do by calling myself a Viz-Ability marketing specialist. (See Figure A.4 to see how Raleigh presents herself on her own Web site.)

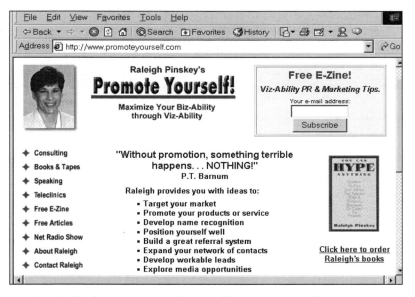

FIGURE A.4: Raleigh Pinskey's **PromoteYourself.com** site clarifies her identity as a self-promotion specialist.

What can freelancers do to create a brand identity online?

I don't believe anyone should call himself or herself a freelancer. The word conjures images of someone who is unemployed and unreliable. I advocate that everybody should use a business name. Pick a business name that incorporates your name and what you do, such as Bill Smith Graphic Design.

When picking a domain name for a Web site, it should be short and include a benefit, like GetYourArtworkHere.com. When your most defining keyword is part of your domain name, you do far better with search engine placement. So brand yourself with a keyword of what you do or a benefit. Let's say your name is John Jones. If someone has already registered JohnJones.com as a domain name, see if JohnJonesArtist.com or JohnJonesKarateExpert.com is available. It may end up being an even better choice from a branding standpoint.

How important is specialization?
You can't focus too much. Your brand should reflect your level of knowledge. For instance, I specialize in showing people how to promote themselves. Under that umbrella fall media relations, direct mail, using the Internet, and so on. But some experts specialize only in teaching people how to get on talk shows. Therefore, people who want information on talk show promotion gravitate toward them.

Should self-promoters still market themselves offline?
People need to understand that the Web is not the end all and be all of promotion. You have to promote yourself and reach people with your message in all sorts of ways—through speeches, post card campaigns, trade shows, and by printing your Web address and contact information on everything.

Any final thoughts on branding?
People either remember you for what you do or for who you are. Branding allows you to combine and cover both bases.

Jim Daniels

Jim Daniels is the Webmaster of **BizWeb2000** (http://www.bizweb2000.com/), a site that offers advice to people wanting to make money or run a business online. He also publishes an e-zine called the *BizWeb e-Gazette* and is the author of *Insider Internet Marketing* and *Make a Living Online*. Jim has been featured in *Entrepreneur* and *Smart Computing* magazines. Reach him by e-mail at jim@bizweb2000.com.

What's the best way to sum up your brand identity?
It can be summed up as Jim Daniels, the guy who's been there and done it on the Internet and can help you do the same. That's what I hear most from my prospects and clients. They come to me when they've had enough with the business opportunities on the Web and they are ready to build their own business.

How did you determine that identity?
It sort of determined itself as I helped hundreds of people via e-mail every week. That's one thing that lots of other business owners do not do: personally answer all their e-mail. It's one of the things that has enabled me to remain in touch with folks trying to make a living online.

How important is your e-zine to your online success?
My e-zine is probably the number one component in my business. It keeps me in touch with my best potential clients and it grows by 1,000 or so new subscribers every week. Nothing in the real world comes close to what an e-zine can do for online businesses.

What are some of the most effective ways you increase the number of subscribers?
I give away a free e-book called *Beginner's Guide to Starting a High-Income Business on the Internet*. It's a big hit, and every one comes with a complimentary subscription to my newsletter. Visitors get a great free e-book and I get another subscriber and potential customer.

How important is writing style to conveying your personality online?
Extremely important. Lots of people through the years have written to thank me for telling it like it is. I prefer a no-fluff style that talks to my readers rather than at them. I share with them what is working for my online business and why. They love that kind of stuff when it is written in a style they understand and enjoy.

Geoffrey Kleinman

Geoffrey Kleinman and his wife, Heather, run four different Web sites. Geoffrey founded *The Kleinman Report* newsletter and its accompanying Web site, **Kleinman.com** (http://www.kleinman.com/), in 1995 as a resource for new Internet users. The following year, Heather launched **Heather Kleinman's Cosmetic Connection** (http://www.CosmeticConnection.com/) and a newsletter called *The Cosmetic Report*, both of which feature cosmetic product reviews and makeup advice. Soon after, Heather also started **The Makeup Diva** (http://www.makeupdiva.com/), a weekly beauty and makeup advice column that has garnered considerable media exposure. In 1999, Geoffrey launched **DVD Talk** (http://www.dvdtalk.com/), a news and information resource about DVD movie releases. Reach Geoffrey by e-mail at geoff@kleinman.com.

You and Heather juggle various sites and newsletters with different identities. What is the importance of focus and specialization?

Focus is extremely important. Even though **Kleinman.com** covers very different specialized areas, we are set up so that each of the two principles of our company focuses on its own area. Heather runs the two makeup sites and I run **DVD Talk** and **The Kleinman Report**. We often discuss where our sites and company are heading and we always try to make sure we're keeping within the scope of our audience. It's clear to us why people come to our sites, and we owe a lot of that to the fact we are so focused. It would be easy for me to expand **DVD Talk** to cover all things movie-related, or even the broad world of entertainment. But I know that our customers come to **DVD Talk** because they want DVD information and don't want to sift through other, less-relevant information to find what they are looking for.

Being focused also gives our sites simple value propositions for our customers. My background is in film and I was always told that if you can't yell the plot of a script across a parking lot in one or two sentences, then you probably wouldn't be able to sell it. It's the simplicity of *why* you come to one of our sites that makes it so compelling. You know you're going to get exactly what you heard about.

Heather readily attaches her name to the cosmetics and makeup sites. Why? Heather's sites are really advice sites, and she deals with almost an exclusively female audience. When she started the site, she had a clear vision of what she wanted—a place where people could get no-nonsense advice about makeup and cosmetics. She also wanted visitors to feel that, even though they were on a Web site, they were communicating with a close friend.

Heather is approached in public frequently by fans, and when we talk to them you get a real sense that they feel a bond with her. Attaching her name humanizes what she does and who she is. In her own way, she's famous. People don't ask for her autograph, but she has many of the same experiences as someone who stars on a TV show or in a movie.

For my part, I attach my name to **The Kleinman Report** for many of the same reasons as Heather. I want to make the Internet more personal and create a relationship with my readers.

What are some of the ways you create a brand image for your sites?
The first thing I did with **DVD Talk** was give it a distinct look. I created a style that I wanted to carry over to every page on the site. I have a specific color I use—which I call "DVD Talk blue"—and a specific style of layout and writing. I also established a consistent editorial tone. While I have many people who contribute to the site, everyone is in tune with the site's overall editorial style. (See Figure A.5 for a glimpse of the DVD Talk look.)

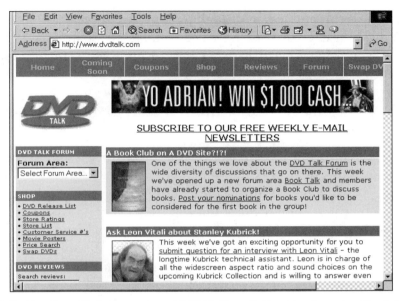

FIGURE A.5: Geoffrey Kleinman gives **DVD Talk** a distinct look and editorial style that is consistent throughout the site.

Also, I treat the community forum like it's the TV show *Cheers*. Everyone is welcome to come and be themselves. When people become members of our site, even if they just sign up for one of our free newsletters, they are treated as part of the tribe. I work hard to make that mean something. Whether it's giving them a collective voice to the studios or offering a special giveaway, being a DVD member means something—and that translates into a real brand image for **DVD Talk**.

For Heather Kleinman's **Cosmetic Connection**, she's more of a stickler about her brand. She is brutally honest with her advice and reviews, even if a company is an advertiser, a friend, or an acquaintance. It's that fierce editorial integrity that has created her brand image over anything else she's done.

How important is it for people to make their brands a reflection of their true selves?

Whether it's your personality or the personality you've created for your business, I think it's critical to the success of any site to be true to your site's personality. For Heather it's been extremely key. She's the brand. Heather Kleinman and Cosmetic Connection are seen as the same thing, so she has amazing brand power to do other related things in this space, and people follow.

What role does an e-zine play in online branding success?
I am a firm believer in e-zines and have been publishing them since 1995. I don't think a site would last long if it didn't have some sort of e-mail component. People are just too busy to remember to come back to a site. An e-zine is a nice reminder that you're still around, plus it provides people with a digested version of what's on the site. This year we launched three new e-zines on DVD Talk and I've got plans for at least two more.

What are some of the most effective ways you increased your number of subscribers or Web site visitors?
Number one is word of mouth. There's nothing better than someone telling someone else that they should check out our sites. How do we do this? It starts with working hard to be a place people want to tell their friends about, which is a gargantuan task, but it creates a specific focus for us. We are always looking at the needs of our users, always making our sites a place worth telling other people about. We constantly ask for feedback and constantly fine-tune our sites to fit people's needs. Also, we ask our users to tell their friends. If you never ask, they may never think of it.

What are some creative things people can do to keep readers coming back to their Web sites or e-zines?
Give your audience a crack at winning something they want and people will come back to your site. Also, provide relevant content. If people want info on upcoming DVDs, give them info on upcoming DVDs. If they want reviews, offer great reviews. Remember *why* people come to your site in the first place, give them more of it, and they're likely to return.

What publicity have you garnered?
Heather's been featured in *People* magazine and I've been on ABC News. That's not bad exposure given our size, since we don't have a publicist and don't send out a lot of press releases. The best publicity we've received has come from reporters who are working on a story and need an expert opinion or quote. They usually hear about us from people they talk to, which wouldn't happen if we didn't establish our brands. After using one of us as a source, media people often get interested in our sites and do a full story on us.

What do you consider the most important things an individual can do to create a brand identity online?
Be clear about what your brand is and what it stands for. Know it like you know yourself. Once you've created your brand, be true to it. Measure everything you do against what your brand promises. Don't mess with your brand; in the end

it's the most valuable asset you've got. Also, make some room and let your fans in. Give people an opportunity to feel an association with your brand. Do that and your brand can mean so much more.

Carla Hall

Carla Hall is a singer-songwriter who has released CDs of her original music on her own record label. She is the author of *The DIY (Do-It-Yourself) Guide to the Music Biz* and frequently presents music business seminars in the New York City area. Her Web site, **CarlaHall.com**, can be found at http://www.carlahall.com/. Reach her by e-mail at Carla@carlahall.com.

What's the best way to describe your brand identity and how did you determine it?
DIY Diva—advocate of the independent musician. It was an extension of the things I was already doing: giving advice to musicians starting out. At first it was just for friends who wanted to create press kits. That soon mushroomed into classes and articles.

How did you get involved with doing business online?
I had an offline music business newsletter, called *The Soulflower*, for about five years. After getting online, I subscribed to a few music business e-zines, including your *Buzz Factor*. I realized that I could take my newsletter online, reach more people, and spend less money. What a concept!

How important is your e-zine to your online success and what are some of the most effective ways you increased the number of subscribers?
It's how I keep in touch with lots of people on a regular basis. When subscribers like what they read, they forward it to others who might like it. Some of my readers cut and paste the columns into other e-mails, giving me credit with a hot link to my site.

The articles that I've published online have been really successful. The blurb at the end always includes a link to my site. I get a good number of new subscribers after visitors look around my site. Using an e-mail signature is also good. I always include mine when I meet someone online. Since it's a hot link, my site is only a click away.

How important is networking?
All of us are busy with our lives, and we want to feel that we're not just a number or a demographic. I like to reach out to people every now and then just to say hello, without a sales pitch of any kind. For example, I try to keep current with what's

going on in the music industry. When I see interesting articles, I forward them to people I know will be interested. This works offline and online to build relationships.

Do you think most people are too introverted to contact people in their industry or they feel unworthy of communicating with authors, experts, and media people?
I call it the Who Do You Think You Are? Syndrome. Many musicians are afraid to promote themselves to the people who actually need them. For example, a music journalist needs to report on new music, whether it's a new CD or a local concert. Musicians need people to know that they exist. Once you realize that a journalist or a prominent person in your industry needs you too, it becomes a win-win situation.

How important is it to convey your personality when branding yourself online?
People like to connect with other people, not with a corporation or a slogan. In my writing, I write like I speak—slang and all. People seem to connect with that and feel that they know who I am. I'm a friendly, positive person and that comes through.

What do you consider the most important things an individual can do to create a brand identity online?
Personality, consistency, and patience.

In what ways have you generated publicity for yourself?
Giving lectures has been an excellent way of getting exposure as an expert. When I give classes at The Learning Annex in New York City, they provide a great ad with my picture in their glossy magazine at no cost to me. This free brochure is distributed at stands all over New York and has a circulation of over 25,000.

Offering classes for local industry organizations is another great way to self-promote. Even if these organizations cannot pay you for a class, they usually have online and offline newsletters in which they promote the class; some will also run articles you submit.

Writing a book or booklet is another way to brand yourself as an expert. There will always be wannabes and newbies in every field. Offering a guide demonstrates your expert status. And selling a book after a class helps you break even when you're giving a free lecture.

What else is important about online branding?
The importance of patience. When creating a brand, it takes repeated exposures before people remember who you are. If you give up too soon, you'll never know how close you were.

A 12-Month Action Plan

This appendix is designed to give you a one-year plan for branding yourself online. Consider it a road map filled with suggestions regarding the steps you should follow to carve a memorable identity on the Internet. Of course, your mileage may vary. You may have already mastered some of the preliminary stages and can therefore skip ahead to more advanced parts of the plan and move things along in less than 12 months. On the other hand, you might be pursuing your branding goals on a part-time basis and may choose to stretch this plan to 18 months or more.

While each month is filled with suggested steps, many basic activities that you should engage in regularly are not listed. For instance, you should check your e-mail and send necessary responses every day. Once you launch your free e-zine, you should deliver new issues on a consistent schedule. Also, every week, you should keep your eyes open for new exposure opportunities and new contacts to add to your database. Still, you should consider this 12-month action plan a rough draft of your branding blueprint. Tailor it to your situation and make it your own.

Month One

This first month is when you lay the foundation upon which your future activities are built. You decide what your brand identity is, soak up some useful knowledge, and collect the basic tools you need to enter the online world.

- Read this entire book once through quickly to get a feel for the entire process and philosophy behind online branding.
- Read Chapter 1, "The Brand Called You," through Chapter 3, "Developing Your Online Branding Arsenal," in detail while taking notes and doing any suggested exercises.
- Search your soul and consider your various identity options (Chapter 2, "Crafting Your Best Brand Identity").

- Refine your identity and determine your ideal specialty and focus (Chapter 2).
- Ask yourself, "Whom will I serve?" and "How would I describe my ideal fan?" (Chapter 2).
- Determine your current needs regarding your computer's processor, RAM, hard drive space, and other hardware aspects (Chapter 3).
- Purchase or upgrade your computer hardware, monitor, keyboard, and so on (Chapter 3).
- Determine your computer software needs regarding word processing, database management, and so on (Chapter 3).
- Read articles on how the Internet works (Chapter 3).
- Read articles that cover branding-related issues (Chapter 2).
- Spend time visiting Internet business sites and getting a feel for the state of business online (Chapter 3).
- Consider using one of the news filter services that e-mail you customized articles (Chapter 3).
- Consider your Internet access options: ISP, online service, phone or cable company (Chapter 3).
- Consider your connection choices: telephone modem, DSL, cable, and other options (Chapter 3).

Month Two

This month you refine your identity, register a domain name, and begin learning HTML. You also begin planning the content and design of your e-zine and Web site.

- Read Chapter 4, "Maximizing E-mail for Brand Delivery," through Chapter 7, "Publishing an E-mail Newsletter," in detail.
- Give serious thought to the name you want to use to brand yourself online (Chapter 3, "Developing Your Online Branding Arsenal").
- Search for the availability of potential domain names (Chapter 5, "Creating Your Personal Brand Web Site").
- Make a final decision on the brand name and domain name you want to use (Chapter 3).
- Register your chosen domain name using one of the low-cost registrars (Chapter 5).
- Determine your Brand Identity Statement (Chapter 2, "Crafting Your Best Brand Identity").

- Write a first-draft version of your branding goals and game plan (Chapter 14, "Setting Online Goals and Reaching Them").
- Design and print business cards, letterhead, and any other printed materials you deem necessary (Chapter 13, "Exploiting Offline Branding Strategies").
- Select an e-mail client, whether it comes with your ISP or is a stand-alone program such as Eudora (Chapter 4).
- Consider your e-zine delivery options and select one (Chapter 7).
- Experiment with your e-zine content and format (Chapter 7).
- Learn HTML basics (Chapter 5).
- Choose an HTML editor or select a Web designer (Chapter 5).
- Determine your Web site sections and type of content (Chapter 6, "Designing Your Web Site for Brand Impact").
- Decide whether your Web site identity would be best served by using how-to articles, interviews, picture galleries, success stories, news story roundups, reviews, opinion pieces, and/or humor (Chapter 6).
- Begin writing the words for each Web page (Chapter 6).
- Experiment with your Web site design (Chapter 6).
- Consider your Web site hosting options—free services, ISP, Web store, and so on—and make a decision (Chapter 5).

Month Three

During this third month you start writing the articles that demonstrate your expertise while building your database of online contacts. You also begin promoting your e-zine and hone the final design elements of your Web site.

- Read Chapter 8, "Exploiting E-zines and Web Sites of Others," and Chapter 9, "Self-Publishing to Disperse Your Expertise," in detail.
- Read articles about how to write effective how-to articles (Chapter 8).
- Start writing the free articles you want to offer other Web sites and e-zines (Chapter 8).
- Brainstorm on a topic and title for your first free e-book or e-mail workshop (Chapter 9).
- Commit time to thoroughly searching the Internet for sources related to your field (Chapter 3, "Developing Your Online Branding Arsenal").
- Using your database software, compile a list of Web sites, e-zines, link directories, discussion forums, newsgroups, free classified pages, and more (Chapter 3).

- Refine the content and format of your e-zine; write the first two issues (Chapter 7, "Publishing an E-mail Newsletter").
- Craft a short, attention-getting description of your e-zine (Chapter 7).
- Submit your e-zine to the e-zine directories and announcement lists (Chapter 7).
- Fine-tune the words and design of your Web pages (Chapter 6, "Designing Your Web Site for Brand Impact").
- Make sure your Web pages make good use of headlines, subheads, bullet points, lists, bold text, and other visual techniques (Chapter 6).
- Run a spellcheck on your Web site words and have other people proofread your pages (Chapter 6).
- Conduct some informal usability research regarding your Web site (Chapter 6).
- Ask objective people and yourself the following questions:
  1. Does my Web site make my identity clear?
  2. Does my site have a consistent look and feel on all pages?
  3. Is my site quick to load and easy to navigate?
  4. Have I included enough interactivity on my site, such as polls, quizzes, message boards, contests, and giveaways?
  5. Is the content on my site enticing enough to make potential fans stick around and return? (Chapter 6)
- Upload files to your Web host and go live with your site (Chapter 5, "Creating Your Personal Brand Web Site").
- Refine your branding goals and game plan, then make a commitment to act on them (Chapter 14, "Setting Online Goals and Reaching Them").

Month Four

This month you turn yourself into a media-friendly publicity hound and get busy promoting your free articles to other Web sites and e-zines. In addition, you submit your Web site to the top search engines and deliver your first e-zine issue.

- Read Chapter 10, "Branding Yourself through Online Networking," and Chapter 11, "Exposing Your Identity Through Online Publicity," in detail.
- Search for discussion forums and join discussion mailing lists related to your area of expertise; then lurk on these forums and lists to determine those where it would be best for you to have a presence (Chapter 10).

- Compile a list of writers, editors, reviewers, columnists, and other media contacts (Chapter 11).
- Start putting together an online media kit that includes a bio, comments from media and industry people, samples of your work, and a section for media releases (Chapter 11).
- Begin crafting an attention-getting media release that promotes your brand while addressing a media-friendly subject (Chapter 11).
- Write more free articles you want to offer other Web sites and e-zines (Chapter 8, "Exploiting E-zines and Web Sites of Others").
- Craft an enticing, benefit-rich author blurb that will accompany every article written by you and run on other Web sites or in other e-zines (Chapter 8).
- Post your collection of free articles on your Web site along with your author blurb and a notice regarding free reprint rights (Chapter 8).
- Consider making your articles available via autoresponders (Chapter 8).
- Go through your database and send personal e-mails to Web site owners and e-zine editors to make them aware of your free articles (Chapter 8).
- Submit your articles to the free-content sites (Chapter 8).
- Submit information about your articles to the free-articles announcement mailing lists (Chapter 8).
- Submit your Web site to the top 12 search engines and Web directories (Chapter 5, "Creating Your Personal Brand Web Site").
- Send your first e-zine issue to your subscribers, however few their numbers may be (Chapter 7, "Publishing an E-mail Newsletter").
- Write and design your free e-book or e-mail workshop (Chapter 9, "Self-Publishing to Disperse Your Expertise").

Month Five

This fifth month is a busy one as you promote your new free e-book or e-mail workshop, distribute your first press release, and submit your Web site to more search engines and directories. This month you also solicit incoming links, communicate with other experts, and design your printed marketing materials.

- Read Chapter 12, "Other Online Branding Tools and Techniques," and Chapter 13, "Exploiting Offline Branding Strategies," in detail.
- Make a list of the other online techniques and offline strategies that most appeal to you (Chapters 12 and 13).

- Refine and post your online media kit (Chapter 11, "Exposing Your Identity Through Online Publicity").

- Start promoting your free e-book or e-mail workshop on your Web site and in your e-zine; you might also consider making this the hook for the media release you distribute this month (Chapter 9, "Self-Publishing to Disperse Your Expertise," and Chapter 11).

- Refine the media release you wrote last month and submit it to the free or paid submission services (Chapter 11).

- E-mail your media release along with a personal note to select contacts in your field (Chapter 11).

- Submit your Web site to a dozen or more secondary search engines and Web directories (Chapter 5, "Creating Your Personal Brand Web Site").

- Submit your Web site to as many industry-specific link directories as you can find (Chapter 5).

- Send personal e-mails to the owners of related but noncompeting Web sites and request a link (Chapter 12).

- Get busy interacting a few times a week on high-priority discussion forums and mailing lists (Chapter 10, "Branding Yourself Through Online Networking").

- Select 10 to 20 other experts and important people in your field; then send a personal e-mail to each and try to start a professional relationship (Chapter 12).

- Solicit positive testimonials from your e-zine subscribers, paying customers, and prominent people in your field; start using the positive quotes you collect in promotional materials (Chapter 11).

- Conceive, design, and print a post card that promotes your Web site or free e-zine (Chapter 13).

Month Six

In addition to continuing your post card and media-release efforts, this month you consider setting up shop at an expert Web site and investigate becoming a regular columnist. During this sixth month, you also contemplate offering a for-sale e-book, lining up public-speaking events, and attending trade shows and conferences related to your field.

- Read Chapter 14, "Setting Online Goals and Reaching Them," and Appendix A, "Online Success Stories," in detail.

- Mail the promotional post card you created last month to your own or a rented list of targeted people (Chapter 13, "Exploiting Offline Branding Strategies").

- Visit the many expert Web sites and determine whether one of them is a good potential home for your expertise (Chapter 8, "Exploiting E-zines and Web Sites of Others").

- Keep your eye open for a highly traveled Web site that may be in need of a regular columnist (Chapter 8).

- Consider writing and producing a for-sale e-book or printed special report (Chapter 9, "Self-Publishing to Disperse Your Expertise").

- Research public-speaking opportunities and set up as many events as you can over the next two months (Chapter 13).

- Write, design, and print a tip sheet or similar pamphlet that you can hand out after public-speaking events (Chapter 13).

- Consider joining a Web ring to draw more people to your site (Chapter 3, "Developing Your Online Branding Arsenal").

- Take a look at trade shows and conferences in your industry that are scheduled within the next six to nine months; consider attending one or two of them (Chapter 13).

- Develop an elevator speech that quickly communicates who you are and what you do (Chapter 13).

- Craft a new, attention-getting media release that promotes your brand through a fresh, media-friendly angle (Chapter 11, "Exposing Your Identity Through Online Publicity").

- Evaluate the progress you've made over the past three months; determine what's working and what's not (Chapter 14).

- Refine your branding goals and game plan, then make a renewed commitment to act on them (Chapter 14).

Month Seven

This month you add to your promotional arsenal by submitting your site to various online awards, exploring message boards and free classified ad pages, and pursuing radio and TV interviews. If you're still feeling ambitious, you can also consider posting your credentials at talent Web sites and determine whether your site and e-zine could stand a redesign.

- Refine the media release you wrote last month and submit it to the free or paid submission services (Chapter 11, "Exposing Your Identity Through Online Publicity").

- E-mail your media release along with a personal note to select Web site owners, e-zine editors, and media people in your field (Chapter 11).
- Submit your Web site to several appropriate online awards sites (Chapter 12, "Other Online Branding Tools and Techniques").
- Search for message boards and free classified ad pages that are in line with your area of expertise; post appropriate brand-related messages and ads to these sources (Chapter 10, "Branding Yourself Through Online Networking").
- Research radio and TV interview opportunities, craft a noteworthy publicity angle, and set up as many interviews as you can over the next two months (Chapter 13, "Exploiting Offline Branding Strategies").
- Take a fresh look at your Web site and consider adding new features or redesigning it (Chapter 6, "Designing Your Web Site for Brand Impact").
- Examine your e-zine and consider adding new features or taking a fresh approach (Chapter 7, "Publishing an E-mail Newsletter").
- Consider posting a portfolio of your work on some of the talent Web sites (Chapter 12)
- Conceive, design, and print a new post card that promotes your Web site, free e-zine, or other aspect of your brand identity (Chapter 13).

Month Eight

The eighth month is a good time for a tune-up as you go through all of your articles, e-books, e-mail workshops, and site links to make sure your information is current and that all links still work. This month is also a perfect time to consider presenting your own award to other people and Web sites.

- Mail the promotional post card you created last month to your mailing list (Chapter 13, "Exploiting Offline Branding Strategies").
- Increase Web site traffic by sending personal e-mails to more owners of related but noncompeting Web sites and requesting a link (Chapter 12, "Other Online Branding Tools and Techniques").
- Go through your free articles, e-books, and e-mail workshops to make sure your information and links are still current (Chapter 8, "Exploiting E-zines and Web Sites of Others," and Chapter 9, "Self-Publishing to Disperse Your Expertise").
- Check your Web site for link rot and weed out any bad links (Chapter 6, "Designing Your Web Site for Brand Impact").
- Consider offering your own award related to your brand (Chapter 12).
- Craft a new, attention-getting media release that promotes your brand

through a fresh, media-friendly angle (Chapter 11, "Exposing Your Identity Through Online Publicity").

- Research public-speaking opportunities and set up as many events as you can over the next two months (Chapter 13).

Month Nine

Now that you're making the best use of free resources, this month you should seriously consider paying for search engine keyword ads and select e-zine ads. The ninth month is also a good time to update and add to your database of online contacts, evaluate your progress, and refine your goals.

- Consider bidding on keyword ad placement at search engines that offer it (Chapter 12, "Other Online Branding Tools and Techniques").
- Consider running paid e-zine ads in targeted e-zines (Chapter 12).
- Go through your database of online contacts, remove outdated listings, and search for new sources to add to it (Chapter 3, "Developing Your Online Branding Arsenal").
- Think more about critical-mass exposure and having potential fans hear about you from multiple sources (Chapter 12).
- Refine the media release you wrote last month and submit it to the free or paid submission services (Chapter 11, "Exposing Your Identity Through Online Publicity").
- E-mail your media release along with a personal note to select Web site owners, e-zine editors, and media people in your field (Chapter 11).
- Conceive, design, and print a new post card that promotes your Web site, free e-zine, or other aspect of your brand identity (Chapter 13, "Exploiting Offline Branding Strategies").
- Research radio and TV interview opportunities, craft a noteworthy publicity angle, and set up as many interviews as you can over the next two months (Chapter 13).
- Evaluate the progress you've made over the past three months; determine what's working and what's not (Chapter 14, "Setting Online Goals and Reaching Them").
- Refine your branding goals and game plan, then make a renewed commitment to act on them (Chapter 14).

Month Ten

This month features many of the familiar brand-building activities: mailing a new post card, crafting a fresh media release, setting up public-speaking engagements, and so on. This is also a great month to think about sponsoring a large event, contest, or fundraiser.

- Mail the promotional post card you created last month to your mailing list (Chapter 13, "Exploiting Offline Branding Strategies").
- Submit your Web site to more online awards sites (Chapter 12, "Other Online Branding Tools and Techniques").
- Craft a new, attention-getting media release that promotes your brand through a fresh, media-friendly angle (Chapter 11, "Exposing Your Identity Through Online Publicity").
- Research public-speaking opportunities and set up as many events as you can over the next two months (Chapter 13).
- Consider sponsoring a large event, contest, or fundraiser that would draw attention to your name and identity (Chapter 12).

Month Eleven

The eleventh month has your brand awareness chugging along at a good pace as you continue making connections with people in your industry while pursuing more radio and TV interviews. You may also want to weed out any bad links on your Web site again and send another round of e-mails soliciting incoming links.

- Evaluate the effectiveness of the e-zine ads and search engine keyword ads you started running two months ago; determine whether you should continue running them (Chapter 12, "Other Online Branding Tools and Techniques").
- Check your Web site for link rot and weed out any bad links (Chapter 6, "Designing Your Web Site for Brand Impact").
- Refine the media release you wrote last month and submit it to the free or paid submission services (Chapter 11, "Exposing Your Identity Through Online Publicity").
- E-mail your media release along with a personal note to select Web site owners, e-zine editors, and media people in your field (Chapter 11).
- Conceive, design, and print a new post card that promotes your Web site, free e-zine, or other aspect of your brand identity (Chapter 13, "Exploiting Offline Branding Strategies").

- Research radio and TV interview opportunities, craft a noteworthy publicity angle, and set up as many interviews as you can over the next two months (Chapter 13).
- Increase Web site traffic by sending personal e-mails to more owners of related but noncompeting Web sites and requesting a link (Chapter 12).

Month Twelve

By the twelfth month, you should have an excellent idea of what has and hasn't worked over the past year. At this point, you continue to hammer away at the efforts that bring you the most return while phasing out the activities that are less fruitful. This is also an ideal month to look forward to the upcoming year, brainstorm some new ideas, and develop a plan to take your brand identity to even higher levels of success!

- Mail the promotional post card you created last month to your mailing list (Chapter 13, "Exploiting Offline Branding Strategies").
- Craft a new, attention-getting media release that promotes your brand through a fresh, media-friendly angle (Chapter 11, "Exposing Your Identity Through Online Publicity").
- Research public-speaking opportunities and set up as many events as you can over the next two months (Chapter 13).
- Take a look at trade shows and conferences in your industry that are scheduled within the next six to nine months; consider attending one or two of them (Chapter 13).
- Evaluate the progress you've made over the past three months; determine what's working and what's not (Chapter 14, "Setting Online Goals and Reaching Them").
- Refine your branding goals and game plan, then make a renewed commitment to act on them (Chapter 14).

The Basics: Hardware and Terminology

Let's briefly cover the basics of computer hardware and Internet terminology. Here are some of the components you need to be aware of when you go computer shopping:

Processor—If you think of a computer as a car, the processor is the engine. It powers the activities of the computer and helps determine the speed at which it operates. The processor's speed is noted in terms of megahertz (MHz). Resource: Geek.com's **Chip Geek** page at http://www.ugeek.com/procspec/procmain.htm.

RAM—This acronym stands for random access memory. If the processor is a car engine, RAM is the gasoline that fuels it. The more memory your computer has, the faster and smoother it will operate, especially when you run multiple programs at the same time or work with large graphic files. RAM is expressed in terms of megabytes (MBs). Advice: Get as much memory as you can reasonably afford. Resources: **The Ultimate Memory Guide** at http://www.kingston.com/tools/umg/default.asp and **How Computer Memory Works** at http://www.howstuffworks.com/computer-memory.htm.

Hard Drive—In our car analogy, your hard drive space is the size of your trunk. The bigger the trunk, the more stuff you can fit in your car. On your computer, the hard drive (measured in gigabytes, or GBs) is where you store programs, files, and other data. If you play with music, video, and graphic files, you'll need a lot of hard drive space. Resource: **Why Hard Drives Matter** at http://www.redhill.net.au/hw-drives-matter.html.

Monitor—Bigger is also better when it comes to monitors. Instead of settling for the 15-inch monitor that often comes with a package deal offered through a store or catalog, you'll be happier in the long if you upgrade to a 17- or 19-inch monitor. It'll be easier on the eyes and give you fewer headaches when putting in long hours in front of the screen. Resource:

Monitors—Bigger & Better at http://www.zdnet.com/products/content/ wrapper/monitor.html.

Removable storage—This refers to anything onto which you save a file and take with you, such as a floppy or Zip disk. There are two good reasons to have a removable storage option: It's a good idea to back up your data in the event your hard drive crashes, and you need a way to send larger files to other people. Iomega Zip drives have been the rage for many years; but writable (CD-R) and rewritable (CD-RW) drives have become quite popular. Resource: **Memory and Storage Devices for Desktop Publishing** at http://desktoppub.about.com/ compute/desktoppub/cs/memorystorage/.

As of this writing, many popular home computer systems come with 400 to 600 MHz processors and at least 64 MBs of RAM, along with 10 to 15 MBs of hard drive space and 36x CD-ROM (read only) drives; but those features may not be enough for your needs. Dwight Silverman, a technology columnist and Webmaster of **PC Specs**, at http://www.dwightsilverman.com/minspecs.htm, recommends the following minimum specifications for a basic home/business system:

- 700 MHz processor
- 128 MBs of RAM
- 18 Gigabyte hard drive
- 36x CD-ROM
- 4x4x24 CD-R or CD-RW
- 16 MB video RAM
- 16-bit stereo audio

- 17- to 19-inch color monitor
- 56K fax modem
- 10/100 Ethernet port
- 2 PCI slots
- 2 USB ports
- 1 parallel and 1 serial port

Common Internet Terms and Definitions

This list contains words and phrases that will come up frequently in your journeys on the Internet. Even experienced surfers will find they don't know the exact definitions of all of them. Get to know these definitions and you'll be ahead of the game:

Autoresponder—A program set up to automatically respond by e-mail to anyone who sends a message to a specific e-mail address.

Cookie—Information sent by a Web server to a browser, which saves the information for return visits and other purposes. Cookies allow Web sites to recognize you before you even identify yourself.

Domain name—The part of a Web site address that usually immediately follows *www*. For example, Amazon.com is a domain name, as is TopFloor.com.

E-zine—Internet abbreviation for an electronic magazine or newsletter.

Home page—This commonly refers to the main page, or welcome page, of a Web site. Home page is also used to describe the first site that appears when you launch your Web browser.

Hypertext—This is the primary function that makes the Internet interactive. Hypertext is an underlined bit of text that, when clicked, takes you to another Web page or site.

Internet—Think of the Internet as the whole enchilada—the entire network of interconnected computers that allows people the world over to send e-mail, surf the Web, and a lot more.

Javascript—A programming language that, when inserted into Web pages, allows them to display the current date, show animation, use calculators, and provide other cool features.

Opt-in—A term that refers to the way people sign up to receive mailing lists and newsletters. To subscribe, a person must click a box, fill out a form, or in some way give permission to be added to the list.

Snail mail—Postal mail sent via the old-fashioned method to a physical address.

Spam—Unsolicited e-mail, usually sent in bulk to many recipients who never asked for the information—a big no-no on the Internet.

Web browser—This software application reads the code that makes up HTML (and other) files and displays them as Web pages on your computer screen. Microsoft Internet Explorer and Netscape Navigator are the two most popular Web browsers. You can't surf the Internet without a browser.

Web host—A company that either sells or offers free space on its Web server for you to place your online documents and Web pages.

Web page—A single Web document.

Web server—This is the computer where online documents reside. To view a Web page, a browser must collect and read that Web page's file. To accomplish that, the file must exist on a computer system somewhere. That computer is the Web server. Server can also refer to the software used to send Web page data to a browser.

Web site—A collection of Web pages. They usually share the same root domain name and are connected to each other through links.

World Wide Web—The familiar *www* part of Web site addresses stands for World Wide Web. Although the phrase is often used interchangeably with Internet, the World Wide Web is one aspect of the overall Internet.

However, it's the segment that gets the most attention, because it allows users to surf, view Web pages, and conduct transactions over the Internet.

Know Your Internet Acronyms

People love shortcuts, especially when it comes to tongue-twisting technology terms. Here are some of the more common Internet acronyms:

CGI—Common Gateway Interface. Using a series of code instructions called a script, CGI adds interactivity to Web pages. For instance, you can use CGI to take information entered into an online form and send it to your e-mail account.

FTP—File Transfer Protocol. Allows a user to log onto another computer or Internet site to retrieve or send files. This is the method commonly used to upload Web pages and images to a Web server.

GIF—Graphics Interchange Format. A common file format for images that is especially effective for logos and other artwork made up of solid blocks of color.

HTML—Hypertext Markup Language. The coding language used to create Web pages.

HTTP—Hypertext Transport Protocol. The protocol used for communicating across the Internet.

IMAP—Internet Message Access Protocol. A more recent alternative to POP e-mail access with more advanced features.

IRC—Internet Relay Chat. An Internet feature that allows users to "chat" with each other in real time.

JPEG—Joint Photographic Experts Group. Another image file format that compresses information from multitoned color photos by discarding some of the image data to reduce file size and improve transfer speed among computers.

POP—Post Office Protocol. A standard e-mail system used on the Internet.

TCP/IP—Transmission Control Protocol/Internet Protocol. The basic language all computers use to talk to each other over the Internet and to transmit the tiny bits of information that allow you to view e-mail, Web pages, etc.

URL—Uniform Resource Locator. This is simply another way of saying Internet address.

WYSIWYG—What You See Is What You Get. WYSIWYG is a generic reference to programs that let you create Web pages using a graphical user interface (much like desktop publishing software does). The program then generates the HTML code needed for the Web pages.

INDEX

POOR RICHARD'S WEB SITE
Geek-Free, Commonsense Advice on Building a Low-Cost Web Site, 2nd Edition

Poor Richard's Web Site is the *only* book that explains the entire process of creating a Web site, from deciding whether you really need a site—and what you can do with it—through picking a place to put the site, creating the site, and bringing people to the site. It is full of commonsense advice that Amazon.com called an "antidote to this swirl of confusion" and "straightforward information." Praised by *BYTE magazine*, *Publisher's Weekly*, and *USA Today*, *Poor Richard's Web Site* can save you thousands of dollars and hundreds of hours.

❝Poor Richard's Good Advice. With all great new things comes a proliferation of hucksters and snake-oil salesmen, and the Internet is no exception. The antidote to this swirl of confusion lies in Peter Kent's *Poor Richard's Web Site*. The analogy to Ben Franklin's volume is appropriate: the book is filled with the kind of straightforward information the Founding Father himself would have appreciated."
—Amazon.com

❝We highly recommend that you get a copy."
—Marketing Technology

❝Very well written."   *—Library Journal*

❝Poor Richard's offers clear advice to help you defend against jargon-happy sales people and computer magazines."
—Fortune.com

Poor Richard's Web Site is available in bookstores both online and offline, and at http://www.TopFloor.com/

Poor Richard's Web Site, Second Edition
by Peter Kent   ISBN: 0-9661032-0-3

POOR RICHARD'S INTERNET MARKETING AND PROMOTIONS
How to Promote Yourself, Your Business, Your Ideas Online, 2nd Edition

Much of what you've read about marketing on the Internet is wrong: registering a Web site with the search engines *won't* create a flood of orders; banner advertising *doesn't* work for most companies; online malls *do not* push large amounts of traffic to their client Web sites. . . .

What you really need is some geek-free, commonsense advice on marketing and promoting on the Internet, by somebody's who's actually done it! Most books and articles are written by freelance writers assigned to investigate a particular subject. *Poor Richard's Internet Marketing and Promotions* is written by a small-business person who's been successfully marketing online for a decade.

Poor Richard's Internet Marketing and Promotions uses the same down-to-earth style so highly praised in *Poor Richard's Web Site*. You'll learn how to plan an Internet marketing campaign, find your target audience, use giveaways to bring people to your site, integrate an email newsletter into your promotions campaign, buy advertising that works, use real-world PR, and more.

You'll also learn to track results, by seeing who is linking to your site, by hearing who is talking about you, and by measuring visits to your site.

"Go now as fast as you can and get this book and soon your Web site will reach the heights of the well known."
—About.com

"This book offers readers the ability to discipline themselves and the resources they need to succeed. It's loaded!"
—The Web Reviewer

Poor Richard's Internet Marketing and Promotions is available in bookstores both online and offline, and at http://www.TopFloor.com/

Poor Richard's Internet Marketing and Promotions: by Peter Kent and Tara Calishain ISBN: 1-930082-00-2

POOR RICHARD'S E-MAIL PUBLISHING

Creating Newsletters, Bulletins, Discussion Groups, and Other Powerful Communication Tools

E-mail publishing is a powerful communications medium that anyone with Internet access can use. It's cheap, effective, and very easy to use once you learn the tricks of the trade. Electronic publishing is one of the most efficient ways to promote your products or services online, as well as being an excellent way to drive traffic back to your Web site.

Poor Richard's E-mail Publishing is your complete, step-by-step, guide to the nuts and bolts of creating newsletters and discussion groups via e-mail. Whether you're an e-mail novice or a seasoned professional, this resource belongs on your shelf.

You'll find answers to questions such as:

- How do I set up an HTML newsletter?

- Why is e-mail better than a Web site for distributing information?

- How can I communicate via e-mail without spamming?

- What is the proper e-mail etiquette?

- Where do I find subscribers and then how can I manage them?

- Where can I find a high-powered list service?

- What are the insider's tricks to hosting a successful e-mail discussion list?

- How can I generate income through advertising or ancillary product sales?

POOR RICHARD'S BUILDING ONLINE COMMUNITIES

Create a Web Community for Your Business, Club, Association, or Family

Anyone with Internet access can set up an online community—you don't have to be a rocket scientist or spend thousands of dollars. In fact, you probably already have the programs you'll need. But to have a successful Web community where members actively participate you'll need a bit more information. *Poor Richard's Building Online Communities* explains everything you'll need to know, such as:

- What programs are involved and how to manage them

- Where to promote your community so others can find it

- How to protect the privacy of your members

- Ways of dealing with dissension and needless arguments

- How to provide information that people can use

- How to foster a sense of trust and belonging with your members

You'll also learn about the types of systems you can use (mailing lists, usenet newsgroups, Web-based message boards, etc.). The authors explain the advantages and disadvantages of each system as well as how to create and manage each type of community.

If you decide to host a community that is open to everyone, you'll need to invite people to join. This book offers several ways to promote your community.

Finding and getting to know people who share your interests is one of the most interesting and useful things you can do on the Internet. So start building your online community now!

Poor Richard's Building Online Communities is available in bookstores both online and offline, and at http://www.TopFloor.com/

Poor Richard's Building Online Communities
by Margaret Levine Young and John Levine   ISBN: 0-9661032-9-7

POOR RICHARD'S HOME AND SMALL OFFICE NETWORKING
Room to Room or Around the World

A home office or small business can no longer afford to ignore the cost savings, collaboration, and outreach benefits of networking. If you're not connected, you aren't working at maximum efficiency.

However, a network can't make your business more productive or help you work fast simply because you install one. To truly benefit from a network, you must determine the type you need and learn how to design, protect, and maintain it. This book explains how.

A small network isn't simply a scaled-down version of the networks of large businesses. Because it's an entirely different entity, a small network has its own advantages and challenges. That's where the geek-free, easy-to-follow advice in this book is crucial!

You'll learn lots of low-cost networking techniques, including:

- How to use alternative networks, such as house-wiring systems. Did you know you can use your home's electrical wiring as your network?
- What software and hardware you need to make your network work.
- How to administer and maintain your network with minimal time and effort, and how to tune your network to perform more efficiently.
- How to find and plug holes in your network's security. You can't be too careful today!
- How to use the Internet for remote communications and file sharing, including how to set up a Virtual Private Network.

This book also includes a detailed glossary to help you demystify the techie terminology, plus 50 concise tips on successful networking for small businesses.

Poor Richard's Home and Small Office Networking is available in bookstores both online and offline, and at http://www.TopFloor.com/

**Poor Richard's Home and Small Office Networking
by John Paul Mueller   ISBN: 1-930082-03-7**

POOR RICHARD'S CREATINGE-BOOKS

How Authors, Publishers, and Corporations Get Into Digital Print

The e-book revolution is beginning-and with the information in this book, you'll be one step ahead of the rest. Electronic publishing is an exploding field with plenty of opportunities for authors, self-publishers, entrepreneurs, and other professionals.

But how do you get started? And once you have your content in e-book format, how do you promote it and sell it? With this book, you'll learn every phase of the e-book writing and publishing process-from creating manuscripts and e-book files to marketing and distributing online.

You'll get the essential information that you need to know, including:

- What makes a good e-book. You'll find out what sells, what doesn't, and why.

- How to choose e-book formats. We're a long way from a single e-book format that every e-book reader device and program can read. You'll become familiar with the different formats that are available and the pros and cons of each.

- How to create e-book documents. Once you've selected a format, you'll need to know about the tools available for conversion and how to make your book looks as it should.

- Where to find services for start-up e-publishers. Many people make a business of helping other people start and run their e-publishing businesses. You'll discover how to reach and benefit from them.

- Where to distribute your e-books and how to market them.

- What to look for in e-book publishing contracts and what you need to know about digital rights and copy protection.

Poor Richard's Creating E-Books is available in bookstores both online and offline, and at http://www.TopFloor.com/

Poor Richard's Creating E-Books
by Chris Van Buren and Jeff Cogswell   ISBN: 1-930082-02-9

FREE INFORMATION ABOUT SETTING UP AND PROMOTING A WEB SITE

http://www.TopFloor.com/

If you are setting up a Web site, or if you have a Web site and you want marketing and promotions advice that really works, visit http://www.TopFloor.com/.

You'll find free information of all kinds: questions to ask a hosting company, the top 10 mistakes to avoid when setting up a Web site, 8 reasons why you should create your own online community—plus links to hundreds of Web sites with services that will help you set up and promote your site, several chapters from each book in the *Poor Richard's Series*, and much more.

Also, sign up for the free e-mail newsletter, *Poor Richard's Web Site News*. With more than 48,000 subscribers in over 80 countries, this is one of the most respected newsletters on the subject.

You can read back issues and subscribe to the newsletter at http://www.PoorRichard.com/newsltr/, or to subscribe by e-mail, send an e-mail message to subpr@PoorRichard.com.

The Main Page:
http://www.TopFloor.com/

The Newsletter:
http://www.PoorRichard.com/newsltr/

E-mail Subscriptions:
send a blank e-mail message to subpr@PoorRichard.com

(Continued from the back cover)

You may be asking, "Why do I need to brand myself online? How does it benefit me?" The answer is that branding allows you to take control of your online identity and influence the impression that people have of you, which helps you accomplish the following objectives:

- Establish yourself as an expert in your field
- Connect with like-minded people on a large scale
- Focus your energies on feeding your life's purpose
- Build a solid reputation within your industry
- Become self-employed doing something you enjoy (or gain credibility and be in a better position to land the job you really want)
- Increase your notoriety and improve your perceived value
- Develop your circle of influence within a business niche
- Earn praise and recognition from a growing number of people who embrace your message
- Become a celebrity in your chosen field

If you're an artist, branding helps you connect your name with your technique and attract more fans (and more paying customers). If you're a Web designer, branding allows you to mix your attitude and distinct perspective with your technical skills so more people hire you. If you're a writer, branding paves the way to reaching a loyal readership without having to kiss the feet of a major publisher.

Poor Richard's Branding Yourself Online not only explains *why* you will benefit from establishing a personal brand; it also explains *how* you determine your brand identity. Here are a few questions to ask yourself: What are your personal strengths and weaknesses? What are you passionate about? What are you knowledgeable about? What solutions do you provide?

Once you have learned how to effectively position yourself, define your focus, and develop a "fan-club mentality," the author delves into ways of promoting the brand *you*. You'll find out how to:

- Maximize e-mail for brand delivery—there's more to it than just creating a signature file
- Design your web site for brand impact, including tips on content, design, and interactivity
- Exploit the e-zines and web sites of others